american
popular
illustration

Recent Titles in
American Popular Culture

Series Editor: *M. Thomas Inge*

Film: A Reference Guide
Robert A. Armour

Women's Gothic and Romantic Fiction: A Reference Guide
Kay Mussell

Animation: A Reference Guide
Thomas W. Hoffer

Variety Entertainment and Outdoor Amusements: A Reference Guide
Don B. Wilmeth

Women in Popular Culture: A Reference Guide
Katherine Fishburn

Sports: A Reference Guide
Robert J. Higgs

Play and Playthings: A Reference Guide
Bernard Mergen

American Popular Music: A Reference Guide
Mark W. Booth

american popular illustration

A REFERENCE GUIDE

James J. Best

American Popular Culture

GREENWOOD PRESS

WESTPORT, CONNECTICUT • LONDON, ENGLAND

Library of Congress Cataloging in Publication Data

Best, James J.
   American popular illustration.

   (American popular culture, ISSN 0193-6859)
   Bibliography: p.
   Includes index.
   1. Illustration of books—United States.
2. Magazine illustration—United States. 3. Illustrators—United States. 4. United States—Popular culture.
5. Illustration of books—United States—Bibliography.
6. Magazine illustration—United States—Bibliography.
7. Illustrators—United States—Bibliography.
8. United States—Popular culture—Bibliography.
I. Title. II. Series.

NC975.B45 1984   741.64′0973   83-14150
ISBN 0-313-23389-6

Library of Congress Catalog Card Number: 83-14150
ISBN: 0-313-23389-6
ISSN: 0193-6859

First published in 1984

Greenwood Press
A division of Congressional Information Service, Inc.
88 Post Road West
Westport, Connecticut 06881

Printed in the United States of America

10 9 8 7 6 5 4 3 2 1

This book is dedicated to my wife Lynda, whose interest in books, patience, and support has made this book possible; to Bryan and Brett, who helped their father collect some of the data used in this book; and to the many book dealers, museum curators, librarians, and people interested in illustration, who have taught me much of what I know about American illustration. This is their book as well as mine.

Contents

PREFACE   ix

Chapter 1   A Historical Overview   **3**
The Roots of American Illustration: 1800–1890   3
The Golden Age of American Illustration: 1890–1920   6
The Transition Period: 1920–1945   12
The Illustration Renaissance: 1945–Present   17

Chapter 2   History and Aesthetics of American Illustration   **21**
The History of American Illustration   21
Critiques and Aesthetic Theories of Illustration   35
Bibliography   41

Chapter 3   Major Illustrated Works: Bibliographies and Books   **47**
Bibliographies   47
Illustrated Classics   58
Bibliography   67

Chapter 4   The Major Illustrators   **71**
The First Illustrators: Anderson, Darley, and the "Special" Artists   71
The First Professionals: Charles Parsons and the Staff at Harper's   76
The Golden Age of American Illustration: 1890–1920   84
The Transition Period: 1920–1945   99
The Illustration Renaissance: 1945–Present   105
Bibliography   110

Chapter 5   The Social and Artistic Context of Illustration   **117**
The Social Milieu   117
The Artistic Milieu   123
Bibliography   130

Chapter 6   Illustration Media   **133**
Illustration Techniques   133
Publication Media   140
Bibliography   147

Appendix 1   Magazines and Periodicals   **151**

Appendix 2   Research Collections   **153**

Appendix 3   Bibliography of Illustrated Books   **157**

INDEX   163

Preface

This book represents one person's efforts to determine the limits of what we know (and don't know) about American illustration. My "need to know" stemmed from teaching a course on the history of American illustration, doing research in the field, and collecting illustrated books and magazines. Since I was not trained as an illustrator, art historian, or book collector, my initial efforts to fill gaps in my knowledge were haphazard because I didn't know where the gaps were. In the process of doing the reading and research for this book I have become far more aware of what I don't know.

In my bibliographic search I limited myself to sources that are reasonably accessible, dealing with American illustrators who have made a significant contribution to the body of American illustration. These limitations may disturb those who cannot find their favorite illustrator discussed here. Even with the number of volumes on American illustration and illustrators, the vast majority of illustrators are bibliographically unknown. As I note at various points in the text, some of those "unknowns" deserve artistic and literary recognition. I have also tried to read all the major source materials about American illustrators and illustration. In the process I undoubtedly missed some of the literature, a prospect that has concerned me from the inception of this project but one that I have come to accept.

Once the bibliography was assembled, it had to be organized. The book begins with a historical overview of the field of American illustration to give the reader a sense of perspective for some of the discussion that will follow in succeeding chapters. Chapter 2 analyzes those works that deal with the history and aesthetics of American illustration. Chapter 3 analyzes the major bibliographic sources on American illustration, with an eye toward listing the most noteworthy books in the field. Chapter 4 examines the biographic material on the major American illustrators, seeking to determine some of the important factors in their lives and some of the controversies between their biographers. The premise of chapter 5 is that it is useless to talk about American illustration without understanding the cultural, social, and economic contexts within which it took place. However, there has been little written about this question. Chapter 6 explores the media of illustration, in terms of both illustration techniques and sources of publication. Since I am not an illustrator, it was difficult to evaluate the technique books, so I relied most on people who had written about illustration techniques, who had asked why rather than how. Complete citations of books and articles mentioned in the text are found in the bibliography at the end of each chapter. Illustrated books mentioned in each chapter will be found in appendix 3. In the appendixes I have provided the reader, researcher, and book collector with a list of magazines of interest, research sites to explore for original artwork or major collections of illustrated books, and a list of illustrated book "classics," organized by illustrator.

It would have been impossible to do this book without the assistance of many people. I would like to thank the staff librarians of the interlibrary loan service at Kent State University for their unstinting service in pursuit of hard-to-get books, as well as the staffs of the Kent Free Library, the Akron Public Library, the Cleveland Public Library, the Akron University Library, the Philadelphia Free Library, the New York Public Library, the Library of Congress, and the Archives of American Art who made the research for this book so much easier. I would also like to thank a number of people who have aided and encouraged me in my research on American illustration. Rowland Elzea and his staff at the Delaware Art Museum, Ann Barton Brown and her staff at the Brandywine River Museum, and Terry Brown at the Society of Illustrators were helpful in collecting information and answering questions. A number of book dealers have also been of help. Frank Klein in Akron, Ed Nudelman in Seattle, Milton Riesman in New York City, and JoAnn Reisler in Vienna, Virginia, have spent time talking to me about our common interest in illustrated books, which, in turn, sustained my interest in American illustration. I would be remiss if I did not acknowledge the contributions of members of my class in American illustration, who saw the need for this type of book, encouraged me to write it, and then listened to and critiqued parts of what I had written. For their material support, I would like to acknowledge the assistance of the American Council of Learned Societies for a summer grant, the Research Council at Kent State University for financial assistance, the computer center at Kent State University for computer assistance, and my colleagues in the political science department at Kent State for their support in this endeavor.

american
popular
illustration

CHAPTER I

A Historical Overview

Popular illustration refers to artwork intentionally designed for mass consumption by means of reproduction on paper. Initially, illustrations were limited to books, magazines, and posters, but more recently they have appeared on phonograph album covers, playing cards, and a host of paper ephemera. The job of the illustrator is to create images that can be used in whole or in part to tell stories and recreate events in ways that are intelligible to a mass audience. Unlike the fine artist, who has few constraints on how, what, when, or why he or she paints, the illustrator is constrained by the subject matter, the manner of reproduction, the audience, the art editor supervising the work, and publication deadlines.

To the extent that illustrators have been successful in their task, the vehicles for their illustrations have become art galleries for the mass public. In the days before television and radio, even before photography, illustrations had an enormous impact on American society and culture. Popular illustration requires a literate public, the technology for inexpensive reproduction of artwork, and the means for inexpensive distribution to the public. Because of these requirements the content, techniques, and vehicles for popular illustration have varied through time. As popular tastes and technology have changed so have the popularity of various illustrators, different illustration techniques, and the media for the publication of illustrations. The historical outline that follows will chart many of those changes.

THE ROOTS OF AMERICAN ILLUSTRATION: 1800–1890

The history of popular illustration in the United States dates from the eighteenth century, but illustrations were not widely used until the Civil War era. As with many American cultural phenomena, the roots of American illustration can be traced to England. English newspapers, illustrated magazines, and books, containing illustrations by Thomas Rowlandson, Thomas Bewick, "Phiz," and others, were sold in the United States and served as models and inspiration to early American illustrators. Many of these early English illustrations were "copied" (often without attribution) by less skilled American illustrators or engravers.

Although there is debate as to who was the "first" American illustrator (Paul Revere and Benjamin Franklin are nominees), Dr. Alexander Anderson was the first American illustrator of note, signing or initialling many of his illustrations to differentiate them from the work of copyists. Anderson began his career by imitating Bewick's illustrations for an American audience, but as his skills developed his individual style matured and his subject matter became more clearly American. Once he had established himself, he trained some of the first wood engravers of the postcolonial period. During his seventy-year career (he died at age ninety-five) Anderson produced more than eight thousand illustrations for juveniles, spelling books, and other paper ephemera, very few of which are still in existence. Although prolific, Anderson worked in relative obscurity, and Felix Octavius Carr (F.O.C.) Darley is generally credited with being the first American illustrator of sufficient stature to have his name as illustrator on title pages and covers of books that he illustrated. Through the study of leading English illustrators and through practice, Darley developed his artistic skills to the point that during the period 1840–1860 he was unrivalled in the field of American illustration. As a result, he received commissions to illustrate books by Washington Irving, Francis Parkman, James Fenimore Cooper, and other leading American authors. Darley's illustrations were distinctively "American" in content and style. His scenes of frontier life and Indians were unpretentious but not primitive, demonstrating real virtuosity of line, and were frequently humorous in an earthy way. His line drawings for JUDD'S MARGARET (1856) and Irving's LEGEND OF SLEEPY HOLLOW (1849), while distinctively American in content, were equal in technique to the best European work of the time. His drawings were immediately recognizable to the reading public, and Darley's success insured his livelihood as an illustrator and even merited recognition in American art circles. By 1852 Darley had been elected a member of the prestigious National Academy of Design—a singular honor for an illustrator—and the Century Association in New York City, a social club of the artistic, cultural, and financial elite. Although Darley continued illustrating into the 1880s, it was his early artwork that served to liberate American illustration from its dependence on Britain for inspiration and style. After the Civil War, Darley's role was more inspirational than artistic, although some of his later work still shows the character and artistic control that made him so popular twenty-five years earlier.

While Darley served to liberate American illustration from its British heritage, it was the Civil War that created the demand for American illustration. As a result of educational reforms begun in New England, public education produced a more literate population, and the events of the Civil War created an unprecedented demand for comprehensive coverage of the war in words and pictures. HARPER'S WEEKLY and LESLIE'S ILLUSTRATED WEEKLY responded to this demand by dispatching reporters and artists to cover the major battles, to travel with the troops, and to provide readers with a "feel" for the war, at least from the Northern perspective. People read accounts of major battles and saw pictures of them within weeks of their occurrence. Battlefield "special" artists did rough sketches that were dispatched by boat, train, or horseback to New York, where engravers, using their imaginations to fill in voids in the drawings, translated rough sketches into visual images by carving them onto boxwood. Frequently, a number of engravers would work on the same large sketch, each working on a different part, to meet the newspaper's weekly deadline; when finished, the various pieces of boxwood would be bolted together to make the complete picture. An electrotyped metal impression was then made for printing on rotary presses. The system obviously called for cooperation between the "special" artists and the engravers to produce good quality, accurate illustrations, and as the war progressed the quality of the illustrations improved. The use of boxwood for engraving meant that illustration plates could be locked into presses with movable type, eliminating the need for a second press run for the illustrations and producing durable, inexpensive illustrations. The day of inexpensive reproduction of illustrations for a mass market had arrived. So successful was HARPER'S WEEKLY with its war illustrations that its press run at the peak of the Civil War exceeded 150,000 a week. Not surprisingly, a number of "special" artists, namely Winslow Homer and Thomas Nast, established reputations during the war that endured after it ended. Interestingly, neither of them spent a great deal of time at the front, preferring to make only occasional forays before returning to New York to work from memory and imagination. As a result, few of Homer's or Nast's Civil War illustrations deal with battle scenes; in fact, Nast's best-remembered war illustration is the double-page spread he did for HARPER'S WEEKLY on Lincoln's death. A number of skilled battlefield artists, such as William and Alfred Waud, Edwin Forbes, and Theodore Davis, had only limited success as postwar illustrators.

But the Civil War stimulated the demand for illustrated material. The success of HARPER'S WEEKLY led the House of Harper to expand the use of illustrations in its monthly magazine, HARPER'S MONTHLY; its children's magazine, HARPER'S YOUNG PEOPLE; and in its books. Equally important, Harper's hired Charles Parsons, a successful artist and illustrator, to serve as full-time art editor for the firm's fledgling art department. Under Parsons's direction, the House of Harper recruited a staff of illustrators—most notably Edwin Austin Abbey, A. B. Frost, Alfred Kimble, and Howard Pyle—who became leaders in the Golden Age of American illustration that followed. Parsons created the first commercial art department, and the illustrators who worked for him were the first "professional" illustrators in America, working full time at their craft and receiving adequate compensation for their services. Parsons had two skills that enabled him to build and maintain Harper's artistic preeminence: his ability to spot talent and to nurture it. Pyle and Frost, in particular, were able to hone their skills under Parsons's watchful eye and then, when their skills were widely recognized and competition for their services became intense, they left Harper's and were replaced by other illustrators. As the circulation of the various Harper's magazines, particularly HARPER'S MONTHLY, increased, two other quality illustrated monthly magazines entered the field, CENTURY and SCRIBNER'S. These three magazines dominated the field of quality illustrated magazines during the last twenty years of the nineteenth century, and an illustrator whose work was published regularly in them was a "recognized" illustrator. The establishment of more and more illustrated magazines was a response to increased demand and signalled increased competition between publishing houses for quality artwork from qualified illustrators—which produced a Golden Age of American illustration.

While magazines turned increasingly to illustrations after the Civil War, publishers were more reluctant to use illustrations lavishly in their books. Illustrated books were more costly and there was no guarantee they would sell. The publication of PICTURESQUE AMERICA (1872–1874) and its success convinced many publishers that illustrated books could sell profitably. Indeed, the right illustrations could increase enormously the reputation and sales of a book; A. B. Frost's illustrations for RUDDER GRANGE (1888) and the Brer Rabbit books made them classics. An illustrator's ability to enhance an author's words visually gave more impact to the book. Illustrators, of course, loved to work on books—there were more illustrations than in a magazine story and the material was thematically coherent. Consequently, illustrated books became a showcase for authors' and illustrators' talents. So successful were illustrated books that by 1900 there were very few novels published in America that were not illustrated at least in part, and the increasing success and recognition of illustrators led to books of their illustrations alone being published (most notably those of Howard Chandler Christy, Harrison Fisher, and Frederic Remington).

THE GOLDEN AGE OF AMERICAN ILLUSTRATION: 1890–1920

By 1890 the stage was set for a dramatic growth in the quantity and quality of American illustration. Demand for illustration artwork was increasing, and competition between publishing houses created a need for more illustrators and guaranteed that good-quality illustrators would be well paid. Technological developments in printing, namely the development of high-speed presses and the increased use of halftone plates for photographic reproduction of artwork meant illustration artwork could be better reproduced more cheaply. Halftone illustrations, for example, cost $20 to reproduce as compared with $300 for a comparable wood engraving. Because of these cost savings, and spurred by intense competition, the price of illustrated magazines declined to $.25 or less. At the same time, the development of a truly nationwide network of roads and railroads made rapid distribution of printed materials a reality. Suddenly there was a national market for illustration, and illustration became an art form for the mass public. The demand for illustrated magazines and their large circulations and national distribution made them natural vehicles for advertisers seeking a broader audience. Advertising revenues, in turn, helped underwrite the costs of magazine production, making them increasingly profitable for publishers and illustrators.

The arrival of a Golden Age of illustration was a mixed blessing for illustrators. The demand for illustration artwork meant that well-trained illustrators could find a market for their artwork at a decent price, and the yearly incomes for top illustrators rose to undreamed-of heights. By 1910 a Philadelphia reporter estimated that Harrison Fisher earned $75,000 per year, while another thirteen illustrators earned between $15,000 and $50,000. (These are pre-income tax and pre-inflation dollars.) Individual illustrators were earning more; Charles Dana Gibson and Maxfield Parrish were paid $1,000 or more for their magazine covers, while less well known illustrators were paid from $50 to $500 for individual pieces of artwork. Publishing houses competed with each other to sign illustrators to lucrative, long-term exclusive contracts. Illustrators moved from their garret studios to the suburbs and became part of the society that they drew.

Success was not without costs, however. As the number of illustrators grew and competition for artwork became more intense, an older laissez-faire set of relationships between illustrators and publishing houses and art editors was replaced by more formal sets of agreements and contracts. Aside from questions of pay rates for artwork, a perpetual problem that varied with the financial health of the publishing industry, illustrators were concerned about the ownership of artwork after it had been published. Publishers traditionally kept the artwork after publication, sometimes selling it to help underwrite the cost of illustrations, using it in other formats (frequently without consulting the illustrators), keeping the artwork for personal use, or destroying it.

In 1901 the Society of Illustrators was formed in New York to serve as a club room and meeting ground for illustrators and art editors to discuss common professional problems. The Society never became the professional union that many publishers feared, but it did serve as the vehicle for resolving some common professional problems—such as ownership of artwork. By 1910, for example, contracts for artwork also contained provisions regarding the disposition of the artwork after publication, most of which was returned to the artist.

One of the leading illustrators in America at the start of the Golden Age of illustration was Howard Pyle. Pyle received recognition for his early work at Harper's, but it was the publication of ROBIN HOOD (1883)—a book written, designed, and illustrated by Pyle—that established his reputation as a master of pen-and-ink drawing. Subsequent publication of PEPPER AND SALT (1886), THE WONDER CLOCK (1888), and OTTO OF THE SILVER HAND (1888) established his reputation as the premier illustrator of fantasy and medieval tales for children and juveniles. Whatever the subject, Pyle's figures were realistically portrayed in "heroic" style, which was appropriate for his historical illustrations as well. With the advent of halftone and four-color reproductions, Pyle made the transition from pen-and-ink to oils with great success—a transition that many illustrators did not make, for example, Edwin Austin Abbey.

On the basis of his artwork alone Pyle would have ranked as one of the leading illustrators during the Golden Age. But Pyle had a more important contribution to make. Beginning with twice-weekly illustration classes at Drexel Institute in Philadelphia in 1894, and then moving to Chadds Ford, Pennsylvania, and Wilmington, Delaware, Pyle established the first art school for training professional illustrators, the Howard Pyle School of Art. Pyle accepted few students, and those who finished a program of studies with him had a disproportionate impact on illustration during the latter half of the Golden Age. N. C. Wyeth, Frank Schoonover, Maxfield Parrish, Thornton Oakley, Jessie Wilcox Smith, and Elizabeth

Shippen Green head the alumni roster. Admission was based on Pyle's evaluation of a student's portfolio and meant the student was given studio space, allowed to attend Pyle's classes, and have work critiqued by Pyle. In a letter to his mother (reproduced in Betsy James Wyeth's THE WYETHS [1971]), N. C. Wyeth noted that his first composition class with Pyle was an "eye-opening" experience. Pyle emphasized the need for capturing the essence of the action in a story and involving the reader in the illustration. The illustration had to be historically accurate and realistic as well. This emphasis on an approach to illustration rather than style required that Pyle's students have artistic imagination as well as talent but allowed each one to develop their own artistic style within Pyle's approach. Not surprisingly, many of Pyle's male students emulated his style to a degree, becoming romantic Realists like Pyle. Pyle's women students, on the other hand, developed a more decorative style than their male contemporaries; they were more likely to do pictures of women and children than of pirates or cowboys.

Once his students had completed the fundamentals of their training, Pyle worked to secure commissions for them from various magazine and book publishers. When he was overburdened with commissions Pyle would offer the work of a student as a substitute, but only if he was satisfied that the work was of sufficient merit. Art editors from major publishing firms, recognizing that Pyle would stand behind the quality of his students' work, began to offer them commissions even before they had completed their training. Pyle's success in placing the artwork of his students made his school attractive for promising illustrators, and the quality of his students made easy Pyle's placement of their work. Over a period of time he established solid rapport with various art editors, and HARPER'S MONTHLY, in whose art department Pyle had once worked, became an artistic showplace for the work of Pyle and his students.

Many of Pyle's students, collectively labelled the "Brandywine School" (after the Brandywine River, which flows through Chadds Ford), became major illustrators after leaving his studio. Maxfield Parrish achieved success with his jewel-like illustrations of children's fantasy tales, which combined opalescent color, excellent draftsmanship, and a sense of naive belief that made his work attractive to children and their parents. His illustrations for POEMS OF CHILDHOOD (1904) and THE KNAVE OF HEARTS (1925) epitomize his artistic talent. N. C. Wyeth and Frank Schoonover achieved success in other genres. Following Pyle's advice that an illustrator who had lived an experience could better illustrate it, N. C. Wyeth travelled West and Schoonover traversed the Canadian North Woods for material to illustrate. From these experiences they received their first commissions. Wyeth soon tired of painting the West and went on to explore a variety of themes, doing the illustrations for sixteen juveniles in the Scribner's ILLUSTRATED CLASSICS series, as well as a variety of other book and magazine commissions. Schoonover, on the other hand, continued to depict the world he experienced during his first trip and periodically returned there to refresh himself and his memory. Many of Pyle's other students specialized as well; Stanley Arthurs painted sea scenes while Thornton Oakley concentrated on depicting urban and industrial America.

Comparatively few women studied with Howard Pyle, but three—Elizabeth Shippen Green, Sarah Stillwell, and Violet Oakley—founded their own studio at Cogslea, on the Philadelphia Main Line. Violet Oakley became one of the premier muralists in pre-World War I America and the other two, along with another Pyle student, Jessie Wilcox Smith, became leading illustrators of women and children. Their subjects have a Victorian sweetness and charm that is instantly appealing. It is unfortunate that the Brandywine women illustrators were restricted largely to drawing women and children by editors and publishers who felt those subjects would be more "natural" for them than cowboys or pirates.

Howard Pyle's impact extended far beyond the fifteen-year period during which he taught illustration. Many of his students worked as illustrators long after Pyle's death in 1911; N. C. Wyeth, Maxfield Parrish, Thornton Oakley, and Frank Schoonover were still doing illustration artwork of one sort or another into the 1940s. In addition, several of Pyle's students became teachers as well. One of the most successful, Harvey Dunn, trained Dean Cornwell, who was one of the most popular illustrators of the 1930s and 1940s (and a romantic Realist as well). Even N. C. Wyeth, who became increasingly ambivalent about what he had learned from Pyle, had a few students working with him—the most notable being his son, Andrew, who began his career in his early teens as an illustrator but soon became the fine artist his father always aspired to be.

Pyle's students were not the only successful illustrators during this period. One group of illustrators—Charles Dana Gibson, Harrison Fisher, Howard Chandler Christy, and James Montgomery Flagg, among others—became noted for their depictions of American womanhood. These "American Beauty" illustrators built their careers on creating the idealized American sweetheart—modern, urbane, saucy, independent, flirtatious, yet vulnerable—traits to which American women could aspire but few could achieve. These illustrators drew pictures of society, and their success ensured access to society and influenced what society should look like. The Gibson Girl became the benchmark for womanhood in this era, defining how the "ideal" girl should look and act. Gibson's success as an illustrator could be gauged by the number of women who emulated his drawings; when the Gibson Girl changed hair styles or dress fashions, the reverberations were felt in beauty salons and dress shops across the nation. The Fisher and Christy Girls established standards in their own way, differing from the Gibson Girl because of Gibson's reliance on pen-and-ink rather than the color washes and oils favored by Fisher and Christy. One of the "American Beauty" illustrators, Coles Phillips, combined an ability to draw idealized women with an excellent eye for color and graphic design. The results were illustrations in which the girl's costume was the same color or design as the background, fading away to emphasize her face, hands, and feet. These "Fadeaway Girls" became Phillips's trademark and made his American Beauties distinctive. The women of the American Beauty illustrators were also different from those drawn by the women of the Brandywine School; the former were single, liberated, and modern, while the latter were maternal and Victorian. The one idealized the present and the future, while the other idealized the past.

Other illustrators specialized in depicting "foreign" places, at home and abroad. In the days before television, radio, and motion pictures, illustrations provided most Americans with their most important ideas about the world outside their experience. For many Americans the "wild" West was just as Frederic Remington and Charles M. Russell depicted it. Most Americans were not aware that each man brought different experiences and perspectives to the task of depicting the West and, as a result, the West portrayed by the two illustrators was not the same. Although both were popular, Remington's illustrations showed the drama and violence involved in the struggle to tame the West, while Russell's artwork focused more on the workaday world of the cattlemen, trappers, and Indians with whom he was familiar in the Judith Basin of Montana. Remington was an easterner, visiting the West, experiencing it, but returning to his home in the East to paint what he had seen. To that extent Remington was always an "outsider," forced to use his imagination to recreate events and people about which he had no direct knowledge. Russell, on the other hand, was always the "insider," a cowboy who painted, who used his firsthand knowledge and artistic skill to accurately portray the world around him. As a consequence, Russell's artwork became increasingly melancholy as he watched the familiar West disappear. Regardless of the perspective they brought to bear on their subject, both illustrators met a substantial need in the American public for pictures about the "wild" West.

Still another group of illustrators focused on depicting locales outside the United States. It was not unusual for an illustrator travelling abroad on vacation to make sketches that were published in books or magazines when he returned. Edward Penfield's illustrated books on Holland and Spain and Gibson's illustrated book on his travels in Egypt are typical of the genre. Other illustrators were sent abroad on assignment or chose to live abroad, and their pictures gave Americans insights into foreign lands. Andre Castaigne, for example, seems to have drawn pictures of most of the major buildings and towns in Europe during his illustration career. One of the most stunning series of color illustrations was that done by Jules Guerin of the French chateau country and of the Middle East for CENTURY magazine.

Another group of illustrators specialized in illustrating fictional romances. The artwork of F. W. Taylor, Frederic Dorr Steele, George Wright, F. C. Yohn, William G. Stevens, and Louis Hitchcock appeared frequently on the pages of HARPER'S MONTHLY, CENTURY, and SCRIBNER'S magazines, illustrating stories by Harold Bell Wright, George McCutcheon, and other Victorian romanticists. Unfortunately, neither the fiction nor the illustrations are remembered today. In their day, however, the Victorian romances were soap operas for the mass public, and the illustrators played an important role in delineating character and establishing scene and mood. Envision if you can what television soap operas would be like without the picture, and you can better appreciate the value of illustrators to these books.

A number of other non-Brandywine illustrators made important reputations for themselves. Hugh Seton Thompson and Paul Bramson made names for themselves as illustrators of animal life; Thompson did the original illustrations for Jack

London's animal books. May Wilson Preston and A. B. Frost set standards for comedic art; Preston focused on the foibles of everyday family life, while Frost drew panel after panel of rural humor cartoons for HARPER'S MONTHLY and SCRIBNER'S.

Concurrent with the growth in demand for magazine and book illustrations was the poster craze, which first developed in France in the 1880s, when the posters of Henri de Toulouse-Lautrec and Jules Cheret became popular and collectible. This craze spread to England, where the Beggarstaff brothers and Dudley Hardey were the most successful practitioners, and finally arrived in America in the early 1890s. Formal recognition of the importance of poster art was given by the CENTURY poster contest of 1894, won by J. C. Leyendecker, with second place won by Maxfield Parrish. The initial use of posters in America during the 1890s was to advertise magazines and, as a result, magazine illustrators frequently did the poster art. Most successful of the group were Maxfield Parrish, who did posters for CENTURY, SCRIBNER'S, Kodak cameras, and Jell-o; Edward Penfield, who did a monthly series of posters for HARPER'S MONTHLY; and Will Bradley, whose innovative designs had changed the face of magazine covers, and who also did a series of Art Nouveau posters advertising several small magazines, bicycles, and paper.

The American poster craze of the 1890s died within ten years, but poster art was given a fresh impetus by American involvement in World War I. A number of illustrators, under the leadership of Charles Dana Gibson and the Society of Illustrators, devoted their very considerable energies to creating war posters for the government. Howard Chandler Christy, C. B. Falls, James Montgomery Flagg, J. C. Leyendecker, Joseph Pennell, Coles Phillips, Harrison Fisher, and Gibson (to name but a few) lent their talents to creating over two thousand posters promoting war-bond drives, raising money for the Red Cross, soliciting books for soldiers, "over there," recruiting volunteers for the armed forces, and publicizing German atrocities. One of the most enduring was the simple bearded face in red, white, and blue top hat and cutaway, saying, "Uncle Sam Wants You!"— a self-portrait by James Montgomery Flagg.

Illustration art and poster art during the Golden Age of American illustration seem to have been little influenced by contemporary illustration trends in Europe. American illustration was distinctively American, developing its own subject matter, character, and style. One has only to compare the Romantic Realism of Howard Pyle and his students with the fantasy illustrations of Arthur Rackham, Edmund Dulac, and W. Heath Robinson or the "decadent" illustrations of Aubrey Beardsley, Harry Clarke, or Kay Nielsen. There are several reasons why European and American illustration developed differently. First, the Golden Age of American illustration corresponded with the emergence of the United States on the world stage and a growing appreciation at home and abroad of things American. No longer was European culture automatically accepted as superior because it was "European." Second, the literary and artistic traditions in Europe and America diverged substantially. European literature had a very substantial tradition in nonreality fantasy, and European illustration had developed a very real sophistication in fantasy illustration. The American heritage of children's literature was of shorter duration and of different character. This difference can be seen in the fantasy illustrations of Arthur Rackham for PETER PAN IN KENSINGTON GARDEN (1906) or Edmund Dulac's for STORIES FROM THE ARABIAN NIGHTS (1907), which are quite different from those of Maxfield Parrish for POEMS OF CHILDHOOD (1904) or W. W. Denslow's for the most popular American children's fantasy story of the period, THE WONDERFUL WIZARD OF OZ (1900). Third, the longer and more diverse history of European illustration ensured that its subject matter and style would differ from that in America. The Pre-Raphaelites, the Art Nouveau movement, the Arts and Crafts movement, and the Vienna Secession were artistic winds blowing across Europe that had only minimal impact on American illustration. American illustration, searching for its own separate identity, turned inward, identifying its own historical experience as its major source of inspiration. Howard Pyle's advice to his students that they not study abroad because America was enough inspiration was typical of that spirit. Lastly, the role and status of illustrators in Europe and America were quite different. In much of Europe illustrators were regarded as legitimate professional artists, subject to the same accolades, awards, and criticisms as fine artists. Many American illustrators aspired to be fine artists—William Glackens, John Sloan, Edward Hopper, N. C. Wyeth, and Charles Dana Gibson among them—so that the European influence on their work came from fine artists rather than illustrators.

Poster art is one of the few areas in which one can see the impact of European illustration on American artwork. It is possible to see the impact of Japanese wood-block prints, which made substantial use of outline, large masses, and solid colors, on French and British poster art. At the same time the organic naturalism and sinuous line of the Art Nouveau movement can be seen in British and French poster art. The impact of both these European developments can be seen in American poster art. The simple, colorful posters of Edward Penfield, with flat two-dimensional characters and large masses of color, reflect the Japanese wood-block tradition, while Will Bradley's swirling-line- and vine-decorated borders reflect the influence of the Art Nouveau movement. Nonetheless, for many American poster artists, poster art was merely an extension of illustration art. Maxfield Parrish used many of the same asexual adolescents in his poster art and his illustrations. The American Beauty girls looked much the same in World War I uniforms as they did in the latest high fashion. To the extent that American illustration developed independently of European influence, so did American poster art.

THE TRANSITION PERIOD: 1920–1945

World War I effectively marked the end of the Golden Age of American illustration. The number of illustrated books and magazines declined precipitously after World War I, and the reproduction of color illustration in magazines, except for covers, virtually disappeared by the late 1920s. Why? There were a number of factors. First, the economics of publishing had changed. Increased competition between publishers, higher costs for materials, and declining revenues forced many publishers to save money where they could—by cutting back on the number of illustrations or placing a premium on black-and-white and pen-and-ink illustration, which could be reproduced on the same paper stock as the text. As a result, HARPER'S MONTHLY and SCRIBNER'S magazines were quite different from their predecessors twenty years earlier. After World War I, success was measured by having one's artwork published as a magazine cover, particularly for THE SATURDAY EVENING POST.

A second reason for the decline of illustration was photography increasingly replacing artwork as an illustration medium; advances in color photography soon made it a rival for four-color reproductions. Photography had been used in the reproduction of black-and-white as well as color illustrations, but gradually photographs became the dominant illustration medium. Ease of reproduction and comparative cheapness made them more attractive.

Third, the development of radio and motion pictures opened alternative entertainment media for many people who had earlier relied on books and magazines. Consequently, the numbers of mass market magazines declined and cheaper specialty magazines carved a niche in the publications marketplace. At the same time, public tastes changed: John Held's Flapper Girls were "in" and Gibson Girls were "out." So a whole generation of American Beauty illustrators either adapted to changing standards or faced extinction. Some, such as Charles Dana Gibson, could not accept their change in status. Gibson purchased the financially moribund LIFE magazine at the end of World War I and kept it afloat until 1933. Unfortunately, the Gibson Girls of the 1920s and 1930s, even though dressed in appropriate styles, looked strangely out of place.

Fourth, American society and culture had changed as a result of the war. The era of Victorian innocence had ended, and the emergence of the United States as a world power brought a new realism to the American scene. The muckrakers and Progressives had convinced a nation that there were awesome problems to be dealt with, a conclusion reaffirmed by the economic impact of the Depression. American culture and literature changed, and with it came a need for new illustration content and style. Comparatively few illustrators were able to make the transitions from the prewar period to the 1930s with success. Those who made the transition were those able to adapt their illustration styles to a changing society.

Finally, the nature of the illustration profession changed. Only a small number of illustrators were able to maintain their "high society" life-styles in the 1920s and 1930s, and many survived because they were able to diversify their publication base. Maxfield Parrish, for example, moved into producing art prints in the mid-1920s and into calendar art in the 1930s, which provided him with a life-style comparable to what he had maintained as a book and magazine illustrator. Advertising artwork became an attractive, well-paying alternative for many. In the 1920s and 1930s N. C. Wyeth did advertising art for Coca Cola and Frank Schoonover adapted some of his illustrations for the Colt Firearms Co. New illustrators found it difficult to make a name for themselves since many of the traditional sources for selling artwork were no longer available. A number of them, who could work quickly and under pressure, did cover art for a generation of "pulps," low cost, cheap paper, mass market specialty magazines for science fiction, romance, or detective aficionados.

Several illustrators stand out during the interwar period. N. C. Wyeth continued to illustrate juveniles, most notably DRUMS (1928), DAVID BALFOUR (1924), and THE YEARLING (1939) in the Scribner's ILLUSTRATED CLASSICS series. Wyeth's artwork during this period is more mature, showing more clearly his desire to combine fine art with illustration. This is particularly evident in THE YEARLING, which bears closer resemblance to his fine art of the period than to his illustrations of a decade earlier.

Two other illustrators emerged from the war years and maintained their reputations during the next two decades. J. C. Leyendecker, whose poster art and early illustrations had established his reputation, survived World War I by creating the male equivalent of the Gibson Girl—the Arrow Shirt man—self-possessed, urbane, restrained. During the interwar years, Leyendecker's reputation rested on his advertising art for Arrow shirts; Kuppenheimer and Hart, Shaffner, and Marks suits; Interwoven socks (the accoutrements of the thoroughly modern man); and the bulk of the 321 covers he did for THE SATURDAY EVENING POST. His success was the result of his sense of pictorial design; like Coles Phillips, he was conscious of color and shape and used both to focus attention on key elements of his illustrations or advertisements. Two factors led to Leyendecker's decline in popularity in the late 1930s. He was continually on the edge of financial ruin, arguing that such a condition prodded him to continue working, but it actually left him little margin for survival when commissions were slow to arrive. More important, like Gibson, he was unable to "modernize" his hallmark; the Arrow Shirt man of the 1920s looked increasingly out of place in the 1930s. By the end of the 1930s, Leyendecker's popularity had faded.

Norman Rockwell was a full-time illustrator by age eighteen, the art editor of BOY'S LIFE by nineteen, and in his mid-twenties, shortly after World War I, he was already a rich and famous illustrator. Much of Rockwell's fame rested on his covers for THE SATURDAY EVENING POST, most of which were executed between 1920 and 1945. These covers reflect a variety of themes: boy meets girl; home and family life; Americans at work, at play, and in uniform; and growing up—to name a few. He brought a realistic style to the representation of many values central to the American Dream. But his artwork was not tied to time or place; his ability to emphasize the same social values in different settings is the basis for his longevity. The values he depicted remained the same, the context changed. His ability to portray universal values artistically made him immune to becoming dated; two of his POST covers, "Girl in the Mirror" and "Breaking Home Ties," made statements about adolescents growing up that are as relevant today as when first published. One criticism of Rockwell's artwork is its unreality. The Depression never entered his artwork, his paintings during the war showed no carnage, and his people lived in small towns and suburbs like the one where he lived and worked. The criticism is valid, but irrelevant. Rockwell was an optimist who emphasized the positive side of American life and the American experience, and his artwork was appealing to people for just that reason. In fact, when Rockwell's social conscience became quite apparent in his POST covers of the 1950s and 1960s, when he dealt with problems of racial integration in schools and neighborhoods, his artwork was very strong but his popular appeal declined—he had become "political." Throughout Rockwell's artwork one senses a humor and affection for the people, places, and events that he is depicting, allowing people to empathize with the illustration. It was only when he experimented with style (as he did for a time in the 1930s) or his humor became caricature that his artwork was less effective. Rockwell's ability to work as an illustrator for half a century is ample testimony to the universality of his appeal.

Although Leyendecker and Rockwell made the transition from the prewar period, a number of illustrators made names for themselves during the 1920s and 1930s. John Held, Jr., for example, was the illustrator who best captured the saucy irrelevance of the flapper era, in dress and in spirit. It is interesting to contrast the people of Held's world with those who appeared in Leyendecker's. At the height of the Depression, however, the Flapper Girl had become outdated.

Two of the most politically conscious and artistically gifted of the transition period illustrators were Rockwell Kent and Lynd Ward. Rockwell Kent was one of the few illustrators to combine art and politics. Trained as a fine artist under Paul Henri, he underwent a crisis of conscience that changed his life-style; he became a vegetarian, a socialist, and a traveller, who wrote and illustrated books about his travels. Kent's illustration style aptly suited his writing style and the economics of the publishing trade—stark, linear, black-and-white images that reproduced well and provided artistic counterpoint to the printed page. Once the books on his life and travels in Greenland and Alaska had received highly favorable reviews, publishers during the 1920s and 1930s were anxious to have him illustrate their books. Two of his most powerfully illustrated books during this period were MOBY DICK (1930) and BEOWULF (1932). The pictures of the great white whale leaping into a dark, starry night and the clenched fist of Beowulf holding a broadsword aloft are stunning visual images. During the 1930s, however, Kent became increasingly active politically and too controversial for his peers. With the beginning of the Cold War Kent's artwork received scant recognition and he disappeared from the public eye.

Lynd Ward's "books without words," patterned after his Belgian contemporary Frans Masereel, were also books of social protest. MAD MAN'S DRUM (1930) and GOD'S MAN (1930) are novels in illustration format, one woodcut per page, and strikingly effective. They were not particularly popular, however, and Ward began to concentrate on illustrating children's books, for which he received a Caldecott Award in 1952.

Not surprising, the social unrest of the 1920s and 1930s produced other social protest illustrators, such as Art Young, John Sloan, William Glackens, George

Bellows, Jo Davidson, and Boardman Robinson, whose book and magazine illustrations were frequently nonpolitical but who also did illustrations for MASSES and other socialist newspapers and magazines on a no-fee basis. Many illustrator-activists of this period thus led dual lives—publishing much of their artwork in "straight" magazines and books and saving their political artwork for political magazines.

Even with the decline of traditional markets for illustration artwork, some markets still flourished. Western stories continued to use illustration artwork and Will James and Harold Von Schmidt became leading illustrators of western material. James's books, written with a folksy twang and drawn in a loose pen-and-ink style, were "traditional" western fare—stories of men and their horses, of tenderfeet learning to be cowboys. But they were so popular that Scribner's commissioned James to do a series of color oils so that SMOKY (1928) and THE LONE COWBOY (1930) could be republished in their ILLUSTRATED CLASSICS series. Von Schmidt's western illustrations had a gritty realism, which differentiated them from the artwork of Russell, Remington, and James. For Von Schmidt the West was not necessarily a heroic setting for the working out of America's Manifest Destiny but a stage for the expression of human emotions. Thus, one sees the sadness, loneliness, and weariness of the West in much of Von Schmidt's artwork.

Children's books remained a market for illustration material for experienced illustrators like N. C. Wyeth and for a whole generation of new illustrators. Some, like Meade Schaefer, were illustrators in the realistic tradition of Wyeth and Norman Rockwell. Others, many of whom were European immigrants, adapted their own styles to the needs of an American market and children's book illustration benefited greatly from the synthesis. Wanda Gag, Ludwig Bemelmans, Kurt Weise, Helen Sewell, Roger Duvoisin, Robert Lawson, and Dr. Seuss (Theodor Seuss Geisel) emerged from this period as leaders of the field. Even motion pictures had an impact on book illustration; the Disney Studios adapted their animation cels for book production and the Disney animated features were published in book form shortly after their screen appearance.

As noted earlier, a whole new market opened for illustrators—cover art for pulp magazines and paperback books. "Pulps," the heirs of the dime novel and the Big Little Book market, were interested in cover art that was eye catching, representational, and cheap. Artwork credit was rarely given and aficionados learned to recognize a favorite illustrator by style rather than by name. Frank R. Paul's covers did much to establish the popularity of the first all-science-fiction magazine, AMAZING STORIES, but few people outside the field are aware of his name. The paperback market developed in the late 1930s, with the publication of Pocket Books and Avon Books. The initial cover art sought to emulate the cover art of hardcover dust jackets, but the demands of a mass market and the needs of newsstand sales required cover art more like that of the pulps. During World War II, paper shortages imposed limitations on the market for and types of artwork that could be used for covers. As we shall soon see, the postwar period saw substantial changes in the quality of paperback cover art.

By the beginning of World War II American illustration had undergone a transformation. Book and magazine illustration had declined in importance; pulps, paperbacks, and children's books had become more important. Advertising took an increasingly large share of illustration artwork. The need for color artwork declined except for covers on some quality magazines, pulps, and paperbacks. Even the quality of illustration had declined. This is nowhere more evident than in comparing the posters of World Wars I and II. During World War II there was less need for posters since radio and motion pictures (and even television) could be used as domestic propaganda media. As a result, substantially fewer poster designs were used and fewer posters were printed. In addition, the quality of illustration talent to draw on was less than in the earlier war. John Atherton's posters were visually appealing but where were the contemporary counterparts of Falls, Leyendecker, Gibson, Christy, and Flagg? It is a sad commentary that Flagg was asked to recycle his "Uncle Sam Wants You!" poster, with an older Flagg posing for the national symbol. World War II poster art was "meat-cleaver" art: propaganda art with very little artistic merit but effective in communicating its message.

THE ILLUSTRATION RENAISSANCE: 1945–PRESENT

Illustration in postwar America changed, but very slowly. Unlike the 1920s there was not a sudden and volatile shift in American society and culture; the late 1940s were much like the late 1930s except that people were working. Television was still in its infancy, its impact not to be felt until the early 1950s. Some trends that had appeared in the 1930s continued after the war—mass market magazines still suffered from declining circulation, pulps were still popular, specialty magazines became increasingly popular, and the paperback market began a boom that continues unabated today. The children's book and advertising art markets remained strong, although photography made continuing inroads in advertising art.

The 1950s saw television win societal acceptance, marking the beginning of the "visual" era when pictures would once again serve as vehicles for mass communication. The medium became the message. Illustrators were fearful that television, as a technological medium, would destroy their art; instead, they discovered that television, as a visual medium, created new markets for their art. Illustrators began to realize they were no longer limited to traditional illustration media or styles. Soon illustration artwork was seen everywhere—on matchbooks, record album covers (and, more recently, the record vinyl has been illustrated), and in the host of specialty magazines that replaced the major mass market magazines—magazines like SPORTS ILLUSTRATED, TV GUIDE, PEOPLE, and MS. MAGAZINE replaced THE SATURDAY EVENING POST, LOOK, and LIFE magazines. Even posters experienced a renaissance during the 1960s as vehicles of social protest against the war in Vietnam and environmental degradation. Paperback book cover art underwent an interesting metamorphosis from the sexy covers of the late 1940s (who can forget the cover art for I, THE JURY, for example?) to the "cooler" graphic design and typographically appealing covers of the 1970s.

Several technological changes facilitated the development of illustration after World War II. The airbrush, developed before the war, became a commonly accepted and widely used tool for illustrators, giving them far greater technical and artistic virtuosity. A number of illustrators also began to bridge the gap between art and photography, using photographic images as the basis for their illustration artwork. With photomontages and photorealism used in illustrations it became difficult to tell whether illustrations were photographs, artwork, or both. The impact of the next major technological breakthrough—the use of computers in graphics and illustration—has not been fully felt yet. Computer graphics have been widely used in science and technology but have spread more slowly into the field of illustration. But the sale of computer games, with increasingly sophisticated and realistic graphics, will create a demand for computer-generated graphics and illustration art; the development of color tablets for home computers means that more and more people, as well as illustrators, can become skilled color artists with their own television sets.

Aside from changes in the media and technology of illustration, one of the major changes has been in the structure of the profession. With the diffusion of illustration media, no illustrator or group of illustrators has dominated the field like Howard Pyle and his students during the Golden Age, or Norman Rockwell and J. C. Leyendecker during the transitional period. Nonetheless, the overall quality of illustration has improved dramatically during the past twenty years. Even so, the number of illustrators widely recognized by the public is not very great. Since many illustrators specialize in subject matter, they are frequently familiar to people in that specialty but not outside it. Frank Frazetta, for example, is well known to science fiction fans but not to the lay public, at least by name. Maurice Sendak has a devoted following among readers of children's books; Murray Tinkelman's pen-and-ink illustrations are instantly recognizable by style; David Macaulay's architectural renderings of cathedrals and bridges have made him a favorite of children; and Roger Kastel's cover art for JAWS helped symbolize the threat of the man-eating shark. Some illustrators are known primarily to consumers of a particular publication; James McMullan, for example, is best known for his illustrations in NEW YORK magazine.

Illustrators lack global reputations because there is no one medium that is truly global except for television. For an illustrator to achieve a national reputation he or she must do artwork for a variety of media, in a variety of styles, about a variety of subjects. Instead, most illustrators are freelancers, working through agents to get commissions that fit their skills, interests, and pay rates. Some work for advertising agencies, doing commercial art for a livelihood and illustrations or fine art as a sideline. Increasingly, talented illustrators have organized as studios—Push Pin being the most notable example—that have sought commissions for the studio rather than for the individual illustrator. The studio approach has the advantage of guaranteeing a reasonable wage for the illustrator but at the cost of a personal professional identity. And to the extent that studios subcontract parts of the artwork within the studio, an illustrator may find he or she is specializing in trees or buildings or the like.

Although the profession has changed, in some ways it has remained much the same. The Society of Illustrators still serves as a meeting ground in New York for illustrators and editors; more and more illustrators live outside New York, however, so that many of the advantages of having their own building have been lost. Instead, the Society's newsletter and its annual shows serve a valuable communication function for those who rarely get to New York. There are still complaints over pay rates for illustration artwork. Although pay rates have increased over what they were during the 1940s and 1950s (although they are not much higher than they were in 1908) it is difficult to make a living working as a full-time professional illustrator.

Perhaps the greatest change in illustration since World War II has been the change in illustration styles. Whereas American illustration once was immune to influence by either the fine arts or art movements abroad, this is no longer true. The photorealism of Steve Dohanos has been influenced by Norman Rockwell and the European Realist painters. "Pop" art has had a substantial influence on illustration. René Magritte's hyperrealism can be seen in Robert Guisti's illustrations. Another major influence was the development of the counterculture of the 1960s, which liberated illustration from its more traditional styles and, as the counterculture became part of the dominant culture, legitimized psychedelic graphic designs and colors. A whole generation of Americans became acclimated to this style, and Peter Max and his counterparts found markets for their artwork. Nonetheless, the dominant style of American illustration is still "Realism"—whether "Photo-," "Hyper-," or something else.

American illustration, as a popular art form, has had a history of only a century and a half. During that period the quality has improved dramatically, the numbers of illustrators have increased exponentially, and the media of reproduction have changed a number of times. The audience for illustrations has changed as well. As public education became increasingly widespread, the demand for illustration artwork increased, and as the population became more visually literate, there was a corresponding change in the sophistication of illustration styles.

With the increased demand for illustrations, the nature of the field changed as well. It became a full-time professional occupation, with training ultimately entrusted to art schools and schools of graphic design and illustration. As the profession changed so did the relationship between illustrators and the people they worked for, art editors and publishers, the relationship becoming more formal and contractual. Illustrators became business people with brushes. As illustration became more professional and businesslike, it too became subject to the vagaries of the economy as well as the cultural and artistic whims of the public. The decline of illustration during the interwar period can be attributed to changes in public taste and an economic downturn that made color artwork economically unfeasible as an illustration medium. With the economic upturn of the 1950s and 1960s illustration once again became an important communication vehicle.

Finally, illustration has always been responsive to changes in technology—either developments in illustration technology or publication technology. Wood-block engraving made possible the publication of illustrations for a mass public. The use of halftone and four-color printing freed illustrators from reliance on engravers. And some of the traditional boundaries have disappeared. The airbrush gave them greater control of their color and freedom from the brush. Ultimately, computers will serve as both drawing board and color palette for illustrators, giving them greater artistic freedom but tying them more tightly to the means of reproduction. Changes in the technology of printing—from flatbed to rotary presses and greater reliance on photography as a device for reproducing artwork—also have increased the speed, accuracy, and economy of reproducing illustration artwork. Now illustrators can have their artwork faithfully reproduced.

CHAPTER 2

History and Aesthetics of American Illustration

Although American illustration has been the subject of increased research and writing, little attention has been paid to the history and aesthetics of the field. The lack of comprehensive histories (as opposed to histories of specific illustrators or periods) is no doubt the result of the numbers and diversity of people working in the field, which makes it very difficult to provide an overview of its development. In addition, the growth in publication media during the contemporary period has made it virtually impossible to keep track of all the practitioners in the field.

More surprising is the lack of attention to a theory of aesthetics of illustration, particularly in view of the time art historians devote to the aesthetics of the fine arts. One reason for such a deficiency, of course, is that art historians and others have traditionally viewed illustration as a "popular" art, so that aesthetic values and judgments were irrelevant. The "best" illustrations were those that were the most popular with the public—a reasonable criterion but one that makes judgments across time and space next to impossible. Does the fact that Norman Rockwell, J. C. Leyendecker, and Steve Dohanos each did approximately the same number of covers for THE SATURDAY EVENING POST mean that they were equally popular or that their illustration artwork was aesthetically equal? The decline in Leyendecker's popularity in the 1930s, because of his inability to read popular tastes of the period and change his subject matter and style, would indicate the answer is no.

THE HISTORY OF AMERICAN ILLUSTRATION

There are surprisingly few comprehensive histories of American illustration, although a number of people have written histories of different illustration techniques or periods. Henry Pitz's observation in THE PRACTICE OF ILLUSTRATION (1947) that no one has written a comprehensive history of the economic, sociological, and cultural context of American illustration is still true today.

Henry Pitz's 200 YEARS OF AMERICAN ILLUSTRATION (1977), written to celebrate the seventy-fifth anniversary of the Society of Illustrators, is a brief history of the field combined with a glorious collection of 850 pieces of illustration artwork covering the period. Unfortunately, the history does not match the quality of the artwork. A major defect is its brevity; compressing two hundred years of history into eighty-three pages requires greater writing and organizational skills than Pitz commands. The book is initially organized historically, beginning with discussions of the early years: James Audubon and F.O.C. Darley, the Civil War illustrators, and the early western illustrators. When the book enters the Golden Age of illustration, however, it becomes topical, analyzing the impact of Howard Pyle; pen-and-ink artists; children's book illustrators; illustration as history; humor in illustration; and magazine, poster, and advertising illustration. The book concludes with one short chapter on illustration since 1950. Although brief, the Pitz history is useful for those topics that he knows best, particulary Howard Pyle and the Golden Age. And he does provide some useful analysis of the early American illustrators, like Alexander Anderson, Audubon, and Darley. Some of his evaluations are open to criticism; for example, he spends the bulk of one chapter discussing Charles Dana Gibson, suggesting that James Montgomery Flagg, Howard Chandler Christy, and Harrison Fisher were merely talentless imitators. Although Pitz believed they lacked talent, he offers no explanation as to why they were so popular. Another major criticism of the Pitz history is that its brevity forces it to be too superficial—to hit the "high spots," to cover only the "name" illustrators. This defect is remedied to some extent by including the illustration artwork of many people not discussed in the text; the reader is then left with the task of finding out more about the illustrator without any assistance from the book's author. Even then the author doesn't help, by misnaming several illustrators and mislabelling several of the illustrations. The real value of the Pitz volume comes from the visual overview it gives of the richness and diversity of American illustration, qualities not matched by Pitz's historical introduction.

The Clarence P. Hornung and Fridolph Johnson book, 200 YEARS OF AMERICAN GRAPHIC ART (1976), is broader in scope and more historical in approach. It tries to trace the historical development of American graphic arts, including typography, advertising, and design graphics as well as illustration, from 1640 to 1975, considerably more than the two hundred years promised in their title. Although the book fails to achieve its goal, it has some very real virtues. The idea of viewing illustration as part of the graphic arts enables Hornung and Johnson to discuss the development of American illustration within the developmental context of American graphic arts and American culture in general. Part of their discussion of the Golden Age is set within the context of the Gilded Age of American culture that flowed from the Centennial Exposition of 1876. Within their historical analysis, the authors include portfolios showing examples of the types of graphic work they are discussing; in the chapter dealing with the period 1900–1920, for example, there are portfolios of Will Bradley's typographical designs, early magazine covers, and World War I posters. The book concludes with a selective bibliography of materials on book and magazine publishing, printing history, typography and letterforms, advertising history, design and design graphics, illustration, print making, and posters, which is too brief.

The breadth of coverage is not accompanied by a corresponding depth of analysis. A number of topics are not discussed consistently throughout the book; bookbinding, for example, is analyzed during the 1900–1920 period, although bookbinding flourished before and after those dates. Another weakness is their coverage of the post-1950 period, which does not pay sufficient attention to dust jacket and record album art as graphic art forms of the contemporary scene. These defects notwithstanding, this book is the best one available for a look at illustration and the graphic arts, broadly defined.

Frank Weitenkampf's AMERICAN GRAPHIC ART (1912) is a truncated version of the Hornung and Johnson book, tracing the development of various graphic arts until 1912. As one would expect, Weitenkampf spends more time discussing "early" graphic artists and is more sensitive to the role of illustration in the graphic arts. Consequently, the function of illustration as a graphic art is more closely defined and the leading illustrators—Pyle, Gibson, Christy, and Fisher—are analyzed. Weitenkampf also devotes a substantial amount of space to a discussion and analysis of various graphic arts techniques, particularly the role of wood engraving in the development of American illustration. While this book gives a more intensive view of the turn-of-the-century graphic arts than the Hornung and Johnson book, it is obviously dated. Weitenkampf's later book, THE ILLUSTRATED BOOK (1938), has a narrower focus and more breadth, being a history of book illustration from the fifteenth through the twentieth century. This allows Weitenkampf to put the Golden Age of illustration in better perspective, to examine in detail and from a comparative perspective changes in the reproduction of book illustrations, and to compare British and American book illustrators. Like his earlier work, this one is now dated.

A CENTURY OF AMERICAN ILLUSTRATION (1972), an exhibition catalog of the Brooklyn Museum of Arts and Sciences, attempts to trace the development of American illustration through two periods, 1850–1920 and 1920–1972. Much of the value of this catalog, like the Pitz work, is in its visual presentation of American illustration through the years rather than in its text. The major problem, of course, is that an exhibition catalog does not allow sufficient space for the development, in depth, of themes that are crucial to an understanding of the evolution of American illustration. The argument made in this catalog, for example, that illustration is social and cultural history, rather than an adjunct to fine art, is an important one and deserves a more fully developed explication. This catalog ranks as an important first step in that direction.

Lacking a first-rate book on the history of American illustration, it is surprising to find a monumental effort devoted to the history of the illustrated book in the western world. Such a book is John Harthan's THE HISTORY OF THE ILLUSTRATED BOOK: THE WESTERN TRADITION (1981), which covers book illustration from the illuminated manuscripts of the fourteenth century to the "book beautiful" and beyond, 1880–1980. Given this time span it is not surprising that American illustration is considered only in the last two chapters, which cover the period 1800–1980. Harthan describes the period 1800–1880 as the Romantic period of illustration, and Darley and George Catlin are seen as the two American prototypes, although it is not clear why Catlin is regarded as an illustrator or why Darley is regarded as a Romanticist. In his last chapter, "The Book Beautiful—

And After," Harthan covers the last one hundred years of western illustration in Europe and the United States. The "Book Beautiful" movement—which focused on books produced using medieval traditions and high standards—was a predominately European movement, reflecting the Art Nouveau and Arts and Crafts movements in Europe. The only American exponent of the book beautiful, according to Harthan, was Elihu Vedder—who produced very few books, was primarily a fine artist, and spent much of his professional career in Italy. Such analysis overlooks the role played by Edwin Abbey, Pyle, and Bradley in the development of the American book. The discussion of American illustration is necessarily sketchy and concentrates on men who worked during the Golden Age of illustration—Pyle, A. B. Frost, Abbey, Charles M. Russell, Frederic Remington, Edward Kemble, Gibson, and Maxfield Parrish—but neglects the many illustrators who were their contemporaries or followed them.

Harthan's tome is a monumental and lavishly produced work, which seeks to do for illustration what art history texts have done for that field: to give the field a temporally and geographically global perspective. Unfortunately, that perspective tends to downplay the contributions of American illustration because of its short history and its rather idiosyncratic development. And as is frequently the case with art history books, the history of American illustration becomes the history of the "old masters."

Harthan's book, criticisms notwithstanding, is a substantial improvement over Howard Simon's 500 YEARS OF ART AND ILLUSTRATION (1942), which pays no attention to past American illustration and focuses instead on fifteen contemporary illustrators who worked in black-and-white and are primarily woodcut or wood-engraving illustrators. Four pages of text is far too skimpy a coverage, particularly for some of the illustrators—H. L. Glitenkamp, for example—who are little remembered today. David Bland's THE ILLUSTRATION OF BOOKS (1941) suffers from many of the defects noted in Harthan and Simon—too long a time period and too broad a survey to be very revealing about the illustration of American books.

A number of writers have dealt with some segment of the history of illustration. Some have dealt with limited time periods. Rowland Elzea, in THE GOLDEN AGE OF AMERICAN ILLUSTRATION: 1880–1914 (1972), deals with the causes, manifestations, and leading illustrators of one of the premier periods of American illustration. Elzea's analysis constitutes one of the best brief descriptions and analyses currently available, offering insights that are judgmentally sound. For example, Elzea might argue with Weitenkampf's emphasis on book illustration since Elzea notes that magazines were the major publishing sources of illustrations during the Golden Age. Although Joan H. Gorman's introduction to THE ART OF AMERICAN ILLUSTRATION (1976) would appear to cover a broader time period, it focuses most heavily on the Golden Age of American illustration. Its contribution is a short but meaningful discussion of the impact of technological change on the nature of illustration at the end of the nineteenth century. The exhibition catalog also includes brief biographies of artists whose works were included in the exhibit, useful for lesser known artists such as Thure de Thulstrup and Daniel C. Beard. Rowland Elzea and Ann Barton Brown, curators at the Delaware Art Museum and the Brandywine River Museums, respectively, have made, through their writings and the activities of their museums, important contributions to the study of American illustration. For many illustrators, their exhibition catalogs are the only or the best sources of bibliographical or biographical information.

Henry Pitz, in THE BRANDYWINE TRADITION (1968), provides an analysis of one of the leading illustration schools, its teacher Howard Pyle, and some of his most famous students during the period covered by the Elzea catalog. Thus, there is overlap in the two works. There is far more overlap between this book and Pitz's biography, HOWARD PYLE (1975), since Pitz uses some of the same textual material in the two books. In THE BRANDYWINE TRADITION, Pitz tries to show how Pyle and his illustration style flowed naturally from the history and culture of the Brandywine River Valley of Pennsylvania. In the process, according to Pitz, Pyle developed a truly "American" approach to illustration.

THE AMERICAN PERSONALITY: THE ARTIST-ILLUSTRATOR OF LIFE IN THE UNITED STATES, 1860–1930 (1976), an exhibition catalog for the Grunwald Center for the Graphic Arts at the University of California, Los Angeles, contains an interesting set of essays analyzing various facets of American life as depicted in American illustration. The essays deal with the dime novel, women illustrators, children's literature, "special" artists, depicting Americans at leisure, Afro-American artist-illustrators, depicting urban life, pictures of American immigrants, portraying characters from American literature, and the American frontier. Each essay deals with one aspect of American history and culture as depicted in its illustrations, so the focus of the catalog is cultural rather than historical. As might be expected the essays are uneven; the essays on Afro-American and women artist-illustrators are not as useful as they could have been, while those dealing with the dime novel and immigrants are useful and thought provoking, particularly regarding the social role of illustrations. The catalog contains a representative collection of 226 illustrations, short biographies of 116 illustrators, and a selected bibliography of books and articles dealing with American illustration.

CITY LIFE ILLUSTRATED, 1890–1940 (1980), an exhibition catalog from the Delaware Art Museum, examines those illustrators who depicted the urban scene. Essays deal with the illustrations of the "Philadelphia Four"—William Glackens, George Luks, Everett Shinn, and John Sloan—newspaper illustration from 1890 to 1910, realism in magazine illustration from 1900 to 1920, and some examples of satire in book illustration, as well as a series of short biographies of "urban" illustrators of the period. The catalog suffers from a diffuse focus—part of the exhibition deals with the Philadelphia Four, and part deals with those illustrators who depicted the urban scene. Unfortunately, the two parts do not overlap extensively. Also, there is some question as to whether the Philadelphia Four were primarily concerned with depicting the urban scene, or whether the urban scene was merely the tableaux for their personal or political statements.

THE ARTIST AND THE BOOK: 1860–1960 (1961), an exhibit catalog of the Boston Museum of Fine Arts, examines the work of artists who also illustrated books. This catalog allows the reader to see the evolution of "illustrated" books from those works in which the illustrations are designed to illuminate textual events to "illustrated" books that are hardly books except in format. At the same time it is possible to compare the styles of 203 artist-illustrators who have done book illustrations over a one-hundred-year period, ranging from F.O.C. Darley to Pablo Picasso. In the process we can also compare American book illustrations with those of artists from other countries. If nothing else, this catalog reminds us that we must be careful in delineating what we mean by illustration—for the line between illustration and art is becoming even finer.

Walt Reed's volume, THE ILLUSTRATOR IN AMERICA: 1900–1960 (1966), provides a useful introduction to and an overview of the work of leading American illustrators, arranged by decade. Each chapter begins with an essay written by a major illustrator of the decade discussing illustration during that decade; we have Harold Von Schmidt on the period 1900–1910; Arthur William Brown, 1910–1920; Norman Rockwell, 1920–1930; Floyd Davis, 1930–1940; Al Parker, 1940–1950; Austin Briggs on 1950–1960; and Bernard Fuchs on the decade of the 1960s. This edited work contains brief biographies of over two hundred illustrators, including mentions of where their illustrations appeared, and examples of their artwork. The book allows the reader to trace the evolution of American illustration over a sixty-year period. Unfortunately, the book needs an overview that would place each of the chapter analyses in a comparative perspective and would talk about trends in illustration, the longevity of illustrators, and illustration styles. One must occasionally guess where a long-lived illustrator's work will appear. N. C. Wyeth, for example, is located in the decade 1910–1920, but the bulk of his book illustration occurred during the following decade. Nonetheless, merely skimming through it gives one a sense of the continuity and change within the field of American illustration. Another book in the "great" illustrators tradition is Susan Meyer's AMERICA'S GREAT ILLUSTRATORS (1978). She analyzes in depth ten "great" illustrators—Howard Pyle, N. C. Wyeth, Frederic Remington, Maxfield Parrish, J. C. Leyendecker, Norman Rockwell, Charles Dana Gibson, Howard Chandler Christy, James Montgomery Flagg, and John Held, Jr.— and provides examples of their artwork and a comparative chronology. Obviously, one can argue with her choice of "great" illustrators, but her analysis of these ten is solid, particularly considering the little space available. The introduction to the volume is a rare, and very valuable, comparison of the ten illustrators.

Reed's later book, GREAT AMERICAN ILLUSTRATORS (1979), is a slender volume that provides more information on fewer illustrators than his earlier work, with fewer, but larger, examples of their artwork. The paucity of information makes it less useful than Meyer's AMERICA'S GREAT ILLUSTRATORS (1978) for those illustrators covered in both books. At the same time, GREAT AMERICAN ILLUSTRATORS has fewer illustrators than THE ILLUSTRATOR IN AMERICA:1900–1960 (1966) but provides more information than in that book.

Overall, the size, price, and availability of this later book make it an attractive introductory text in illustration courses, a distinction formerly held by Pitz's 200 YEARS OF AMERICAN ILLUSTRATION (1977), now out of print.

Other works have dealt with specialized facets of the history of illustration. Jeff Dykes, FIFTY GREAT WESTERN ILLUSTRATORS (1975); Peter Hassrick, THE WAY WEST: ART OF FRONTIER AMERICA (1977); and Robert Taft, ARTISTS AND ILLUSTRATORS OF THE OLD WEST, 1850–1900 (1953) all deal with some aspect of "western" illustration. Taft and Dykes deal in a biographical and bibliographical way with the major western artists of the period they are studying; Taft focuses on the last half of the nineteenth century, while Dykes catalogs the later nineteenth and twentieth centuries. Taft biographically recounts the histories of some of the early western illustrators and the work they did, including a critique of much of their work; also included is the interesting and petty controversy between Frederic Remington and Charles Schreyvogel over the accuracy of clothing depicted in Schreyvogel's popular piece, "My Bunkie." Dykes's work is more bibliographical, including catalogs of art exhibitions and galleries where work was displayed, works illustrated by the artists, and articles dealing with the artist and his work. Dykes's book is easily the most comprehensive listing of works by and about western artists but it is curiously uneven; artists whose work was not primarily western are included—A. I. Keller, E. Boyd Smith, and N. C. Wyeth—while Charles Russell is not, because his work has been cataloged by Yost and Renner in A BIBLIOGRAPHY OF THE PUBLISHED WORKS OF CHARLES M. RUSSELL (1971). The entries for those western illustrators included are not complete, although major illustrated works are listed. In addition, there are bibliographical errors in many of Dykes's entries, making them of limited utility for the book collector seeking information on first editions. Nonetheless, Dykes's book still stands as the best starting point for anyone interested in exploring the work of American western illustrators.

Hassrick's book is an attempt to place western art within a larger context; indeed, he argues that western artists were part of the mainstream of fine art, not proponents of a separate discipline. There is a description and brief analysis of a number of western artists, and Hassrick uses various artists' works to show how they treated subjects and events in Western history. The discussion is interesting because of Hassrick's contention that western art is part of the mainstream of American art, and his inclusion of some American illustrators in his analysis, for example, N. C. Wyeth, makes an unintentionally strong case that American illustration falls within the mainstream of American art as well.

The history of children's illustration has received extensive, and generally good, treatment. The Mahoney, Latimer, and Folmsbee volume, ILLUSTRATORS OF CHILDREN'S BOOKS: 1744–1945 (1947) and its supplements—Ruth Hill Viguers, Marcia Dalphin, and Bertha Mahoney Miller, ILLUSTRATORS OF CHILDREN'S BOOKS, 1946–1956 (1958); Lee Kingman, Joanna Foster, and Ruth Giles Lontoft, ILLUSTRATORS OF CHILDREN'S BOOKS, 1957–1966 (1968); and Lee Kingman, Grace Allen Hogarth, and Harriet Quimby, ILLUSTRATORS

OF CHILDREN'S BOOKS, 1967–1976 (1978)—provide the most comprehensive analysis of children's illustration. The initial book includes chapters on illustrated books for children before 1800, nineteenth-century English illustrators, early American illustrators, Howard Pyle and his influence, illustrators of children's classics, and developments of the twentieth-century. Each subsequent book analyzes developments over the previous ten years and analyzes special segments of the field. Overall, the quality of analysis is excellent, giving the reader an understanding of the development of children's illustration in America and abroad, providing insights into specific illustrators, and analyzing some of the major illustrated books. Phillip Hofer's analysis in the 1947 volume of how various illustrators have dealt with the classics is one of the few comparative analyses of illustrations. The value of the book is increased by the inclusion of biographies of major illustrators and bibliographies of illustrators' works and of authors, indicating who illustrated their books.

Barbara Bader's book, AMERICAN PICTURE BOOKS FROM NOAH'S ARK TO THE BEAST WITHIN (1976), takes a different approach. Within a broadly historical perspective she discusses and analyzes the major children's book illustrators and their work. Her analysis is more global in scope and her taste more eclectic than that exhibited in the Mahoney, Latimer, and Folmsbee series; she is not afraid to select heretofore unacclaimed illustrators for praise. For example, she singles out E. Boyd Smith for his children's book illustrations and C. B. Falls for his ABC book, arguing persuasively that both merit attention for the quality of their artwork, even though they had few followers and made no major impact on American illustration. Unfortunately, Bader's book is neither systematic nor comprehensive. She devotes chapters to people—Dr. Seuss—and subjects—Golden Books—that are important elements of children's book illustration, examines topics like social change, books depicting blacks, and children's informational books, but leaves unmentioned important illustrators, such as Nancy Eckholm Burkert. The bibliography included lists some of the more "fugitive" magazine and periodical literature written about the illustrators Bader discusses, and demonstrates the paucity of material on many of them. The Bader book, along with the Mahoney, Latimer, and Folmsbee book, thus provides the researcher with a very sound base for studying the history of children's illustration.

A third approach is found in Joyce Irene Whalley's COBWEBS TO CATCH FLIES (1975), an analysis of various types of early American children's books, which can be read profitably in conjunction with Virginia Haviland and Margaret Coughlan's YANKEE DOODLE'S LITERARY SAMPLER OF PROSE, POETRY AND PICTURES (1974), which provides examples of various types of early American children's books. Using somewhat the same approach but far more uneven is Ruth Freeman's CHILDREN'S PICTURE BOOKS: YESTERDAY AND TODAY (1967). The history of picture books, for example, is covered in one chapter, which argues that pictures in children's books are no longer used to illustrate the text but as an end in themselves. The change in the function of book illustrations may have as much to do with changes in children as with fundamental changes in book illustration, as Freeman suggests. There is an interesting chapter devoted to analyses of major bibliographical works, in which Freeman is critical of the Mahoney, Latimer, and Folmsbee book because the bibliography is organized by illustrator rather than by subject matter. The former approach is more useful if you are interested in which works an illustrator had done, while the latter works best if you are interested in who illustrated a specific genre of children's books. The chapter on public library collections of children's books is useful, particularly to the novice collector, although her analysis of the Rosenbach collection (a major collection of children's books now at the Library of Congress)—"primarily American and much of it could be called Sunday School picture books"—would not be supported by those who have seen and worked with the collection. The latter part of the book is a largely self-serving description of the Ruth S. Freeman collection of children's books. She classifies children's books into ten categories—alphabet books, Mother Goose and related jingles, nature and animals, humor, horror and nonsense tales, historical subjects, activity and adventure tales, family and home stories, seasonal tales, trick pop-up and game books, and fairy or fanciful tales—which she uses to list her collection. The categories are not mutually exclusive (what is the difference between fairy tales, fanciful tales, horror stories, and nonsense tales?), and while the field needs a classification schema, Freeman's is not the one.

There are a number of books that deal with the history of children's books but not in depth. YANKEE DOODLE'S LITERARY SAMPLER (1974), for example, is a picture book of children's books printed in America during the eighteenth and nineteenth centuries and found in the Library of Congress. EARLY CHILDREN'S BOOKS AND THEIR ILLUSTRATION (1975) is a compendium of various types of children's books—ABC's, primers, fairy tales, and so on—housed in the Pierpont Morgan Library, with brief descriptions (and pictures) of exemplars in each category. Since much of the material is pre-1900, the emphasis is more British than American. In both cases, the purpose of the works is not to provide a history of the field, but the description and presentation of the materials does give a historical overview, albeit from the perspective of the books contained within the respective collections. Bertha Woolman's book, THE CALDECOTT AWARD (1978), provides an interesting historical perspective on all the Caldecott Award winners and honor books during the period 1938–1977. The book contains brief biographies and descriptions of the work habits of all award winners—arranged alphabetically—so that one can examine how the nature of children's book illustration, as exemplified by these award winners, has changed, but it requires work to organize them historically. Lee Kingman's books on the Newberry and Caldecott Medal winners (1965, 1975) reprint the speeches of the winners in each decade.

A number of books have dealt with the history of science fiction illustration, but usually as an adjunct to a broader discussion of the history of science fiction literature. David Kyle's book, A PICTORIAL HISTORY OF SCIENCE FICTION (1976), for example, gives an excellent set of book and pulp magazine illustrations along with its discussion of the development of science fiction in general. Several books have focused on the history of science fiction art specifically. Anthony Frewin's ONE HUNDRED YEARS OF SCIENCE FICTION ILLUSTRATION: 1840–1940 (1974) is the best of the group because he weaves his analysis of illustration artwork with the history of science fiction literature. In the process, for example, one becomes aware of how much the success of some of the early writers and editors depended on their illustrators; Hugo Gernsback's success as publisher of AMAZING STORIES during the 1920s was at least partly attributable to the fine illustration artwork of Frank R. Paul. Equally important, the reproduction of a large number of covers enables the reader to study the styles of various illustrators and to see how styles varied by magazine and over time. Ian Summers examines the contemporary scene (1950–1978) in TOMORROW AND BEYOND: MASTERPIECES OF SCIENCE FICTION ART (1978). This book represents the work of sixty-five illustrators, organized by type of illustration, that is, aliens, astronauts, barbarians, and so on. It is interesting to compare the artwork from Summers's book with that of the earlier pulp magazine era as seen in Frewin's book. There are obviously differences in the quality and style of artwork, but the major difference is in the depiction of what constitutes the "unknown" and how it is to be depicted. Once we have sent unmanned spaceships to Mars and Venus and learned they are uninhabited it is difficult to draw Martians as small green humanoids with two heads. Peter Haining uses a somewhat broader context—horror illustrations—for his book, TERROR!: A HISTORY OF HORROR ILLUSTRATIONS FROM THE PULP MAGAZINES (1976), which traces the history of terror illustrations through two hundred years of popular magazines, from the British gothic chapbooks and shilling shockers to the present. Two very long chapters are devoted to the development of pulp magazines and a historical analysis of the first all-fantasy publication, WEIRD TALES. The illustrations used in the book are largely in black-and-white (as they were in the originals), with some covers reproduced in color. Haining's book is useful because of its breadth of outlook and the quality of analysis, which consistently relates the development of pulp magazines and their illustrations to the culture of which they were a part. Unfortunately, the three authors have differing perspectives on the state of the art; Haining sees horror illustration as a dying tradition, Kyle sees the nature of science fiction illustration changing, while Summers finds it at a highly creative period.

The history of paperback art in general also has been the subject of recent books. Geoffrey O'Brien's, HARD-BOILED AMERICA: THE LURID YEARS OF PAPERBACKS (1981), is an excellent effort to relate changes in cultural values with changes in the texts and cover art of "hard-boiled," that is "private eye," paperbacks. In the process, O'Brien also discusses paperback cover art within the status hierarchy of American illustration, suggesting that most paperback illustrators viewed working for paperback firms as a place to start, a way of making a living, on the road to more prestigious assignments with THE SATURDAY EVENING POST. There is an excellent discussion of the leading cover artists—Stanley Metzoff, Leo Manso, James Avati—illustrators little known to the public at large. Piet Schreuders's book, PAPERBACKS, U.S.A.: A GRAPHIC HISTORY, 1939–1959 (1981), has a broader perspective. His concern is with the development of paperback art, regardless of subject matter. This breadth of concern makes his focus different from that of O'Brien; Schreuders's book is more a history of paperback publishing, and his analysis argues that cover art was less responsive to text than to public taste. As a result, trends in cover art are divided into five periods: the war years, the immediate postwar period, the sex era, the beginning of the 1950s, and the modern era of the late 1950s. In the process of analyzing changes in cover art, Schreuders discusses the role of art editors, the technical aspects of cover art production, and the leading contemporary paperback illustrators. The appendixes to this book are not to be overlooked. They include a year-by-year review of paperback book publication; an overview of American paperback publishers; a list of the first one hundred paperbacks published by Pocket Books, Avon, Penguin, Popular Library, Dell, Bantam, and Signet; and an excellent section on collecting paperbacks. But the most useful appendix is the "Who's Who" in cover art—bibliographical and biographical snapshots of 174 cover illustrators, providing information on people little known outside the field, and identifying some of their best artwork sources. As useful as the Schreuders book is, it suffers from its limited time perspective. Certainly the number of paperbacks has probably doubled since 1959 and a whole generation of paperback cover artists have published artwork that is not covered by Schreuders's excellent book.

More recently, Thomas Bonn's UNDERCOVER: AN ILLUSTRATED HISTORY OF AMERICAN MASS MARKET PAPERBACKS (1982) devotes one section to paperback cover art. There is one chapter devoted to the history of paperback art, in far less detail than Schreuders's book but bringing that history up to date. There is also an excellent chapter on the relationship between the art editor, illustrator, and the text. In addition, there are a number of examples of cover art in color. Unfortunately, Bonn's book suffers in comparison with Schreuders's: there is no bibliography, no biographical listing of major paperback artists, nor is there as complete a collection of cover art. The major advantage of the Bonn book is its inclusion of more contemporary cover art.

There are also several histories of emphemeral illustration. Chris Mullen has written one definitive history in CIGARETTE PACK ART (1979), which traces cigarette package design from the World War I period to the present, showing examples of various styles and tracing the evolution of the genre. Kurt Weidemann has edited BOOK JACKETS AND RECORD COVERS: AN INTERNATIONAL SURVEY (1969), which combines a historical overview of the two types of cover illustration. The section on book jackets is short but well written and duplicates some of the points made by Schreuders and Bonn in their discussion of paperback art. Weidemann points out that initially book jackets were to reflect the contents of the book, but more recently book jackets have assumed the same functions as the paperback cover—to meet the advertising methods and aims of the publisher.

The analysis of record covers is briefer (given their shorter history) but suggests that contemporary record covers serve the same function as book jackets—to sell the product. The bulk of the book is devoted to showing 300 book covers and 127 album covers from various countries, most of them contemporary. Brad Benedict and Linda Barton, in PHONOGRAPHICS: CONTEMPORARY ALBUM COVER ART AND DESIGN (1977), focus more intensely on album covers, particularly covers from the late 1950s, tracing their evolution from the drug-inspired rock art of that period to the more abstract and "cool" art of the 1970s.

Surprisingly little has been written about advertising art. Clarence Hornung's HANDBOOK OF EARLY ADVERTISING ART, VOLS. I AND II (1947) was one of the first attempts to trace the development of advertising artwork, particularly the use of wood engravers and the development of job printers to handle much of the burden of early advertising. Volume I focuses on illustration art, and Volume II is devoted to advertising typography and typographical ornaments, in both cases devoting the analysis to pre-Civil War advertising art. Aside from its discussion of early wood engravers, this book is useful for its discussion of the relationship between reproduction processes and the content and style of early advertising art; the cost of creating new typefaces and plates, for example, meant that much of the early advertising art was repetitive, using whatever typefaces and illustration plates the print shop had available at the time. A more recent book by Victor Margolin and Ira and Vivian Brichta, THE PROMISE AND THE PRODUCT: 200 YEARS OF AMERICAN ADVERTISING POSTERS (1979), takes a more comprehensive view of advertising art, tracing its evolution from painted wooden signs in front of colonial inns to highway billboards screaming for our attention as we drive on superhighways. Early posters were designed to provide information, but the bicycle posters of the 1890s were designed as works of art to draw attention to the product and bestow prestige on the manufacturer. The development of the automobile led to the use of billboards as advertising media and the evolution of many of the qualities of contemporary advertising art—simple message and large clear illustrations in bright and contrasting colors. The technological explosion of the post-World War II period, combined with advances in market research, led to changes in the use and look of advertising posters by the late 1960s. Margolin et al. document these changes in their analysis and provide examples of various types of advertising art at different points in history. Although the textual material is excellent, the book suffers from a lack of color reproductions, which would more clearly demonstrate the change from advertising art as an information conveyer to that of a product seller. A similar defect occurs in Atwar, McQuade, and Wright's EDSELS, LUCKIES, AND FRIGIDAIRES (1979). This deficiency in Margolin et al. and Atwar et al. is remedied in Bryan Holme's ADVERTISING: REFLECTIONS OF A CENTURY (1982), a beautifully produced compendium of black-and-white and color advertisements for the period 1880–1980. Each section begins with a historical preface outlining the major cultural and historical events that occurred during each twenty-year period. But there is little effort in the text to tie cultural and historical changes to changes in advertising media and content, a focus that is far more explicit in THE PROMISE AND THE PRODUCT. Together, they make a lovely marriage.

The history of poster art in general has been the subject of several excellent books. Ervine Metzl's book THE POSTER: ITS HISTORY AND ITS ART (1967) and Bevis Hillier's POSTERS (1969) provide the best historical overview of this genre. Both trace the history of American poster art back to the French posters of Jules Cheret and Henri de Toulouse-Lautrec, through the Beggarstaffs in England, and to the American poster artists of the 1890s—Edward Penfield, Maxfield Parrish, J. C. Leyendecker, and Will Bradley. Hillier divides his history into three periods: pre-1914, 1914–1939, and the modern period, post-1939. Within each time period he examines the major poster artists and movements. Hillier has favorites, but he also states why he likes some and not others. He is an admirer of Will Bradley's posters, for example, but he thinks Maxfield Parrish's posters, while they are good art, fail as posters. Hillier also has good discussions of poster art during the two world wars, particularly World War I, and post-World War II poster art.

Metzl's book is also organized historically. He discusses and analyzes the leading European and American poster artists from Cheret through the post-World War II period. His analysis is trenchant but fair; his comparison of Cheret and Toulouse-Lautrec is sound and insightful; and he assigns the premier position in American poster art during the 1890s to Edward Penfield rather than Will Bradley or Maxfield Parrish. But Metzl's major contribution, as we shall soon see, is his effort to develop criteria for judging the quality of poster art, criteria that are then applied in his evaluation of various poster artists.

Max Gallo's book, THE POSTER IN HISTORY (1972), while examining the historical development of posters, concentrates on their social and political role. Thus, his emphasis is on the poster as a popular or political art form and he is less interested in the people who did poster art than in the content of their posters and their impact on society, an interest shared by Gary Yanker in PROP ART (1972), which focuses on post-World War II political posters. Yanker's book thus can be viewed as a continuation and more contemporary version of Gallo's excellent work.

Victor Margolin's book, AMERICAN POSTER RENAISSANCE (1975), takes a narrower time perspective, suggesting that poster art of the 1890s represented a high point in American art, having an important effect on the visual arts because it introduced the American public to the Art Nouveau movement and Post-Impressionism. Margolin differentiates between three different poster styles—the decorative, the descriptive, and illustrative, exemplified by Will Bradley, Edward Penfield, and Maxfield Parrish, respectively—describing the activities of these representative poster artists and providing examples of their products. Looking at much the same period, Larry Freeman in VICTORIAN POSTERS (1969) examines various types of poster art, that is, for clothing, fashion, food, household aids, liquor and tobacco, patent medicines, and the like. This focus on advertising posters during the Victorian era makes this book an interesting adjunct to Margolin's books on poster art and advertising art, as well as Holme's book on advertising. Indeed, Freeman's book acknowledges the dual nature of poster art—he discusses posters as pictorial art forms and as sales devices. The bulk of the book is devoted to showing examples of the latter. Unfortunately, as with the Margolin book on advertising art, the illustrations are in black-and-white, whereas color would have made the distinction between advertising and art posters more clear.

Several writers have analyzed the posters of World Wars I and II. Julian Street's article in McCLURE'S (1918) is one of the best brief summaries and analyses of American World War I posters, giving examples of posters by Wallace Morgan, Henry Raleigh, Neysa McMein, Adolph Treidler, and Gari Milcher—poster artists whose works are rarely seen in modern poster art books. For this reason it is interesting to see artistic judgments made by peers rather than in historical retrospect.

Among the best sources of information on World War I posters are the various biographies of illustrators who worked as poster artists during this period—particularly J. C. Leyendecker, Howard Chandler Christy, James Montgomery Flagg, and Coles Phillips.

Although the poster art of World War II was far inferior to that of World War I, Zbynek Zeman's book, SELLING THE WAR (1978), is a short but useful thematic analysis of those posters. Zeman is not concerned with posters as works of art or as recruiting devices (the draft negated that need), but as propaganda devices that to be effective had to be direct, immediate, and easily understood. Five themes are examined: your country needs you (the appeal to patriotism), you never know who's listening (designed to control gossip), back them up (the campaign for war production), united we are strong (war as an international crusade), and behold the enemy (the enemy as savage barbarians). Examples of each theme are shown.

Post-World War II posters are examined in two quite different books, IMAGES OF AN ERA: THE AMERICAN POSTER 1945–75 (1975) and Gary Yanker's PROP ART (1972). IMAGES is an attempt to give a pictorial overview of postwar poster art, starting with the assumption that World War II represented a watershed in poster art and that postwar posters have been more visual, more graphic, and indeed more photographic than their prewar predecessors. The 275 contemporary posters presented in this exhibition catalog give evidence that there is some merit to this assumption. Gary Yanker suggests the postwar posters have not only become more visual but also more political in content, and that some of the best poster art has been done on behalf of various causes. His symbolic analysis of propaganda posters, mainly from the post-World War II period, suggests certain commonalities as to sponsorship, function, modes of presentation, and symbols. It is interesting to see, for example, that certain ideological symbols appear to be timeless—the flag, the eagle, the cross, peace symbols, and the raised rifle appear in a variety of posters through time. The book also contains an excellent collection of propaganda posters, in color and black and white, to exemplify the various symbolic themes.

We see in poster art the same phenomenon we see in illustration in general during the post-World War II period, the lessening in importance of the "name" poster artist. In poster art, as in illustration generally, the quality of the artwork and its content have become more important than who designed or executed them. The medium has become the message.

Much of the history of post-World War II illustration still waits to be written. The artistic development of the field can be seen in the Annuals of the Society of Illustrators, ILLUSTRATOR, since 1951, and ILLUSTRATORS IN THE THIRD DIMENSION (1978); a fascinating book by the American Institute of Graphic Arts, THE MENTAL PICTURE III: PORTRAITS (1978), which shows how illustration has expanded its boundaries; GRAPHIC DESIGNERS IN THE USA/3 (1972), a presentation of artwork and interviews with leading illustrators; MAGIC AND OTHER REALISM: THE ART OF ILLUSION (1980); and Walt Reed's NORTHERN LIGHTS COLLECTION (1979), as well as books analyzing individual illustrators, such as Alan Cober's COBER'S CHOICE (1979), David Levine's THE ARTS OF DAVID LEVINE (1978), Daniel Kagan's THE IL-LUSTRATIONS OF MURRAY TINKELMAN (1980), and James McMullan's REVEALING ILLUSTRATIONS (1981).

CRITIQUES AND AESTHETIC THEORIES OF ILLUSTRATION

Although a great deal of verbiage has been devoted to various facets of the history of illustration there has not been a corresponding commitment to its analysis and criticism. There are a number of important questions to be asked and answered. What is illustration? How is illustration different from fine art? What is illustration's place in the arts? What criteria can be used for judging illustration? Answers to these questions have been hard to find because the questions, except for the first, have rarely been asked.

F. J. Harvey Darton, in MODERN BOOK ILLUSTRATION IN GREAT BRIT-AIN AND AMERICA (1931), raised a fundamental question for illustrators working with textual material—do you illustrate the text, do the illustrations complement the text, or are the illustrations the artist's projections of the author's ideas? Darton suggests that historically all three views have had credibility. The most traditional view has been that the purpose of illustration is to give a visual image to what the author is saying. The modern view would be that an illustration is an artist's response to the same forces that inspired the author and, as a result, may have little or nothing to say about the text. Given this range of views on the nature of illustration, it is obviously difficult to make aesthetic judgments about the quality of illustrations unless one knows what the illustrator intended them to do.

This artistic functionalism argument has been developed by Alan Gowans in two books, THE UNCHANGING ARTS (1971) and LEARNING TO SEE: HIS-TORICAL PERSPECTIVE ON MODERN POPULAR/COMMERCIAL ARTS

(1981). Gowans differentiates between "high" art, produced by serious artists for exhibition in museums, and "low" art, popular-commercial art used in everyday life. Low art performs four functions for society: substitute imagery, illustration, beautification, and conviction and persuasion. In THE UNCHANGING ARTS Gowans describes illustration as the typical art of the nineteenth-century, and for the period 1890–1930 it was typically done by professional illustrators who considered their work to be totally different from fine art. As we shall later see, there were a number of artist-illustrators who worked at illustration not as a profession but as a way of making a living until they had established themselves as fine artists. And some professional illustrators were torn between their profession and their aspirations to be recognized as fine artists. Building on this set of distinctions in LEARNING TO SEE, Gowans argues that low or popular-commercial art always reflects the society in which it is embedded. "Avant-garde arts belong in histories OF art. If you want to write about history IN art, then for our times, the documents to use are its popular/commercial arts" (p.23). If the initial assumption is correct—that popular-commercial art reflects the society of which it is a part— then a number of hypotheses can be derived. First, and foremost, what is chosen to be illustrated constitutes an assertion of values. Unfortunately, it is not clear whose values are being asserted—the author's, the illustrator's, the publisher's, or the public's, which serves as a market for the illustrator's work. Gowans's answer seems to be that it is the illustrator responding to the public's values in ways that appeal to them. Taken to its logical conclusion one could argue that the "best" illustrations (those that embody societal values) are those that are published in successful magazines, and that the "best" illustrators are those who have their artwork most widely published. Such an argument has the advantage of freeing us from comparing illustrators of different cultures or historical periods, except in terms of their comparative popularity in their cultures or time periods.

Unfortunately, Gowans does not follow this logical thread. Instead, he has other ends. In the concluding chapter of LEARNING TO SEE, he develops a comprehensive framework for the analysis of all art—high, low, primitive, even children's. In a tabular finale he ties together temporal age, social functions of children's art, characteristic art forms, thought processes, corresponding stages of developmental psychology, and corresponding types of time awareness into a global framework that attempts to correlate children's mental and creative growth with historic arts of the ancient world: a possible ontogeny repeats phylogeny paradigm. But this paradigm raises more questions than it answers. The social functions of art—substitute imagery, illustration, beautification, and persuasion and conviction—are a function of age and psychological development. But the age and psychological development of what? Children? No. More logically, the paradigm would appear to be relevant for an understanding of how and when various facets of popular-commercial art develop within societies. If that is the case we have an argument that the development pattern of children parallels the artistic development of societies. Gowans argues that there is substantial evidence that the parallelism does exist. I am far more impressed with Gowans's discussion of the social functions of art than I am comfortable with his presentation of Jean Piaget's theories (which acknowledges none of the criticism of Piaget's work). However, by presenting this global paradigm in the last chapter, with only minimal discussion of the developmental psychology material on which the theory rests, there is little space to develop his argument. Charitably, one can say that his "possible paradigm" is just that—possible. Whether it is a paradigm, in the Kuhnian sense of the word, is another question.

Other authors have attempted to explain the development of American illustration in less global terms. Much of their attention has been focused on the Golden Age of American illustration in an attempt to explain why it occurred, when, and how it did and to understand its importance. John Tomsich, in A GENTEEL ENDEAVOR: AMERICAN CULTURE AND POLITICS IN THE GILDED AGE (1971), attempts to lay the groundwork for understanding the development of American culture through the late nineteenth and early twentieth-centuries. Tomsich characterizes the period as a conflict between those cultural conservatives of the Genteel Tradition and their critics. This cultural elite—which commanded the major cultural institutions of the period—sought to protect and promote Culture among the masses; they were pessimistic about human nature, feared democracy, and valued order, discipline, scholarship, and tradition. In his book, Tomsich focuses on eight men who were part of this cultural elite and shows the extent to which they thought and acted alike. Unfortunately, Tomsich does not spend as much time on those imperilling the cultural elite. Implicitly they were urban, Catholic ethnics who had not gone to the "right" schools or shared the same background as the cultural elite. They were not a "counter"-elite, seeking to displace the traditional elite while maintaining the same values but an elite of "new" men, with a new and different set of cultural values. Subsequently, the threat they posed was revolutionary rather than evolutionary.

In HERE THE COUNTRY LIES: NATIONALISM AND ART IN TWENTIETH CENTURY AMERICA (1980), Charles Alexander focuses more narrowly and insightfully on the conflict between the Genteel Tradition and its attackers within the arts. Alexander's book defines the Genteel Tradition more clearly than that of Tomsich, assigning to the cultural elite two roles: to erect barriers against the increased vulgarity of the democratic age, and to inspire and uplift, to enlighten and teach those whose standards made the art of the democratic age so vulgar. The insurgents, led by Van Wyck Brooks, Frank Lloyd Wright, Robert Henri, Alfred Stieglitz, and Scott Joplin, attacked the defenders of the Genteel Age on the grounds that the contemporary arts had no relevance for contemporary American life. The rebellion lasted, according to Alexander, from 1900 to 1914 and produced in art and illustration the romantic nationalism of the 1920s and 1930s and the modernism of the 1940s.

Jerome Mellquist (THE EMERGENCE OF AN AMERICAN ART [1942]) would agree with Alexander on the general developmental outline but would disagree somewhat on specifics. For Mellquist, the artistic revolt against the Genteel Tradition was led by the "Realists" of the "Ash Can" school, under the tutelage of Robert Henri. At the same time there was a "Realist" revolt in illustration, which produced a "Silver Age" of American illustration (1905–1915) to follow the "Golden Age." The Silver Age introduced a gritty Social Realism into illustration, with Boardman Robinson, Arthur Dove, Henry Raleigh, Wallace Morgan, and F. R. Gruger as its leading proponents. It is interesting that the Delaware Art Museum exhibition catalog, CITY LIFE ILLUSTRATED, 1890–1940 (1980), makes much the same argument about the rise of Social Realism in illustration but includes a somewhat different set of illustrators as its proponents. Among this set of Social Realist illustrators are William Glackens and John Sloan, members of the Ash Can school of art.

By 1915 the Silver Age of illustration had ended, according to Mellquist. Some of the more ambitious illustrators had become painters, others began working for advertisers to make more money from their artwork, and still others went with the mainstream of American illustration. But Alexander and Tomsich would argue that the Silver Age ended because the revolutionaries had won—the mainstream of American art and illustration now included their work. While this might be true in the fine arts, the revolutionaries did not carry the day in illustration. If we examine the leading illustrators of the postwar period, it is hard to envision Norman Rockwell and J. C. Leyendecker as revolutionaries. And the heirs of Boardman Robinson, Arthur Dove, and F. R. Gruger were not the leaders of the next generation of illustrators; Lynd Ward and Rockwell Kent were always on the fringes of legitimate illustration rather than in the mainstream. All too few books have attempted to compare a group of illustrators working in the same time period or working on the same material. The introduction to Susan Meyer's AMERICA'S GREAT ILLUSTRATORS (1978) includes her effort to compare and contrast the life styles and artistic styles of ten of America's "great" illustrators from the Golden Age of illustration. Her conclusions, while interesting, are not startlingly insightful. These "greats" were American—by birth, temperament, and subject matter—and they played an important role in making Americans conscious of their nationhood. Their greatness was translated into lavish incomes (one reason why their period is called the "Golden" Age of illustration) and corresponding life styles, even for the more rural-living types like Pyle and Wyeth. They had a common wariness of too much emphasis on technique—subject matter was more important. They were all hard workers (is that a sign of their greatness or a cause?), and they were not in total agreement about the value of illustration nor were they committed to illustration as a career—Pyle and Harrison Fisher were committed to illustration as a profession, while Wyeth and Remington aspired to be fine artists. Less important than Meyer's conclusions is her attempt to say something about the nature of illustrators and illustration by directly comparing a number of illustrators. Far too little of this type of analysis has been done; instead, the focus has been on exploring one illustrator at a time, in depth. As a result we know a great deal (much of it unimportant) about very few people. Of real value in her introduction is the two-page chronology she constructed to compare what each illustrator was doing at the same point in time; from it one can see the reason why the period was truly "golden."

If there has been a lack of comparative research on illustrators there has been some analysis of how various illustrators have dealt with the same theme or material. In 1964, for example, the Metropolitan Museum of Art held an exhibition of illustrations for Aesop's fables, resulting in the exhibition catalog compiled by John J. McHendry, AESOP: FIVE CENTURIES OF ILLUSTRATED FABLES (1964). Aesop's fables were chosen as a focal point because they have been illustrated so frequently over time that the illustrations serve as a history of illustration itself, and the diversity of illustration styles provided a useful starting point for a comparison of how the same material was treated by various illustrators. Unfortunately, the exhibit catalog does little of the comparison except historically, so little is said about why one set of illustrations was more effective than others. John Lewis, in THE TWENTIETH CENTURY BOOK (1967), does a comparative analysis of ten different illustrated versions of TREASURE ISLAND, ranging from F. T. Merrill's original illustrations (1884) through those of N. C. Wyeth (1911) to Robert Micklewright (1963). Grahame Ovendon's little book, THE ILLUSTRATORS OF ALICE IN WONDERLAND AND THROUGH THE LOOKING GLASS (1972), is a brief history of the original Alice and the John Tenniel illustrations, a critique of various illustrated editions since Tenniel, and examples of how various illustrators have handled Alice on a chapter-by-chapter basis. His selections for the best illustrators may surprise: in addition to himself, Ovendon chooses Lewis Carroll, Arthur Rackham, Mervyn Peake, Ralph Stedman, Salvador Dali, Max Ernst, and William Blake. Quite a diverse group! What they have in common is a fresh or different perspective on how to deal with Alice and her wonderful world.

Several writers have analyzed the illustration of children's books in a somewhat broader perspective. Peter Bennett's book, THE ILLUSTRATED CHILD (1979), for example, is a survey of 450 years of children's illustration that includes nice analyses of how various illustrators have treated Heinrich Hoffman's SLOVENLY PETER, ALICE IN WONDERLAND, and Christina Rossetti's THE GOBLIN MARKET.

In a delightful little book, Welleran Poltarness (ALL MIRRORS ARE MAGIC MIRRORS [1972]) attempts to say some important things about children's book illustration. His theme: "The illustrator, when he reads, must see. The great illustrator sees rightly" (p. 5). The best book is the one in which words and pictures work complementarily, producing a new whole that is superior to either words or pictures alone. Within this theme he presents examples of various illustrators' works, that is, how Kate Greenaway, Tomi Ungerer, Jean deBrunhoff, E. H. Shepard, and Edward Ardizonne portrayed scenes of domestic happiness. Poltarness also has an interesting analysis of those occasions where there can be no union between artwork and words and how the illustrator deals with the problem. The illustrator, under those circumstances, has two options—to ignore the words and use artwork that is personally satisfying but irrelevant for the text, for example, Kate Greenaway with THE PIED PIPER OF HAMLIN, or to illustrate the words exactly as written, for example, Arthur Rackham and Edgar Allan Poe's TALES OF MYSTERY AND IMAGINATION.

Selma Lanes, in DOWN THE RABBIT HOLE (1971), has several chapters in which she compares "odd couples" of illustrators—Kate Greenaway and Joan Walsh Anglund, Arthur Rackham and Maurice Sendak on their perceptions of childhood. She argues that Rackham and Sendak look at childhood through opposite ends of the telescope; Rackham's illustrations are lighthearted and fantasy-oriented, whereas Sendak's represent the memories of a solemn and somber child. For Lanes, Rackham's power came from his writing, his illustrations serving as a lightweight and gratuitous accompaniment. In a concluding chapter there is an analysis of the Oz books as American fairy tales, in which L. Frank Baum's characters seek personal improvement—courage, knowledge, and adventure—rather than material possessions. Each of the chapters in the Lanes book is stimulating but they seem to have no focus except their analysis of various children's book illustrators.

Several of the authors in part one of Lee Kingman's THE ILLUSTRATOR'S NOTEBOOK (1978) focus on the relationship between illustration artwork and text. Warren Chappell argues that the illustrator must work around the main passages of a story—which are frequently overdescribed by the author. Hilda Van Stockum suggests that one of the author's responsibilities is to provide a good story with plenty of action and character and opportunity for the illustrator to fill in the descriptive holes. With these points in mind, Marcia Brown suggests that illustrations can be evaluated by asking, How appropriate are the illustrations to the spirit as well as the facts of the story? Lee Kingman suggests that if the illustrations are successful they must clarify or decorate the text and change or intensify one's perceptions of reality. The principal criterion for evaluating illustration becomes its emotional impact—its ability to affectively complement an author's text. "Bad" illustrations are those to which we have no emotional response, those that leave us "cold."

Ervine Metzl developed a similar taxonomy for classifying posters: posters can be judged on their artistic merits and as advertising devices. As a result we can have four classes of posters: those that are good advertising and good art, good advertising and bad art, bad advertising and good art, and bad advertising and bad art. But what determines "good" or "bad" art? Metzl suggests criteria developed by the French poster artist Jules Cheret: a poster should not be overburdened with detail, should not be too literal, must enlist the viewer as a participant, must imply a world of continuing action, and must sell its product or idea. The last criterion, of course, is the critical criterion for judging a poster's advertising merit. With these criteria—quality of advertising and quality of art—Metzl then evaluates a number of renowned poster artists, and his conclusions are somewhat surprising. For example, he gives the Beggarstaffs high marks for their artwork but argues their posters were not good advertising. Edward Penfield, on the other hand, did posters that were strong and simple (artistically good) and the lettering advertising the product (HARPER'S MAGAZINE) was designed to enhance the effectiveness of the whole poster (good advertising). Metzl's criteria provide him with a sounder basis for his judgment of the Beggarstaffs than Bevis Hillier in POSTERS, who judges the Beggarstaffs to be the finest posterists of the period. Metzl would agree with that judgment on artistic but not advertising grounds.

Steven Brown, in his empirical research on how people respond to illustrations or poster art (1976, 1979), found that Metzl was both right and wrong. Using examples of posters from Yanker's book, PROP ART, Brown had people evaluate a set of posters on the basis of their appeal; he found that posters were evaluated on the basis of their content (advertising appeal), their color (artistic appeal), or both. Thus, the Beggarstaffs' posters would appeal to some people but not to others. Brown would agree with Metzl's argument that the best posters are those that are both good art and good advertising, but because such posters appeal to all three groups that Brown found in his study.

As we have seen in the foregoing analysis, a number of people have written bits and pieces of the history of American illustration or facets thereof, but no one has yet tackled the monumental, yet vital, task of tying all the disparate pieces together. Until that is done we may not know whether and why (or why not) poster art developed in relation to American illustration of the same period. It is apparent, for example, that American posters at the turn of the twentieth century were far more heavily influenced by Japanese wood-block prints. Until we can answer these questions in a systematic fashion, the history of American illustration will continue to be fragmented, incomplete, and inconclusive.

The lack of aesthetic theories that can be applied to American illustration is also a hindrance to the development of the field. Without an ability to compare illustrations across time and media we are left to judge each illustrator and his or her artwork in splendid isolation. Perhaps we should use the most fundamental standards available—those illustrators who sell their artwork are the most successful, financially and aesthetically.

BIBLIOGRAPHY

Alexander, Charles. HERE THE COUNTRY LIES: NATIONALISM AND ART IN TWENTIETH CENTURY AMERICA. Bloomington, Indiana University Press, 1980.

American Institute of Graphic Arts. THE MENTAL PICTURE III: PORTRAITS. New York, American Institute of Graphic Arts, 1978.

THE AMERICAN PERSONALITY: THE ARTIST-ILLUSTRATOR OF LIFE IN THE UNITED STATES, 1860–1930. Los Angeles, Grunwald Center for the Graphic Arts, UCLA, 1976.

THE ARTIST AND THE BOOK: 1860–1960: IN WESTERN EUROPE AND THE

UNITED STATES. Boston, Museum of Fine Arts and Harvard University Library, 1961.

THE ART OF AMERICAN ILLUSTRATION. Chadds Ford, Pa., Brandywine River Museum, 1976.

Atwar, Robert, Donald McQuade, and John W. Wright. EDSELS, LUCKIES, AND FRIGIDAIRES. New York, Delacorte Press, 1979.

Bader, Barbara. AMERICAN PICTURE BOOKS FROM NOAH'S ARK TO THE BEAST WITHIN. New York, Macmillan, 1976.

——— THE NEWBERRY AND CALDECOTT MEDAL BOOKS, 1966–1975. Boston, Horn Book, 1975.

Benedict, Brad, and Linda Barton, eds. PHONOGRAPHICS: CONTEMPORARY AL-BUM COVER ART AND DESIGN. New York, Collier Books, 1977.

Bennett, Peter. THE ILLUSTRATED CHILD. New York, G. P. Putnam's Sons, 1979.

Blanck, Jacob. PETER PARLEY TO PENROD. New York, R. R. Bowker, 1939.

Bland, David. THE ILLUSTRATION OF BOOKS. London, Faber and Faber, 1941.

Blechman, Robert O. BEHIND THE LINES. New York, Hudson Hills Press, 1980.

Bonn, Thomas L. "American Mass Market Paperbacks." In Jean Peters, ed., COLLEC-TIBLE BOOKS. New York, R. R. Bowker, 1979, 118–51.

——— UNDERCOVER: AN ILLUSTRATED HISTORY OF AMERICAN MASS MARKET PAPERBACKS. New York, Penguin, 1982.

Brewer, Francis J., ed. BOOK ILLUSTRATION: PAPERS PRESENTED AT THE THIRD RARE BOOK CONFERENCE OF THE AMERICAN LIBRARY AS-SOCIATION IN 1962. Berlin, Gebr. Verlag, 1963.

Brown, Ann Barton. THE ART OF AMERICAN ILLUSTRATION. Chadds Ford, Pa., Brandywine River Museum, 1976.

——— HOWARD PYLE, A TEACHER. Chadds Ford, Pa., Brandywine River Museum, 1980.

Brown, Steven R. "Observational Standpoints in the Study of Political Communication." Paper presented at the annual meeting of the International Communication As-sociation, Portland, Oreg., 1976.

——— "Perspectives, Transfiguration, and Equivalence in Communication Theory: Re-view and Commentary." In Dan Nimmo, ed., COMMUNICATIONS YEAR-BOOK 3. New Brunswick, N.J., Transaction Books, 1979, 51–65.

A CENTURY OF AMERICAN ILLUSTRATION. Brooklyn, Brooklyn Museum of Arts and Sciences, 1972.

CITY LIFE ILLUSTRATED, 1890–1940. Wilmington, Delaware Art Museum, 1980.

Cober, Alan. COBER'S CHOICE. New York, E.P. Dutton, Unicorn Books, 1979.

THE COWBOY. San Diego, Calif., San Diego Museum of Art, 1981.

Darracott, Joseph, ed. THE FIRST WORLD WAR IN POSTERS. New York, Dover, 1974.

Darton, F. J. Harvey. MODERN BOOK ILLUSTRATION IN GREAT BRITAIN AND AMERICA. New York, Studio Limited, 1931.

Dykes, Jeff. FIFTY GREAT WESTERN ILLUSTRATORS: A BIBLIOGRAPHIC CHECKLIST. Flagstaff, Ariz., Northland Press, 1975.

EARLY AMERICAN BOOK ILLUSTRATORS AND WOOD ENGRAVERS: 1670–1870. Princeton, N.J., Princeton University Press, 1958.

EARLY CHILDREN'S BOOKS AND THEIR ILLUSTRATION. Boston and New York, Pierpont Morgan Library and David R. Godine, 1975.

Ellis, William Richardson. BOOK ILLUSTRATION. Kingsport, Tenn., Kingsport Press, 1952.

Elzea, Rowland. THE GOLDEN AGE OF AMERICAN ILLUSTRATION: 1880–1914. Wilmington, Delaware Art Museum, 1972.

Freeman, Larry, comp. VICTORIAN POSTERS. Watkins Glen, N.Y., American Life, 1969.

Freeman, Ruth S. CHILDREN'S PICTURE BOOKS: YESTERDAY AND TODAY. Watkins Glen, N.Y., Century House, 1967.

Frewin, Anthony. ONE HUNDRED YEARS OF SCIENCE FICTION ILLUSTRATION: 1840–1940. London, Jupiter Books, 1974.

Gallo, Max. THE POSTER IN HISTORY. New York, American Heritage, 1972.

Gowans, Alan. LEARNING TO SEE: HISTORICAL PERSPECTIVE ON MODERN POPULAR/COMMERCIAL ARTS. Bowling Green, Ohio, Bowling Green State University Popular Press, 1981.

——— THE UNCHANGING ARTS. New York, J. B. Lippincott, 1971.

GRAPHIC DESIGNERS IN THE USA/3. New York, Universe Books, 1972.

Gunn, James. ALTERNATE WORLDS: THE ILLUSTRATED HISTORY OF SCIENCE FICTION. Englewood Cliffs, N.J., Prentice-Hall, 1975.

Haining, Peter. TERROR!: A HISTORY OF HORROR ILLUSTRATIONS FROM THE PULP MAGAZINES. N.p., A and W Visual Library, 1976.

Harthan, John. THE HISTORY OF THE ILLUSTRATED BOOK: THE WESTERN TRADITION. London, Thames-Hudson, 1981.

Hassrick, Peter. THE WAY WEST: ART OF FRONTIER AMERICA. New York, Henry Abrams, 1977.

Haviland, Virginia, and Margaret N. Coughlan. YANKEE DOODLE'S LITERARY SAMPLER OF PROSE, POETRY AND PICTURES. New York, Thomas Y. Crowell, 1974.

Hillier, Bevis. THE DECORATIVE ARTS OF THE FORTIES AND FIFTIES. New York, Clarkson N. Potter, 1975.

——— POSTERS. New York, Stein and Day, 1969.

Hockney, David. DAVID HOCKNEY. New York, Henry Abrams, 1976.

Holme, Bryan. ADVERTISING: REFLECTIONS OF A CENTURY. New York, Viking Press, 1982.

Hornung, Clarence P. HANDBOOK OF EARLY ADVERTISING ART. VOLS. I, II. New York, Dover Publications, 1947.

Hornung, Clarence P., and Fridolph Johnson. 200 YEARS OF AMERICAN GRAPHIC ART. New York, George Brazillier, 1976.

IMAGES OF AN ERA: THE AMERICAN POSTER, 1945–75. Washington, D.C., National Collection of Fine Arts, Smithsonian Institution, 1975.

Kagan, Daniel, ed. THE ILLUSTRATIONS OF MURRAY TINKELMAN. New York, Art Directors Book Co., 1980.

Kingman, Lee. NEWBERRY AND CALDECOTT MEDAL BOOKS, 1956–1965. Boston, Horn Book, 1965.

——— NEWBERRY AND CALDECOTT MEDAL BOOKS, 1966–1975. Boston, Horn Book, 1975.

——— ed. THE ILLUSTRATOR'S NOTEBOOK. Boston, Horn Book, 1978.

Kingman, Lee, Grace Allen Hogarth, and Harriet Quimby. ILLUSTRATORS OF CHILDREN'S BOOKS, 1967–1976. Boston, Horn Book, 1978.

Kingman, Lee, Joanna Foster, and Ruth Giles Lontoft. ILLUSTRATORS OF CHIL-
DREN'S BOOKS, 1957–1966. Boston, Horn Book, 1968.

Koch, Robert. "Artistic Books, Periodicals and Posters of the 'Gay Nineties.' " ART
QUARTERLY, no. 25 (1962), 370–83.

Kyle, David. A PICTORIAL HISTORY OF SCIENCE FICTION. New York, Hamlyn
Publishing Group, 1976.

Lanes, Selma G. DOWN THE RABBIT HOLE. New York, Atheneum, 1971.

Levine, David. THE ARTS OF DAVID LEVINE. New York, Alfred A. Knopf, 1978.

Lewis, John. THE TWENTIETH CENTURY BOOK. London, Studio Vista, 1967.

McHendry, John J. AESOP: FIVE CENTURIES OF ILLUSTRATED FABLES. New
York, Metropolitan Museum of Art, 1964.

McKay, G. L. "American Artists as Reporters, 1851–1900." AMERICAN COLLECTOR,
November 1947, 6–8.

McMullan, James. REVEALING ILLUSTRATIONS. New York, Watson-Guptill, 1981.

MAGIC AND OTHER REALISM: THE ART OF ILLUSION. New York, Society of
Illustrators, Visual Communications Books, 1980.

Mahoney, Bertha E., Louise Latimer, and Beulah Folmsbee. ILLUSTRATORS OF CHIL-
DREN'S BOOKS: 1744–1945. Boston, Horn Book, 1947.

Margolin, Victor. AMERICAN POSTER RENAISSANCE. New York, Watson-Guptill,
1975.

Margolin, Victor, Ira Brichta, and Vivian Brichta. THE PROMISE AND THE PRODUCT:
200 YEARS OF AMERICAN ADVERTISING POSTERS. New York, Macmillan,
1979.

Mehlman, Robert. "Posters of the Nineties." AMERICAN ARTS AND ANTIQUES,
November/December 1978, 53–61.

Mellquist, Jerome. THE EMERGENCE OF AN AMERICAN ART. New York, Charles
Scribner's Sons, 1942.

Metzl, Ervine. THE POSTER: ITS HISTORY AND ITS ART. New York, Watson-
Guptill, 1967.

Meyer, Susan E. AMERICA'S GREAT ILLUSTRATORS. New York, Henry Abrams,
1978.

Miller, Bertha Mahoney and Elinor Whitney Field. CALDECOTT MEDAL BOOKS,
1938–57. Boston, Horn Book, 1957.

Mullen, Chris. CIGARETTE PACK ART. New York, St. Martin's Press, 1979.

O'Brien, Geoffrey. HARD-BOILED AMERICA: THE LURID YEARS OF PAPER-
BACKS. New York, Van Nostrand, 1981.

Ovendon, Grahame, ed. THE ILLUSTRATORS OF ALICE IN WONDERLAND AND
THROUGH THE LOOKING GLASS. New York, St. Martin's Press, 1972.

Pitz, Henry C. "Book Illustration Since 1937." AMERICAN ARTIST, April 1967, 64–
71, 101.

——— THE BRANDYWINE TRADITION. New York, Weathervane Books, 1968.

——— HOWARD PYLE. New York, Clarkson N. Potter, 1975.

——— THE PRACTICE OF ILLUSTRATION. New York, Watson-Guptill, 1947.

——— A TREASURY OF AMERICAN BOOK ILLUSTRATION. New York, American
Studio Books and Watson-Guptill, 1947.

——— 200 YEARS OF AMERICAN ILLUSTRATION. New York, Random House
and the Society of Illustrators, 1977.

Poltarness, Welleran. ALL MIRRORS ARE MAGIC MIRRORS. La Jolla, Calif., Green Tiger Press, 1972.

Price, Matlack. "War Posters That Get Action." AMERICAN ARTIST, April 1942, 8–11, May 1942, 21–23, 40.

Reed, Walt. GREAT AMERICAN ILLUSTRATORS. New York, Abbeyville Press, 1979.

———— ed. THE ILLUSTRATOR IN AMERICA: 1900–1960. New York, Reinhold Publishing Co., 1966.

———— ed. NORTHERN LIGHTS COLLECTION. Westport, Conn., Northern Lights Publishing Co., 1979.

Schreuders, Piet. PAPERBACKS, U.S.A.: A GRAPHIC HISTORY, 1939–1959. San Diego, Calif., Blue Dolphin Enterprises, 1981.

Simon, Howard. 500 YEARS OF ART AND ILLUSTRATION. Cleveland, Ohio, World Publishing Co., 1942.

Society of Illustrators. ILLUSTRATORS IN THE THIRD DIMENSION. New York, Hastings House, Visual Communications Book, 1978.

THE STANFORD LOW MEMORIAL COLLECTION OF AMERICAN ILLUSTRA-TION. New Britain, Conn., New Britain Museum of American Art, 1980.

Street, Julian. "Our Fighting Posters." McCLURE'S MAGAZINE, July 1918, 12–13, 34.

Summers, Ian. THE ART OF THE BROTHERS HILDEBRANDT. New York, Ballantine Books, 1979.

———— ed. TOMORROW AND BEYOND: MASTERPIECES OF SCIENCE FICTION ART. New York, Workman Publishing Co., 1978.

Taft, Robert. ARTISTS AND ILLUSTRATORS OF THE OLD WEST, 1850–1900. New York, Charles Scribner's Sons, 1953.

Tomsich, John. A GENTEEL ENDEAVOR: AMERICAN CULTURE AND POLITICS IN THE GILDED AGE. Stanford, Calif., Stanford University Press, 1971.

Viguers, Ruth Hill, Marcia Dalphin, and Bertha Mahoney Miller. ILLUSTRATORS OF CHILDREN'S BOOKS: 1946–1956. Boston, Horn Book, 1958.

Weidemann, Kurt, ed. BOOK JACKETS AND RECORD COVERS: AN INTERNA-TIONAL SURVEY. New York, Praeger, 1969.

Weitenkampf, Frank. AMERICAN GRAPHIC ART. New York, Henry Holt and Company, 1912.

———— THE ILLUSTRATED BOOK. Cambridge, Harvard University Press, 1938.

Whalley, Joyce Irene. COBWEBS TO CATCH FLIES. Berkeley, University of California Press, 1975.

Woolman, Bertha. THE CALDECOTT AWARD. Minneapolis, T. S. Dennison, 1978.

Yanker, Gary. PROP ART. New York, Darien House, 1972.

Yost, Karl, and Frederick G. Renner. A BIBLIOGRAPHY OF THE PUBLISHED WORKS OF CHARLES M. RUSSELL. Lincoln, University of Nebraska Press, 1971.

Zeman, Zbynek. SELLING THE WAR. London, Orbis, 1978.

CHAPTER 3

Major Illustrated Works: Bibliographies and Books

The numbers of illustrators and the amount of artwork produced, in all formats and for all media, have made the compilation of a comprehensive listing of illustrated works virtually impossible. Thus, the problem of defining "major" illustrated works, which depends on a complete list of all works, is nearly insurmountable. For many of the most important illustrators we lack complete bibliographies of their work, and even the existing bibliographies are often incorrect. In the following pages comprehensive and limited bibliographies of illustrated works will be discussed. Most of these suffer from at least one major defect—a lack of attention to magazine illustrations—a serious defect for those illustrators from the Golden Age when magazines were a major publication source.

Even if there were a complete listing of all illustrations, the numbers of illustrations and the changing tastes of the American public over the past one hundred years would make it difficult to determine the "best" illustrated works. Not only have tastes changed during the past century but illustration media have changed as well; how can one compare a series of book illustrations from the 1890s with a record album cover from 1975?

In the following sections bibliographies of work done by major illustrators also will be examined. From these bibliographies and some other sources "major" illustrated works by "major" illustrators also will be examined. Given the unevenness of bibliographic coverage, which tends to cover only those illustrators described as major today, we find that some of the most popular works of their day are neglected. For that reason, other criteria have been used. One of the most useful in determining "greatness" is the economics of the antiquarian book marketplace—what illustrated books are now in greatest demand, which have retained their appeal through the years?

BIBLIOGRAPHIES

There is no comprehensive bibliography of all illustrations. Several people have attempted bibliographies of various segments of the field, and some biographers have compiled useful bibliographies of individual illustrators. Theodore Bolton's book, AMERICAN BOOK ILLUSTRATION (1938) is a bibliographical checklist of book illustrations for 123 American illustrators. It stands as a useful starting point in a bibliographic search, but it has defects. The book is now dated since the coverage of illustrators whose careers ended or began after 1938 is incomplete or missing entirely. The selection of illustrators is also uneven. Some of Howard Pyle's more important students are not included while several illustrators of minor importance have been included. Comparatively few women are listed, a glaring omission in a field where women have played an important role. The most important defect, however, is the incomplete coverage of those illustrators chosen. There is no listing of magazine illustrations except insofar as they were incorporated as illustrations in books. And the book bibliographies for many illustrators are not complete—one would do well to look elsewhere for more complete bibliographies for Charles M. Russell and N. C. Wyeth, for example. Nonetheless, because of the breadth of coverage (in numbers of artists listed) the Bolton volume is still the first one that comes to hand when searching for bibliographic information on American book illustrators.

Recognizing the enormity of the task, several writers have constructed bibliographies of selected segments of the field. Jacob Blanck's PETER PARLEY TO PENROD (1939) is a bibliographic checklist of leading juveniles published in the United States, with first edition points and other important bibliographic information. Whitman Bennett's book, A PRACTICAL GUIDE TO NINETEENTH CENTURY COLOR PLATE BOOKS (1949), for example, is designed to be a comprehensive bibliography of American color plate books of the period. The coverage of the early nineteenth century is adequate, but the increasing number of illustrated books in the 1890s made a complete catalog virtually impossible. Nonetheless, this is a useful guide to hand-colored illustrated books from the nineteenth century. Jeff Dykes's FIFTY GREAT WESTERN ILLUSTRATORS (1975) provides a bibliography of works illustrated by each artist as well as articles dealing with the artist and his art. In addition, the bibliography lists various editions and reprints of each book, but the list is frequently incomplete or bibliographically incorrect. The inclusion and exclusion of some illustrators is curious; Thomas Fogarty, A. I. Keller, E. Boyd Smith, and N. C. Wyeth, all of whom did some but not a great deal of western illustration, are included. Frederic Remington is included but Charles M. Russell is not. In the latter case Dykes argues that the Yost and Renner bibliography, A BIBLIOGRAPHY OF THE PUBLISHED WORKS OF CHARLES M. RUSSELL (1971), is so comprehensive as to preclude the need for his inclusion. That same logic, however, would apply to the Allens' bibliography of N. C. Wyeth's work (N. C. WYETH [1972]), John Carroll's bibliography of Nicholas Von Schmidt (VON SCHMIDT: THE COMPLETE ILLUSTRATOR [1973]), and Harold McCracken's bibliographical checklist of Remington's work (FREDERIC REMINGTON: ARTIST OF THE OLD WEST [1947]), all of whom are included in Dykes's book. Given the number of illustrators cataloged and the amount of work they did, it is not surprising that Dykes restricts himself to their book illustrations. That makes a far more manageable universe of material. As noted elsewhere, even the book bibliographies are incomplete. In addition, many western artists published a substantial segment of their illustration artwork in magazines and, as of yet, there remains no bibliography of that important material. These criticisms notwithstanding, Dykes's book remains a useful entry into the field, so long as the reader is aware of its general deficiencies.

There have been a number of efforts to catalog illustrated works in the field of children's literature. One of the early ones was Elva Smith's ILLUSTRATED EDITIONS OF CHILDREN'S BOOKS (1923). Smith's work is useful because it is an annotated bibliography, complete with reviewer's comments, of a number of books from the early 1920s. From the same period we have Louise Latimer's ILLUSTRATORS: A FINDING LIST (1929), a bibliography prepared for the Washington, D.C., public library. Unfortunately, it is confined to listing books in English and in print as of 1929 so it is of greatest use for illustrators of the 1920s, particuarly those who were popular then but less well known today. The books are indexed by illustrator and author but the only information given is the title, author, illustrator, and publisher. Much more useful is the Junior Authors and Illustrators series. Stanley J. Kunitz and Howard Haycroft began the series with THE JUNIOR BOOK OF AUTHORS (1934, revised in 1951); the 1934 edition contained biographies and bibliographies of 268 authors and author-illustrators of children's books, while the 1951 edition contained biographies and bibliographies of 289 people, 129 of them new, having come into prominence in the field since 1934. Muriel Fuller edited MORE JUNIOR AUTHORS (1963), which contains biographical and bibliographical material on 268 authors and illustrators, most of whom had become prominent since 1951. Doris De Montreville and Donna Hill edited the THIRD BOOK OF JUNIOR AUTHORS (1972) and De Montreville and Elizabeth Crawford edited the FOURTH BOOK OF JUNIOR AUTHORS AND ILLUSTRATORS (1978), each of which adds to the information generated in the previous books. Together, these five books provide biographical and bibliographical information on almost one thousand authors and illustrators. One must exercise some care in using these sources, however. It is occasionally difficult to determine in which volume a given illustrator is to be found, particularly if he or she has had a long career. And the biographical and bibliographical material is of limited utility; the biographies are very short and the bibliographical material is not comprehensive—it represents high points in the illustrator's book illustration career. In addition, the earlier books in the series include only those illustrators who wrote children's books; those who merely illustrated them were not included. Martha Ward and Dorothy Marquardt's IL-LUSTRATORS OF BOOKS FOR YOUNG PEOPLE, Second Edition (1975) provides 750 brief biographies of book illustrators, many of them contemporary, and most of them drawn from the biographies in the first three volumes of the ILLUSTRATORS OF CHILDREN'S BOOKS series mentioned below. As with the AUTHORS AND ILLUSTRATORS series, the coverage is very uneven and the biographies are sketchy at best.

The preeminent resource work in the field of children's book illustration is still Bertha Mahoney et al., ILLUSTRATORS OF CHILDREN'S BOOKS: 1744–1945 (1947), supplemented by Ruth Hill Viguers, Marcia Dalphin, and Bertha Mahoney Miller, ILLUSTRATORS OF CHILDREN'S BOOKS: 1946–1956

(1958); Lee Kingman, Joanna Foster, and Ruth Giles Lontoft, ILLUSTRATORS OF CHILDREN'S BOOKS: 1957–1966 (1968); and Lee Kingman, Grace Allen Hogarth, and Harriet Quimby, ILLUSTRATORS OF CHILDREN'S BOOKS, 1967–1976 (1978). In addition to useful articles on various aspects of children's illustration, each book contains a number of biographies and bibliographies of books illustrated by each illustrator. The bibliographies, while not comprehensive, are representative of each illustrator's book illustrations. As with most other bibliographies of a field, there is no attention paid to magazine illustration, so that aspect of an illustrator's work is unrecorded.

The number of children's book illustrators and the growth in the numbers of biographies and bibliographies led Adele Sarkissian to construct a useful bibliography of biographies and bibliographies, CHILDREN'S AUTHORS AND ILLUSTRATORS, Second Edition (1978), that can serve as a gateway to this massive material. In looking up an illustrator in Sarkissian, one can discover which of the several hundred books covered contain material on that illustrator, thereby saving untold hours of fruitless searching. Unfortunately, Sarkissian's book is merely a reference tool; its utility is based on the quality of the material contained in the books that she surveys and her ability to continually update and expand her material. In addition, her work is a survey of other surveys, a tertiary reference to secondary source materials. It would be nice if she could include primary biographical and bibliographical material as well. As a survey of secondary materials published over time there is redundancy and incompleteness. It would be helpful, for example, if she would indicate which bibliographies and biographies she felt were most useful for each illustrator. These criticisms notwithstanding, the book is a very useful research tool. If someone would do for the entire field what Sarkissian has done for children's book illustrators, research in the field would be immeasurably easier.

Interestingly, only one person has cataloged the illustrators whose work has appeared in a single publication source. Best (1980) found almost five thousand illustrations by over 250 illustrators in CENTURY, HARPER'S, and SCRIBNER'S, so the task can be monumental. For that reason, John Shaw's POEMS, POETS AND ILLUSTRATORS OF ST. NICHOLAS MAGAZINE (1965), a catalog of illustrators and when they appeared during the history of that important children's magazine, is a signal achievement. The task seems to have exhausted Shaw, however, since the next step—an analysis of who those illustrators were, what they illustrated, and how often—was not included as part of this work.

Bibliographies of artwork done by individual illustrators are available for some illustrators. For the early illustrators Benjamin Lewis's A GUIDE TO ENGRAVINGS IN AMERICAN MAGAZINES: 1741–1810 (1959), Everett Duyckinck's A BRIEF CATALOGUE OF BOOKS ILLUSTRATED WITH ENGRAVINGS BY DR. ALEXANDER ANDERSON (1885), and Theodore Bolton's THE BOOK ILLUSTRATIONS OF FELIX OCTAVIUS CARR DARLEY (1952) provide bibliographical source material on two of America's earliest illustrators, Alexander Anderson and F.O.C. Darley. These bibliographies cover only book illustrations, a defect particularly for Anderson's work, which appeared in a number of sources beside books. Duyckinck catalogs Anderson's book illustrations, listing how many and which illustrations in each book were done by Anderson—an invaluable aid since illustrations were rarely signed nor were illustrators given credit for their work in books. Lewis's book lists Anderson's contributions (among others) to fifty-nine American magazines published during the period 1741–1810, covering Anderson's early illustrations. In the HANDBOOK OF EARLY ADVERTISING ART, VOL. I (1947), Hornung suggests that many of Anderson's illustrations were used for advertising purposes and in textbooks and religious tracts; if so the Duyckinck and Lewis bibliographies are, of necessity, incomplete and the frailty of many of the early publications means that a complete bibliography of Anderson's work may now be impossible. Bolton's bibliography of F.O.C. Darley's work is now the standard work on this illustrator, but it lacks any mention of his magazine work—important work since he started as a magazine illustrator and some of his earliest work was done for GRAHAM'S MAGAZINE when Edgar Allan Poe was still editor—and there is little of the bibliographic detail that is of real utility to book collectors. Thus, Darley's SKETCHES ABROAD WITH PEN AND PENCIL (1868) comes in green or blue bindings; are these variant bindings or does one precede the other, indicating a first printing of the first edition? Bolton provides no help. Christine Anne Hahler's exhibition catalog . . . ILLUSTRATED BY DARLEY (1978) merely provides a checklist of his illustrated books, adding little to Bolton's bibliography.

Since most of the Civil War "special" artists published their illustrations in the newspapers of the time, there is no bibliography of their published work. The books written about these men include examples of their work, but little more. The best sources are still the pages of HARPER'S WEEKLY and LESLIE'S ILLUSTRATED. The only Civil War artist whose work has been cataloged is Winslow Homer. Winslow Homer's illustrations are cataloged in Gordon Hendricks's THE LIFE AND WORK OF WINSLOW HOMER (1979) and Phillip C. Beam's WINSLOW HOMER'S MAGAZINE ENGRAVINGS (1979). Both books contain checklists of his magazine illustrations, with Beam's book giving such bibliographic detail as how the illustrations were signed and who the engraver was, in addition to listing where and when they were published. Hendricks's book includes a chronology of Homer's life; a checklist of works by Homer in public collections, cataloged by state and city; a checklist of published graphics, listed by year; and an extensive bibliography of books and articles written about Homer, many by his contemporaries.

There is a dearth of bibliographic material about the published works of many of the first professionals who worked with Charles Parsons at the House of Harper. Bolton's bibliography provides a useful starting point in a search for the book illustrations of Edwin Austin Abbey, Edward Kemble, C. S. Reinhart, and A. B. Frost. The lack of biographic and bibliographic material on these early professionals is particularly critical, given their importance in the historical development of the field and the overall quality of their work. Frost's long career—from the

1880s through the 1920s—cries for a comprehensive biography and bibliography of his work. To study their magazine illustrations, however, one must turn to the pages of HARPER'S MONTHLY and WEEKLY during the period 1875–1910 to see their magazine work at its peak.

The artwork of Howard Pyle, in contrast, has been competently cataloged by Willard S. Morse and Gertrude Brinckle in HOWARD PYLE: A RECORD OF HIS ILLUSTRATIONS AND WRITING (1920, 1979). This monumental effort lists virtually all of the artwork published by Pyle in magazines, books, and other formats, including dates of publication, type of artwork (color or black-and-white), size of the artwork in published form, location within the book or magazine, and whether it is a republication of earlier published artwork. The book includes materials of Pyle's reprinted up to ten years after his death; SAINT JOAN OF ARC (1919), for example, was the republication in book form of a story Pyle had illustrated in 1904 for HARPER'S MONTHLY. Morse and Brinckle's book provides testimony to the prodigious output of Pyle during his half-century career. Subsequent Pyle biographies, notably by Pitz (HOWARD PYLE [1975]), add very little to the Morse and Brinckle bibliography except by eliminating much of the detail and making publication checklists that are easier to use.

Bibliographic material regarding Pyle's students is abundant, at least for the most popular among them. The bibliography in Douglas Allen and Douglas Allen, Jr.'s N. C. WYETH (1972) is amazingly complete, listing Wyeth's magazine and book illustrations, as well as his murals, advertisements, and other ephemera. The illustrations are also cross-listed so one knows, for example, that some of his book illustrations also appeared in articles written about Wyeth, and which of his magazine illustrations subsequently were republished in which books. Given the volume and diversity of Wyeth's published artwork, this bibliography rivals that of Morse and Brinckle in its comprehensiveness, accuracy, and utility. The major defect is that it is frequently difficult to know in which category to look for a particular work; it is useful to remember, for example, that many of Wyeth's illustrations first appeared in magazines before their appearance in book form. The chapter in Jeff Dykes's FIFTY GREAT WESTERN ILLUSTRATORS: A BIBLIOGRAPHIC CHECKLIST (1975) dealing with Wyeth is not as complete as the bibliography of Allen and Allen but it does include more information on articles dealing with the Wyeths and gallery showings of N. C. Wyeth's artwork. A book catalog of Wyeth's published works by Richard P. DeVictor (1975) gives some additional bibliographical information on some of Wyeth's miscellaneous artwork, as well as prices of a large segment of Wyeth's illustrated work. Book catalog prices should be viewed with some skepticism, however, since they are prices that a dealer hopes to realize and they are out of date as soon as the next auction is held or book catalog is published.

The best bibliography of Maxfield Parrish's work is found in Coy Ludwig's book, MAXFIELD PARRISH (1973). This book includes a bibliography of works about Parrish, many written by his contemporaries, and a catalog of selected works based on Parrish's records and the author's research. The result is the most complete record extant of his book and magazine illustrations (including the name of the artwork, date of completion, and location within the published work), catalog and program covers for noncommercial institutions, advertisements and posters, calendars and greeting cards, color reproductions, portfolios or collections of reproductions including Parrish's work, designs for theatrical scenery, book-plates, murals or panels painted for a specific architectural setting, miscellaneous commissioned works, works commissioned but not used, commissioned works of which publication is uncertain, studies and preliminary drawings, and miscellaneous items. There is no sure way of knowing how complete this bibliography is (although its breadth is staggering), since Parrish's records were incomplete, but the listing of magazine illustrations and calendar art make this an invaluable research tool.

Frank Apgar's bibliography in FRANK SCHOONOVER, PAINTER-ILLUS-TRATOR: A BIBLIOGRAPHY (1969) provides the most comprehensive bibliography of Schoonover's book illustrations. Cortland Schoonover's bibliography in FRANK SCHOONOVER: ILLUSTRATOR OF THE NORTH AMERICAN FRONTIER (1976) includes a listing of many of Schoonover's magazine illustrations. Jeff Dykes's chapter on Schoonover in FIFTY GREAT WESTERN ILLUSTRATORS: A BIBLIOGRAPHIC CHECKLIST (1975) includes a listing of books and articles dealing with Schoonover's work as well as galleries that have held exhibitions of his work and published catalogs.

Cathryn Connell Stryker's exhibition catalog, THE STUDIOS AT COGSLEA (1976), provides a preliminary bibliography of the book illustrations of the three women who worked at Cogslea near Chadds Ford, Elizabeth Shippen Green, Violet Oakley, and Jessie Wilcox Smith. It is not complete, omitting all magazine illustrations, calendar art, and other ephemera. S. Michael Schnessel's biography, JESSIE WILCOX SMITH (1973), contains a more refined bibliography than Stryker's but still omits some of her magazine illustrations and all her advertising artwork. Ruth Freeman's biography, JESSIE WILCOX SMITH: CHILDHOOD'S GREAT ILLUSTRATOR (1977), is a bibliographic nightmare; it contains none of her magazine illustrations and does not include all of her illustrated books. A more comprehensive bibliography of Smith's published illustrations is currently being prepared.

Unfortunately, we do not have similarly comprehensive bibliographies detailing the published illustrations of Elizabeth Shippen Green, Sarah Stillwell, or a host of other Pyle students. The librarians at the Brandywine River Museum and the Delaware Art Museum have been compiling bibliographies of magazine and book illustrations by Pyle and his students, information that has been invaluable in the writing of several of their exhibition catalogs, particularly for some of Pyle's lesser-known students. Elizabeth Hawkes's BERTHA CORSON DAY BATES: ILLUSTRATOR IN THE HOWARD PYLE TRADITION (1978) contains a partial list of her book, magazine, and poster artwork. WHALERS, WHARVES, AND WATERWAYS (1973) contains an incomplete listing of Clifford Ashley's illustration output. Nonetheless, there are no comprehensive bibliographies for some of Pyle's most accomplished students; to understand or study the impact of Pyle on the work of his students it is imperative that we have some grasp of what work they did, and where it was published. Elzea and Hawkes's A SMALL SCHOOL OF ART (1980) is the definitive effort by the Delaware Art Museum to list all of Howard Pyle's students, provide at least some bibliographic information about most of them, give examples of their artwork, and provide some details regarding how and where their artwork was published. This is particularly useful for Pyle's less well known students. From this base the user can begin his or her catalogs of works by less well known illustrators. Reed's THE ILLUS-TRATOR IN AMERICA: 1900–1960 (1966) can serve the same function for other illustrators.

There are outstanding bibliographies for the two major western illustrators during the Golden Age, Frederic Remington and Charles M. Russell. Harold McCracken's biography, FREDERIC REMINGTON: ARTIST OF THE OLD WEST (1947) contains a bibliographical checklist of 2,739 pieces of Remington's work that appeared in print. Unfortunately, McCracken was not very critical when examining artwork attributed to Remington, some of which is in question. Jeff Dykes's chapter on Remington in FIFTY GREAT WESTERN ILLUSTRATORS (1975), on the other hand, is a more critical listing of his major book illustrations, as well as articles dealing with Remington and his work and galleries where his work has been exhibited, but his bibliography is incomplete. The Karl Yost and Frederic G. Renner book, A BIBLIOGRAPHY OF THE PUBLISHED WORKS OF CHARLES M. RUSSELL (1971), began as a response to what the authors perceived as a very meager listing of Russell's work in the 1938 Bolton bibliography. They have expanded Bolton's initial listing to a bibliography of thirty-five hundred citations of Russell's books (including various editions and reprints), gallery catalogs, periodical and newspaper illustrations, portfolios and sets, color and black-and-white prints, postcards and Christmas cards, advertising art, and ephemera. This book must stand as the definitive work on Russell's printed artwork, a claim accepted by Dykes since he did not attempt a bibliography of Russell's work for his volume.

We also lack comprehensive bibliographies for most of the "American Beauty" illustrators. Bolton's bibliography lists the major book illustrations of Charles Dana Gibson, Harrison Fisher, Howard Chandler Christy, and James Montgomery Flagg; since much of their artwork appeared in magazines, this bibliography misses much of their important work. Fairfax Downey's biography of Gibson, POR-TRAIT OF AN ERA AS DRAWN BY C. D. GIBSON (1936); Susan Meyer's biography of Flagg, JAMES MONTGOMERY FLAGG (1974); and Michael Schau's book, ALL-AMERICAN GIRL; THE ART OF COLES PHILLIPS (1975) do little to remedy the defects of the Bolton bibliography. In fact, Bolton does not list Phillips among his 123 illustrators. Fortunately, some of the better magazine illustrations of Gibson, Fisher, Christy, and Flagg were brought together by their publishers and reissued as folio-size books. Thus, the book bibliographies do, inadvertently, pick up some of the more important magazine illustrations of these men. The republication of much of their artwork—as "picture" books, calendars, postcards, playing cards, and even wallpaper—makes the need for comprehensive bibliographies of all their published work even more imperative but also highlights the difficulty of tracking down much of the published miscellany through which these illustrators, particularly Harrison Fisher, made their livings.

Although bibliographic material on children's book illustrators has been discussed above, one of the most popular children's book illustrators at the turn of the century merits individual attention. The biography of the first Oz illustrator, W. W. DENSLOW (1976), by Douglas Greene and Michael Hearn, contains an excellent bibliography of his illustrations for books, book covers, magazines, newspapers, posters, and prints and a good bibliography of works written about Denslow, particularly his relations with Elbert Hubbard and L. Frank Baum. This bibliography is particularly useful for tracing down the various reprints of some of Denslow's more obscure works, which were occasionally combined by reprint publishers into another book with a new title. Complete bibliographical information on the Oz series can be found in the Michael P. Hearn (1973) and Hanff and Greene (1976) bibliographies, while information on non-Oz books illustrated by the Oz illustrators can be found in L. FRANK BAUM AND RELATED OZIANA (1978).

Lack of bibliographical information on interwar period illustrators continues to be a problem. J. C. Leyendecker's career as a cover artist, illustrator, and advertising artist is admirably detailed in Michael Schau's biography, J. C. LEYENDECKER (1976), but the book lacks a complete bibliography—an unfortunate defect for an illustrator whose major works did not appear in book format and therefore are not listed in book illustration bibliographies like Bolton. Such is not the case with Leyendecker's friend and contemporary, Norman Rockwell. Donald and Marshall Stoltz in three volumes of NORMAN ROCKWELL AND THE SATURDAY EVENING POST (1976); Christopher Finch in NORMAN ROCKWELL: 332 MAGAZINE COVERS (1979); and Thomas Buechner's NORMAN ROCKWELL: ARTIST AND ILLUSTRATOR (1970) each show, in black-and-white or color, all of Rockwell's SATURDAY EVENING POST covers. Finch goes further to include Rockwell's non-POST covers, while Buechner provides the most comprehensive list of Rockwell's cover art, magazine and book illustrations, advertisements, Boy Scout calendars, and murals and posters. Although Buechner provides the most comprehensive list, it is of limited value since it omits much of the standard bibliographic detail, particularly for Rockwell's book illustrations. The coverage of his artwork for the Boy Scouts is limited as well. A better listing of his scouting illustrations can be found in Hillcourt's NORMAN ROCKWELL'S WORLD OF SCOUTING (1977). Mary Moline's NORMAN ROCKWELL ENCYCLOPEDIA (1979) is a reasonably successful attempt to catalog his magazine covers, magazine illustrations, book illustrations, advertisements, portraits and self-portraits, greeting cards, calendars, posters, and miscellaneous artwork, as well as biographical books and articles. All the material is organized by year, with the magazine covers and illustrations cataloged by publication source within each year. While this is the most complete checklist of Rockwell's artwork (and it is nothing more) it is still incomplete.

The standard of western art bibliographies established by McCracken and Yost and Renner continues with Hutchinson's excellent bibliography of W.H.D. Koerner's published material in THE WORLD, THE WORK, AND THE WEST OF W.H.D. KOERNER (1978), which lists Koerner's magazine illustrations by magazine and year and does a very nice comparison of when he published his artwork with which magazines. Given the length of his career and the number of magazine illustrations published, this is a very helpful graphic if the researcher is interested in which magazines Koerner was publishing in at a given time or during which periods Koerner was publishing in a specific magazine. John M. Carroll's book, VON SCHMIDT: THE COMPLETE ILLUSTRATOR (1973), contains an extensive bibliography of his illustrations in books, book dust jackets, pamphlets, bulletins, newspapers, catalogs, advertising art, and magazines.

Several other illustrators from the 1920s and 1930s have had excellent bibliographies of their published works compiled. Gail Levin's book on Edward Hopper's illustration career, EDWARD HOPPER AS ILLUSTRATOR (1979), contains an excellent bibliography of his magazine illustrations and advertising art. Fridolph Johnson's book, THE ILLUSTRATIONS OF ROCKWELL KENT: 231 EXAMPLES FROM BOOKS, MAGAZINES AND ADVERTISING ART (1976), contains a useful bibliography of his illustrated books but neglects his magazine and advertising art, surprising given the subject matter of the book. Kent's book, ROCKWELLKENTIANA (1933), contains a bibliography of his writing and illustration to that date, but since his career extended beyond 1933 it is of limited utility except for the earlier material. Lynd Ward's book, STORYTELLER WITHOUT WORDS (1974), serves as a useful bibliography of his book illustrations in his "books without words." His transition to a children's book illustrator means, however, that anyone seeking a complete bibliography of Ward's work would do well to begin with some of the comprehensive children's book bibliographies discussed earlier.

The shift in emphasis in book illustration to children's books has made it somewhat easier to research more contemporary illustrators, particularly in that area. The children's book bibliographies listed earlier are adequate for most purposes. It is only when one wants information on an illustrator who operates in other venues besides book illustration that problems arise. For that reason Selma Lanes's bibliography in THE ART OF MAURICE SENDAK (1980) is particularly useful.

Once we move beyond children's book illustrators it is far more difficult to trace the artistic efforts of various contemporary illustrators. Although there may be picture books of their "best" work there are no bibliographies of all their work; this is not surprising considering that most of them are still working as professional illustrators. Nonetheless, this makes it very difficult to determine who has done what artwork in which media and with what success. It is only when the Society of Illustrators' annual awards are published that we can see who has been doing what type of quality work and where—and has been judged "best" by their peers. But if we seek to look at all of an illustrator's work to date it is virtually impossible. Books dealing with contemporary illustrators are hard to find and those that are available, for example, Daniel Kagan's THE ILLUSTRATIONS OF MURRAY TINKELMAN (1980), Steve Dohanos's AMERICAN REALIST (1980), and James McMullan's REVEALING ILLUSTRATIONS (1981) provide only examples of the illustrator's work rather than complete catalogs. Review articles of leading illustrators that appear in PRINT, GRAPHIS, U&LC and other media magazines may give an indication of the range of an individual's work but rarely a complete listing. For some contemporary illustrators perhaps only their agents know where they have published what artwork (and how much they were paid).

If a prerequisite for judging the best illustrators or the best illustrated works is an inventory of all the work done by the best illustrators, we may never be in a position to make those qualitative judgments. The lack of bibliographic material falls into three major areas. First and foremost, many very competent illustrators, even those about whom books have been written, do not have complete bibliographies of their published works. Sadly, the deficiencies are worse the further back in time one goes. Aside from Anderson and Darley there are no really good illustration bibliographies for illustrators working before 1870. Howard Pyle and some of his more popular students have benefited from bibliographic research, but of the 160 students listed in Elzea and Hawkes's A SMALL SCHOOL OF ART (1980) there are bibliographies for the works of less than one-fifth. Even Bolton's incomplete and dated bibliography of book illustrations for 123 American illustrators merely scratches the surface. Thus, a basic deficiency is the dearth of information regarding who illustrated what, when, and how. Second, even among the published bibliographies there is a serious lack of attention paid to magazine illustrations—a major publication media prior to World War II. This is easy to understand. Prior to the Golden Age of illustration magazine illustrators were infrequently credited for their artwork, so it is difficult to tell who did which illustrations. Then, during the Golden Age the number of illustrated magazines grew so large and magazines entered and left the market so quickly that it is virtually impossible to find a complete inventory of magazines published in a given year during this period, let alone determine who did the illustrations. Even the Library of Congress, the repository of copyrighted material, has been unable to keep up with all published materials during this peak publishing period. As a result it is very difficult to trace the illustrations done by major illustrators that appeared in the mass-market magazines of the day. Without this information a comprehensive bibliography of the most important magazine illustrations is impossible. Third, the diversity of illustration media, particularly since World War II, has made it difficult to compile bibliographies for even the most popular and successful contemporary illustrators. When illustrators publish their work on record album covers, in magazines, and as subway posters how can anyone keep track? Furthermore, the rise of illustration studios has made it difficult to determine who actually did the artwork; when Push-Pin Studio does an illustration is the credit to be awarded to the illustrators working collectively?

ILLUSTRATED CLASSICS

Even when we know which illustrators did which illustrations it is difficult to judge which illustrated works are best. Since illustrations are designed for a mass market it would be easy to say that the best illustrations are those that are the most popular in their day, but that leaves the definition of best in temporal limbo. Are the popular illustrators of a bygone era still popular—have they stood the test of time? One criterion could be that only those illustrators and their works that have exhibited popular appeal over time can be thought of as classics.

Comparatively few early American (pre-Civil War) works have retained popular appeal, certainly not like those by contemporary British illustrators such as George Cruikshank and Thomas Bewick. F.O.C. Darley's role in American illustration is now widely recognized but few of his illustrated books have retained popular appeal; his illustrations from THE SKETCHBOOK OF GEOFFREY CRAYON (1848), COMPOSITIONS IN OUTLINE FROM JUDD'S MARGARET (1856), and SKETCHES ABROAD WITH PEN AND PENCIL (1868), which were popular in their day, only now are beginning to command attention from book collectors and art historians. Winslow Homer's graphic works, concentrated largely in magazines and weekly newspapers, are now receiving the public attention they deserve and that they merited in the late 1800s. It is interesting that the illustrations of Homer and many other artist-illustrators of the late nineteenth and early twentieth centuries are only now being recognized for their merits.

Of the early professional illustrators only the work of Howard Pyle has retained its popularity. THE MERRY ADVENTURES OF ROBIN HOOD OF GREAT RENOWN, IN NOTTINGHAMSHIRE (1883) was a classic in its day and has been reprinted innumerable times since. The combination of Pyle's mastery of pen-and-ink technique, story-telling ability, and the total design of the book produced a unique work, which has compelling unity of style. Few of Pyle's later books match ROBIN HOOD in design and execution. Although PEPPER AND SALT (1886) and THE WONDER CLOCK (1888) added to Pyle's reputation, it is the earlier work that still stands out. None of Pyle's color illustrations are as appealing as those done in pen-and-ink. THE ONE HOSS SHAY (1892, 1905) was initially done by Pyle in pen-and-ink, and color was added after four-color reproduction became feasible. The color version depends for much of its impact, however, on Pyle's pen-and-ink technique, highlighted by the color washes. Some of his most successful color works were the six oils he did for "The Fate of a Treasure Town," (HARPER'S MONTHLY, 1906), which combine his love for pirates with good graphic design and color sense. In these six illustrations he demonstrates an ability to capture action and mood in color as well as in pen-and-ink; the scenes shift from a group of pirates on a beach to the questioning of townspeople about their gold to the attack on a galleon at sea by a pirate longboat.

Some of the best of Pyle's pirate and historical stories and illustrations were compiled by Merle Johnson in HOWARD PYLE'S BOOK OF PIRATES (1921) and HOWARD PYLE'S BOOK OF THE AMERICAN SPIRIT (1923). These books are excellent showpieces for Pyle's pen-and-ink as well as color techniques and his story-telling ability.

Beside Howard Pyle's classics very few illustrated books from the 1870s or 1880s are remembered today. PICTURESQUE AMERICA (1872–1874), the book that convinced publishers that large-scale illustrated books were economically viable, has been reprinted and the original edition is in demand by book collectors. Edwin Abbey's books, with the exception of SELECTIONS FROM THE POETRY OF ROBERT HERRICK (1882)—one of the first Art Nouveau design books—have had limited appeal. A. B. Frost, who first achieved success with his illustrations of Frank Stockton's RUDDER GRANGE (1885)—no longer remembered today—achieved lasting success with his southern rural illustrations for Joel Chandler Harris's UNCLE REMUS, HIS SONGS AND SAYINGS (1895) and TAR BABIES AND OTHER RYMES OF UNCLE REMUS (1904). Some of Frost's hunting illustrations have sustained their appeal, but his cartoons, for example, now look poorly drawn and flat to a generation acclimated to Walt Disney and Doonesbury. One of Frost's contemporaries (and an earlier illustrator of Brer Rabbit), Edward Kemble, was popular for his illustrations of blacks in such books as KEMBLE'S COONS: DRAWINGS OF COLORED CHILDREN AND SOUTHERN SCENES (1896), A COON'S ALPHABET (1898), and COMICAL COONS (1898), which helped perpetuate social stereotypes of rural and southern blacks.

The Golden Age of illustration produced not only a number of good illustrators but an exceptional number of illustrated classics. Some of the books by Howard Pyle's students dominate this list. Maxfield Parrish's book illustrations, from L. Frank Baum's FATHER GOOSE IN PROSE (1899) to Louise Saunder's THE KNAVE OF HEARTS (1925), demonstrate his growth and mastery of the medium. Coy Ludwig (in MAXFIELD PARRISH [1973]) argues that THE GOLDEN AGE and DREAM DAYS represent a near complete accord between author and illustrator in their treatment of the subject. Eugene Field's POEMS OF CHILDHOOD (1904) was one of the best-known children's books in its day and is still quite popular; "Dream Castles" is a classic Parrish illustration, widely reprinted today. His illustrations for Saunder's THE KNAVE OF HEARTS represent one of his most lavish undertakings and are an ideal example of "dynamic symmetry" in action. The book was popular with everyone but the publisher; the oversize book did not sell well, although Parrish made his profits from republication of many of the book's illustrations. Some of his subsequent art prints—"Daybreak" and "The Garden of Allah"—were immensely popular in their day; sales figures seem to indicate that no parlor was complete without a Parrish print on the wall. But their appeal has not been sustained, except for those who collect Parrish's work, regardless of quality.

Much of Parrish's best work can be seen in the covers he did for COLLIER'S magazine between 1905 and 1910, covers that Ludwig labels as some his most imaginative and ingenious. Certainly the cover design of a young man trying to learn arithmetic in a sea of numbers (September 30, 1911) has universal appeal. Parrish's posters, the vehicles by which he initially gained artistic success, have also remained popular, partly because of the asexual innocence of a boy or girl sitting in a pastoral scene, such as "Century Midsummer Holiday Number, August" (April 1896) and "Scribner's Fiction Number, August" (June 1897).

N. C. Wyeth's illustrated work also has remained popular. Much of his work had an attractive showcase, however. Of the thirty-four books in the Scribner's ILLUSTRATED CLASSICS series published between 1904 and 1940, Wyeth illustrated sixteen, beginning with TREASURE ISLAND in 1911 and ending with THE YEARLING (1940). In the process his illustration talents were coupled with the literary talents of Robert Louis Stevenson in TREASURE ISLAND (1911), KIDNAPPED (1913), THE BLACK ARROW (1916), and DAVID BALFOUR (1924); Jules Verne in THE MYSTERIOUS ISLAND (1918) and MICHAEL STROGOFF (1927); and James Fenimore Cooper in THE LAST OF THE MOHICANS (1919) and THE DEERSLAYER (1925). Wyeth's illustrations for the ILLUSTRATED CLASSICS series have remained among his most popular, with Scribner's periodically reprinting some of his illustrated books in the series.

Among Pyle's women students, two of the most successful were Jessie Wilcox Smith and Elizabeth Shippen Green. Green's illustrations for Richard LeGalliene's AN OLD COUNTRY HOUSE (1902) and Norman Duncan's THE SUITABLE CHILD (1909), along with her many illustrations for HARPER'S MONTHLY (with whom she had a contract until 1924), give scope to her impressive range of decorative skills. Jessie Wilcox Smith was best known for her illustrations for Robert Louis Stevenson's A CHILD'S GARDEN OF VERSES (1909)—another Scribner's ILLUSTRATED CLASSIC—and Charles Kingsley's WATER BABIES (1916). The former shows Smith's real skill in depicting children (see her series in SCRIBNER'S titled "A Mother's Day" [1902] as well), while the latter shows her ability to depict a fantasy world, with children as a central theme once again. But a substantial amount of Smith's continuing public popularity stemmed from the many cover designs she did for GOOD HOUSEKEEPING magazine during the years 1918–1932, most of which depicted children, with or without their mothers.

Other illustrators during this period also produced good-quality work. Those illustrators who portrayed "American Beauties" did much of their work for the illustrated monthly magazines of the period, particularly SCRIBNER'S and COLLIER'S. James Montgomery Flagg, who felt that having his illustrations published in SCRIBNER'S was like winning an art competition, published seventy black-and-white illustrations in that magazine during the period 1906–1910. Charles Dana Gibson's "Gibson Girl" appeared regularly in LIFE and JUDGE during the first two decades of the twentieth century. Their illustrations also appeared in book form. Gibson's drawings were republished in folio size books that became quite popular, particularly THE SOCIAL LADDER (1902), THE WEAKER SEX

(1903), EVERYDAY PEOPLE (1904), and THE GIBSON BOOK: A COLLEC-
TION OF THE PUBLISHED WORKS OF CHARLES DANA GIBSON (1906).
Flagg's CITY PEOPLE (1909) is one of a few of his illustrated books, while
Howard Chandler Christy, on the other hand, illustrated many.

Like the American Beauty illustrators, many western illustrators published their
work in magazines. As a result the few books that they did illustrate were popular
and have remained in demand to the present. Remington's illustrations for Theodore Roosevelt's RANCH LIFE AND THE HUNTING TRAIL (1888) helped
establish the reputations of both men. PONY TRACKS (1895) and DONE IN
THE OPEN (1902) are collections of some of the best of Remington's western
art. Charles Russell did fewer book illustrations than did Remington, his best
being those he did for his friend Frank Linderman's books, INDIAN WHY STO-
RIES (1915) and INDIAN OLD MAN STORIES (1920). For both illustrators,
magazines were a major media for the presentation of their artwork. Remington's
series, "Western Types," in SCRIBNER'S (October 1902), presents visual images
of a variety of westerners. In his magazine illustrations one can also see the changes
in Remington's artistic style, from his early Realism to later Impressionism, in
which figures, colors, and mood are his predominant concerns.

Several illustrators established reputations as nature illustrators during this period. Charles Livingston Bull illustrated the first edition of Jack London's classic,
THE CALL OF THE WILD (1903), while Paul Bramson did the illustrations for
a 1912 edition. Both did a number of animal books in addition, with Bramson
being active in this field into the 1940s. Perhaps the best known and most popular
nature writer and illustrator during the Golden Age was Ernest Thompson Seton
(also listed as Ernest Seton-Thompson in some of his books), whose WILD AN-
IMALS I HAVE KNOWN (1898), THE TRAIL OF THE SANDHILL STAG
(1899), and LIVES OF THE HUNTED (1901) are the best examples of his work.
These people were the Marlin Perkins and the Joan Embrys of their day, introducing the public to the animal kingdom through the mass media.

Several illustrators during this period served to introduce the public to foreign
or exotic places. Edward Penfield, better known for his poster art and as art editor
at HARPER'S, wrote and illustrated several travel books, HOLLAND SKETCHES
(1907) and SPANISH SKETCHES (1911). In these books Penfield applied his
poster techniques—large masses of pastel colors outlined in black—to the depiction of foreign scenes and was particularly successful with his illustrations for
HOLLAND SKETCHES. Jules Guerin did a number of illustrations for CEN-
TURY magazine that were subsequently republished in Marie Horner Lansdale's
CHATEUX OF TOURAINE (1906) and Robert Smythe Hichens's EGYPT AND
ITS MONUMENTS (1908). Both books are testaments to Guerin's ability as a
colorist; his color illustrations are muted monochromes with occasionally startling
color contrasts. Within the monochrome, however, one can see the subtle color
and detail of Guerin's artwork. Even Charles Dana Gibson did a travel book,
SKETCHES IN EGYPT (1899), that demonstrates the versatility of his pen-and-
ink technique, evident even when not drawing beautiful women.

A number of illustrated children's books have also remained popular. Undoubtedly the most familiar is L. Frank Baum's THE WONDERFUL WIZARD OF OZ (1900), illustrated by W. W. Denslow, the first of forty books in the Oz series written by Baum and later by Helen Plumley Thompson and Jack Snow and illustrated by Denslow, John R. Neil, and others. Little of Denslow's other artwork rivals his Oz books, but his illustrations for Baum's FATHER GOOSE, HIS BOOK (1899) and DENSLOW'S MOTHER GOOSE (1901) are good examples of the quality of his artwork. Unfortunately, after his split with Baum (over who was more responsible for the success of THE WONDERFUL WIZARD OF OZ and how the royalties from the successful Broadway production of their book should be divided, among other things) Denslow's artwork declined in quality as he sought desperately to show that he could be a success without Baum.

The poster art of a number of people who worked during this period is still popular. The Art Nouveau movement has experienced a renaissance amongst collectors, and turn-of-the-century poster art, still one of the best expressions of that movement, has become as popular now as it once was. Edward Penfield's HARPER'S MAGAZINE posters from 1896, Will Bradley's posters for THE INLAND PRINTER (1896) and THE CHAP BOOK (1894–1895), and the swirling Art Nouveau decorations of Louis Rhead are in great demand today. Less popular today, because of the subject matter rather than the artwork, are the World War I posters of James Montgomery Flagg, Howard Chandler Christy, Harrison Fisher, C. B. Falls, Coles Phillips, and J. C. Leyendecker.

Although poster art from this period is attracting more popular and scholarly attention, as evidenced by the skyrocketing prices for these posters and the number of books devoted to the subject, no one has yet written a complete bibliography of posters printed during the entire period or for any one poster artist. The numbers of posters involved probably precludes a complete bibliography but the lack of bibliographic material makes research and writing on the subject difficult except for the most well-known examples of the art and the most popular artists.

After World War I the number of illustrated books and magazines declined. Nonetheless, quality artwork was published; during the period 1920–1940 twenty-four of the thirty-four books in the Scribner's ILLUSTRATED CLASSICS series were published, ten of which were illustrated by N. C. Wyeth. In addition to his drawings of flappers for magazines, Peter Hurd also did a series of Norse legend illustrations for THE STORY OF ROLAND (1930) and THE STORY OF SIEGFRIED (1931). Western illustration remained popular too. Will James's illustrated books, SMOKY (1929) and THE LONE COWBOY (1932), were published as trade editions with black-and-white drawings and as ILLUSTRATED CLASSICS with additional color artwork.

The success of the ILLUSTRATED CLASSICS series spawned numerous imitators and competitors. Several publishing houses started series with black covers and a color plate on the front cover similar to the Scribner's format. Although none of these other series were as popular they did provide an attractive format for the artwork of several illustrators. Other publishers brought out series of illustrated books. Two of Norman Rockwell's best illustrated books, TOM SAW-YER (1936) and HUCKLEBERRY FINN (1940), were published by Heritage Press as part of their series of "illustrated classics."

For two of the leading illustrators during the interwar period—J. C. Leyen-decker and Norman Rockwell—their best artwork appeared on the covers of THE SATURDAY EVENING POST, Leyendecker's during the 1920s and Rockwell's during the late 1930s. According to Christopher Finch (NORMAN ROCKWELL [1979]) the years 1938–1942 marked a turning point in Rockwell's cover art, after which his work became more contemporary and documentary in nature and the quality became more consistently excellent. Thus, one can view his POST covers as fitting into two broad developmental patterns: from 1916 to 1938 and from 1939, when he moved his family to Vermont, to 1962. Leyendecker's masculine art shared the POST covers with Rockwell's innocent adolescents in the early 1920s; as Rockwell's subjects and cover art matured, Leyendecker's declined. Throughout the period between the wars the covers of THE SATURDAY EVENING POST were art galleries for the work of these two men.

Pulp fiction magazines, such as BLACK MASK and ASTOUNDING SCIENCE FICTION, were also major media for illustrators, but very little of that work has been bibliographically cataloged. There are several excellent histories of the genre but no one has attempted to comprehensively list which illustrators did which illustrations for which pulp magazines. The emphemeral nature of the magazines themselves, arising and disappearing from one month to the next, and the fact that much of the illustration artwork was unsigned makes cataloging next to impossible.

There were major illustrated books outside of those published in series format. Adapting Frans Masereel's "book without words" format to an American audience and topics, Lynd Ward did GOD'S MAN (1929) and MAD MAN'S DRUM (1930). These books, powerful in artistic style and content, were not widely popular in their day, and Ward ultimately achieved popular recognition for his illustrated children's book THE BIGGEST BEAR (1953 Caldecott Medal winner), which is done in an entirely different style and format. Rockwell Kent produced two types of important illustrated books—books written and illustrated by him describing his travels and experiences in the Arctic and his illustrations for other pieces of classical literature. In the former group are WILDERNESS: A JOUR-NAL OF QUIET ADVENTURE IN ALASKA (1920) and N BY E (1930), while in the latter are Melville's MOBY DICK (1930) and BEOWULF (1932). Together, Rockwell Kent and Lynd Ward returned black-and-white illustration in America to the artistic pinnacle that it had enjoyed in the late nineteenth century.

Given the decline in illustrated books and magazines, some of the best illustrated books during the interwar period were children's books. Some of these were done by immigrant illustrators. Maude and Miska Petersham, for example, were very popular during the 1920s and their book MIKI (1929) was a vivid depiction of Miska's Hungarian childhood. Ludwig Bemelmans's MADELINE (1939) suc-ceeded because of his ability to combine naturalistic drawings and text into a story that children could read and enjoy. German-born Kurt Weise did the illustrations for several popular books of the period—Felix Salten's BAMBI (1928), whose visual images defined the story's subject until the Disney feature, and his story and color illustrations for LIANG AND LO (1930), a fantasy story about two Chinese children. Roger Duvoisin, born in France, began his career in the 1930s with DONKEY-DONKEY (1933), showing how the donkey hero looked with his ears in a variety of configurations. His mature illustration style did not emerge, however, until after World War II; his illustrations for Alvin Tresselt's WHITE SNOW, BRIGHT SNOW (1947) won him the Caldecott Award that year, while PETUNIA (1950) is still one of his simplest but most enchanting books.

American-born illustrators also left their mark on children's book illustration during this period. Robert Lawson's illustrations for Margery Bianco's THE HURDY-GURDY MAN (1933) and Munro Leaf's THE STORY OF FERDI-NAND (1936) are among the best black-and-white illustrations of the era. THE HURDY-GURDY MAN illustrations are reminiscent of W. Heath Robinson or Daniel Vierge at their best, a generation earlier. THE STORY OF FERDINAND, done in a heavier black-and-white style, became a children's favorite. Boris Artz-ybasheff brought his own vision and style to Padraic Colum's THE FORGE IN THE FOREST (1925) and his own POOR SHAYDULLAH (1931) and SEVEN SIMEONS (1937), producing three books that are stylistically different but artfully weave text and pictures into a unified whole. Some of Artzybasheff's post-World War II fantasy books are not children's books but psychological picture books.

The changed nature of American illustration since World War II makes it difficult to determine the best "contemporary" illustrators. The Caldecott Awards, begun in 1937, have produced a number of excellent illustrated children's books, but like the Academy Awards, the award winner is frequently not the best or most popular book of the year. Ludwig Bemelmans's MADELINE was a 1940 runner-up, but is today better remembered than the medal winner, ABRAHAM LIN-COLN, illustrated by Ingri and Edgar Parin d'Aulaire. Dr. Seuss (Theodor Geisel) has been one of the most prolific and popular author-illustrators of children's books for the past forty years, but only one of his books, IF I RAN THE ZOO, was named as an Honor book in 1951. Maurice Sendak's IN THE NIGHT KITCHEN, Nancy Eckholm Burkert's SNOW WHITE AND THE SEVEN DWARFS, and David Macaulay's CATHEDRAL and CASTLE were runners-up in 1971, 1973, 1974, and 1978, respectively, but each may be more popular than the Medal winners in each of those years. One reason for these discrepancies may be that the basis for awarding the Caldecott is wrong. The distinction between picture books and illustrated books (the Caldcott Medal is for the former) is too narrow; it excludes illustrated fiction other than picture books, poetry, and non-fiction—areas in which good illustration is done.

The Society of Illustrators has selected the best illustrations of the year (see Gerald McConnell, TWENTY YEARS OF AWARD WINNERS [1981]), and the choices fit into a consistent pattern. During the twenty-year period, a small group of illustrators have won the award more than three times, and twelve—

Alan Cober, John Collier, Etienne Delessert, Mark English, Bernie Fuchs, Milton Glaser, Brad Holland, Wilson McLean, Bob Peak, Charles Schorre, David Schwartz, and Edward Sorel—have won it five or more times. This illustration "elite" are significantly different from their professional counterparts a half century earlier. There is only one woman. These illustrators publish their work in a variety of sources, many of which are specialty magazines, such as TV GUIDE and SPORTS ILLUSTRATED, or advertisements and, as a result, they are better known to their colleagues than to the public at large. Consequently, determining the "best" illustrators or illustrations under these circumstances is not to be done by "the public" but by one's professional peers. The public may be aware of an illustrator's style or technique, and may be able to recognize it when they see it, but may be totally unaware of what work the illustrator has done, or where it was done.

With the decline of book and magazine illustration, other media have become consumers of illustrations. Paperback books, which now outsell hardback books, have become increasingly dependent on good cover art for sales in a highly competitive market. A number of little known but excellent cover artists work in this field, and their artwork constitutes the "best." James Avati is probably the cover artist most widely respected by his peers, and his sultry cover designs for Signet paperbacks during the 1940s and 1950s are classics of their type, particularly those for Horace McCoy's KISS TOMORROW GOOD-BYE (1949) and Theodore Dreiser's AN AMERICAN TRAGEDY (1949). His more contemporary work seems dated and less appealing. A contemporary and peer of Avati was Robert Jonas, whose artwork was more abstract than the Realism of Avati; his cover designs for Carson McCullers's THE HEART IS A LONELY HUNTER (1946) and John Gearon's THE VELVET WELL (1947) are simple but symbolically striking. To see the differences in approach between Avati and Jonas one has only to compare the cover designs both did for the Penguin and Signet paperback editions of James M. Cain's SERENADE (1947 and 1950, respectively). There are and have been other excellent paperback cover artists, but Avati and Jonas represent the best of two different schools—the "sexy Realism" approach and the graphic design approach—that have so heavily influenced paperback cover art since World War II.

If paperback cover artists work in obscurity, record album artists are known only to their employers, families, and a few devotees. Brad Benedict and Linda Barton (PHONOGRAPHICS [1977]) nominate Robert Grossman (who also does cover art for TIME magazine), Peter Lloyd, Peter Palombi, Charles White III, David Willardson, Mick Haggerty, John Van Hamersveld, and design firms AGI, Rod Dyer, Inc., Gribbitt!, and Hipgnosis as the best contemporary record album artists. Although unknown to the general public by name the artwork of these people must be good to sell records. And the graphic design and photorealism of Peter Palombi's cover for CURTIS MAYFIELD—THERE'S NO PLACE LIKE AMERICA TODAY (1975) and Mick Haggerty's cover for THE JAMES MONT-GOMERY BAND (1977) are the equals of the POST covers of Rockwell and Dohanos.

For the books listed above, particularly from the Golden Age of American illustration, there has been a consistent demand in the antiquarian book trade. Certainly Pyle, Wyeth, and Parrish have sold very well and the Oz books have showed surprising strength (see L. FRANK BAUM AND RELATED OZIANA [1978]). Of course there may be a circularity here: book collectors tend to collect books for which there are adequate bibliographies and the best bibliographies are available for the most collectible illustrators.

Justin Schiller's survey of eleven antiquarian book dealers of the classics in the field of modern illustrated juveniles (A. B. BOOKMAN [November 13, 1978]) reveals that the most desirable books from the nineteenth and twentieth centuries are those done by the British illustrator Arthur Rackham, whose illustrated editions of J. M. Barrie's PETER PAN IN KENSINGTON GARDEN (1906), Shakespeare's A MIDSUMMER NIGHT'S DREAM (1908) and THE TEMPEST (1926), and Kenneth Grahame's THE WIND IN THE WILLOWS (1940) are in great demand, as are Kay Nielsen's EAST OF THE SUN AND WEST OF THE MOON (1914) and Edmund Dulac's STORIES FROM THE ARABIAN NIGHTS (1907). Probably the most desirable, and one of the scarcest, is William Timlin's THE SHIP THAT SAILED TO MARS (1923). Only three American illustrators were mentioned by these book dealers—Maxfield Parrish's THE KNAVE OF HEARTS (1925), Rockwell Kent's three volume edition of Herman Melville's MOBY DICK (1930), and Will Bradley's very rare PETER POODLE, TOYMAKER TO THE KING (1906). It is not clear why there are no more American illustrated books listed. The comparative scarcity of British illustrated books in the United States makes them more attractive to dealers and collectors and more expensive. Nonetheless, it appears that many very good American illustrated books have gone relatively unnoticed by the antiquarian book trade.

This phenomenon has led Steve Heller (PRINT [January 1983]) to suggest that there are hundreds of lesser "great" illustrators whose work has suffered unwarranted neglect. Heller's favorite "forgotten" illustrators are Harrison Cady, Art Young, Peter Newell, Oliver Herford, and Arthur Szyk—men whose books cost far less than their better-known colleagues. Indeed, every collector of illustrated books has some "forgotten" illustrator whose work he or she admires and who, it is hoped, will someday be remembered.

The breadth of the field of American illustration makes bibliographic research difficult, at best. Unfortunately, the quality of some of the extant bibliographies makes bibliographic research even harder. Aside from errors of commission— and few bibliographies are immune from these—almost every bibliography is deficient in its coverage, particularly of magazine and ephemeral illustrations. Bibliographers must remember that much of an illustrator's income historically has come from magazine illustrations and subsidiary reprints of the original artwork; a complete bibliography of an illustrator's work must take note of these published appearances if we are to have a complete understanding of an illustrator's artwork.

Without complete bibliographies we run the risk of overlooking the greatness of an illustrator whose work appeared in nontraditional sources, or accept as a measure of their greatness only those illustrations published in books. As noted above, some of the best illustrations done by a number of illustrators—Remington, Russell, Phillips, and Rockwell, to name a few—have appeared in magazines. And if we expand our definition of greatness to include some illustrators now "forgotten," the need for complete bibliographies becomes even more imperative.

Even the label "classic" risks becoming outmoded with the passage of time. Will the Scribner's ILLUSTRATED CLASSICS still be regarded as classics in the twenty-first century? As suggested in my discussion of children's books, popularity does not mean nor ensure greatness; many of the Caldecott winners have been neither popular nor great, and many books that have never received the Caldecott have nonetheless merited artistic recognition. Thus, my listing of books as "illustrated classics" should be viewed as suggestive rather than definitive.

BIBLIOGRAPHY

Allen, Douglas, and Douglas Allen, Jr. N. C. WYETH. New York, Bonanza Books, 1972.

Apgar, Frank P. FRANK SCHOONOVER, PAINTER-ILLUSTRATOR: A BIBLIOGRAPHY. Morristown, N.J., author, 1969.

L. FRANK BAUM AND RELATED OZIANA. New York, Swann Galleries Auction Catalog 1118, November 2, 1978.

Beam, Phillip C. WINSLOW HOMER'S MAGAZINE ENGRAVINGS. New York, Harper and Row, 1979.

Benedict, Brad, and Linda Barton, eds. PHONOGRAPHICS: CONTEMPORARY ALBUM COVER ART AND DESIGN. New York, Collier Books, 1977.

Bennett, Whitman. A PRACTICAL GUIDE TO NINETEENTH CENTURY COLOR PLATE BOOKS. New York, Bennett Book Studios, 1949.

Best, James J. "The Brandywine School and Magazine Illustration, HARPER'S, SCRIBNER'S and CENTURY, 1906–1910." JOURNAL OF AMERICAN CULTURE, no. 3 (1980), 128–44.

Blanck, Jacob. PETER PARLEY TO PENROD. New York, W. W. Bowker, 1938.

Bolton, Theodore. AMERICAN BOOK ILLUSTRATION: BIBLIOGRAPHICAL CHECKLIST OF 123 ARTISTS. New York, R. R. Bowker, 1938.

——— THE BOOK ILLUSTRATIONS OF FELIX OCTAVIUS CARR DARLEY. Worchester, Mass., American Antiquarian Society, 1952.

Buechner, Thomas. NORMAN ROCKWELL: ARTIST AND ILLUSTRATOR. New York, Henry Abrams, 1970.

Carroll, John M. VON SCHMIDT: THE COMPLETE ILLUSTRATOR. Fort Collins, Colo., Old Army Press, 1973.

De Montreville, Doris, and Donna Hill. THIRD BOOK OF JUNIOR AUTHORS. New York, H. W. Wilson, 1972.

De Montreville, Doris, and Elizabeth D. Crawford, eds. FOURTH BOOK OF JUNIOR AUTHORS AND ILLUSTRATORS. New York, H. W. Wilson, 1978.

DeVictor, Richard P. N. C. WYETH: A COLLECTOR'S CATALOGUE. Trenton, N. J., 1975.

Dohanos, Steve. AMERICAN REALIST. Westport, Conn., Northern Lights Publishing Co., 1980.

Downey, Fairfax. PORTRAIT OF AN ERA AS DRAWN BY C. D. GIBSON. New York, Charles Scribner's Sons, 1936.

Duyckinck, Everett A. A BRIEF CATALOGUE OF BOOKS ILLUSTRATED WITH ENGRAVINGS BY DR. ALEXANDER ANDERSON. New York, Thompson and Moreau, 1885.

Dykes, Jeff. FIFTY GREAT WESTERN ILLUSTRATORS: A BIBLIOGRAPHIC CHECKLIST. Flagstaff, Ariz., Northland Press, 1975.

Elzea, Rowland, and Elizabeth H. Hawkes. A SMALL SCHOOL OF ART: THE STUDENTS OF HOWARD PYLE. Wilmington, Delaware Art Museum, 1980.

Finch, Christopher. NORMAN ROCKWELL'S AMERICA. New York, Henry Abrams, 1975.

——— NORMAN ROCKWELL: 332 MAGAZINE COVERS. New York, Random House, Abbeyville Press, 1979.

Freeman, Ruth S. JESSIE WILCOX SMITH: CHILDHOOD'S GREAT ILLUSTRATOR. Watkins Glen, N.Y., Century House, 1977.

Fuller, Muriel, ed. MORE JUNIOR AUTHORS. New York, H. W. Wilson, 1963.

Greene, Douglas G., and Michael Patrick Hearn. W. W. DENSLOW. Mt. Pleasant, Clarke Historical Library, Central Michigan University, 1976.

Hahler, Christine Anne. . . . ILLUSTRATED BY DARLEY. Wilmington, Delaware Art Museum, 1978.

Hanff, Peter, and Douglas Greene. BIBLIOGRAPHIA OZIANA. N.p., International Wizard of Oz Club, 1976.

Hass, I. "Bibliography of the Works of Lynd Ward." PRINT, December 1936, 84–91.

Hawkes, Elizabeth H. BERTHA CORSON DAY BATES: ILLUSTRATOR IN THE HOWARD PYLE TRADITION. Wilmington, Delaware Art Museum, 1978.

Hearn, Michael Patrick. THE ANNOTATED WIZARD OF OZ. New York, Clarkson N. Potter, 1973.

Heller, Steve. "Forgotten Illustrators." PRINT, January 1983, 47–53.

Hendricks, Gordon. THE LIFE AND WORK OF WINSLOW HOMER. New York, Henry Abrams, 1979.

Hillcourt, William. NORMAN ROCKWELL'S WORLD OF SCOUTING. New York, Henry Abrams, 1977.

Hornung, Clarence P. HANDBOOK OF EARLY ADVERTISING ART, VOLS. I, II. New York, Dover Publications, 1947.

Hutchinson, W. H. THE WORLD, THE WORK, AND THE WEST OF W.H.D. KOERNER. Norman, University of Oklahoma Press, 1978.

Johnson, Fridolph, ed. THE ILLUSTRATIONS OF ROCKWELL KENT: 231 EXAMPLES FROM BOOKS, MAGAZINES AND ADVERTISING ART. New York, Dover Publications, 1976.

Kagan, Daniel, ed. THE ILLUSTRATIONS OF MURRAY TINKELMAN. New York, Art Directors Book Co., 1980.

Kent, Rockwell. ROCKWELLKENTIANA. New York, Harcourt Brace, 1933.

Kingman, Lee, Grace Allen Hogarth, and Harriet Quimby. ILLUSTRATORS OF CHILDREN'S BOOKS, 1967–1976. Boston, Horn Book, 1978.

Kingman, Lee, Joanna Foster, and Ruth Giles Lontoft. ILLUSTRATORS OF CHILDREN'S BOOKS, 1957–1966. Boston, Horn Book, 1968.

Kunitz, Stanley J., and Howard Haycroft. THE JUNIOR BOOK OF AUTHORS. New York, H. W. Wilson, 2d rev. ed., 1951.

Lanes, Selma G. THE ART OF MAURICE SENDAK. New York, Henry Abrams, 1980.

Latimer, Louise P., comp. ILLUSTRATORS: A FINDING LIST. Boston, F. W. Faxon, 1929.

Levin, Gail. EDWARD HOPPER AS ILLUSTRATOR. New York, W. W. Norton, 1979.

Lewis, Benjamin M. A GUIDE TO ENGRAVINGS IN AMERICAN MAGAZINES: 1741–1810. New York, New York Public Library, 1959.

Ludwig, Coy. MAXFIELD PARRISH. New York, Watson-Guptill, 1973.

McConnell, Gerald, ed: TWENTY YEARS OF AWARD WINNERS. New York, Society of Illustrators, 1981.

McCracken, Harold. FREDERIC REMINGTON: ARTIST OF THE OLD WEST. New York, J. B. Lippincott, 1947.

McMullan, James. REVEALING ILLUSTRATIONS. New York, Watson-Guptill, 1981.

Mahoney, Bertha E., Louise Latimer, and Beulah Folmsbee. ILLUSTRATORS OF CHILDREN'S BOOKS: 1744–1945. Boston, Horn Book, 1947.

Meyer, Susan E. JAMES MONTGOMERY FLAGG. New York, Watson-Guptill, 1974.

Moline, Mary. NORMAN ROCKWELL'S ENCYCLOPEDIA. Indianapolis, Curtis Publishing Co., 1979.

Morse, Willard S., and Gertrude Brinckle. HOWARD PYLE: A RECORD OF HIS ILLUSTRATIONS AND WRITING. 1921. Reprint. Detroit, Singing Tree Press, 1979.

Pennell, Joseph. PEN DRAWING AND PEN DRAUGHTSMEN. New York, Macmillan, 1920.

Pitz, Henry C. HOWARD PYLE. New York, Clarkson N. Potter, 1975.

Reed, Walt, ed. THE ILLUSTRATOR IN AMERICA: 1900–1960. New York, Reinhold Publishing Co., 1966.

Richardson, J. A. "Illustration and Art: Thematic Content and Aesthetic Standards." BRITISH JOURNAL OF AESTHETICS, no. 11 (1971), 354–68.

Sarkissian, Adele, ed. CHILDREN'S AUTHORS AND ILLUSTRATORS, 2nd ed. Detroit, Gale Research Co., 1978.

Schau, Michael. ALL-AMERICAN GIRL: THE ART OF COLES PHILLIPS. New York, Watson-Guptill, 1975.

———— J. C. LEYENDECKER. New York, Watson-Guptill, 1976.

Schiller, Justin. "Collecting Modern Illustrated Juveniles." A. B. BOOKMAN, November 13, 1978, 2915–22.

Schnessel, S. Michael. JESSIE WILCOX SMITH. New York, Thomas Y. Crowell, 1973.

Schoonover, Cortland. FRANK SCHOONOVER: ILLUSTRATOR OF THE NORTH AMERICAN FRONTIER. New York, Watson-Guptill, 1976.

Shaw, John M. POEMS, POETS, AND ILLUSTRATORS OF ST. NICHOLAS MAGAZINE. Tallahassee, Florida State University Press, 1965.

Smaridge, Nora. FAMOUS AUTHORS-ILLUSTRATORS FOR YOUNG PEOPLE. New York, Dodd, Mead, 1973.

Smith, Elva, ed. ILLUSTRATED EDITIONS OF CHILDREN'S BOOKS. Pittsburg, Carnegie Library, 1923.

Stoltz, Donald R. NORMAN ROCKWELL AND THE SATURDAY EVENING POST, VOL. I. New York, Four S Corp., 1976.

Stoltz, Donald R., and Marshall L. Stoltz. NORMAN ROCKWELL AND THE SAT-

URDAY EVENING POST, THE LATER YEARS, 1943–1971. New York, Four S Corp., 1976.

——— NORMAN ROCKWELL AND THE SATURDAY EVENING POST, THE MIDDLE YEARS, 1928–1943. New York, Four S Corp., 1976.

Stryker, Cathryn Connell. THE STUDIOS AT COGSLEA. Wilmington, Delaware Art Museum, 1976.

Viguers, Ruth Hill, Marcia Dalphin, and Bertha Mahoney Miller. ILLUSTRATORS OF CHILDREN'S BOOKS: 1946–1956. Boston, Horn Book, 1958.

Ward, Lynd. STORYTELLER WITHOUT WORDS. New York, Henry Abrams, 1974.

Ward, Martha E., and Dorothy A. Marquardt. ILLUSTRATORS OF BOOKS FOR YOUNG PEOPLE, 2d ed. Metuchen, N.J., Scarecrow Press, 1974.

WHALERS, WHARVES, AND WATERWAYS: AN EXHIBITION OF PAINTINGS BY CLIFFORD W. ASHLEY. Chadds Ford, Pa., Brandywine River Museum, 1973.

Yost. Karl, and Frederick G. Renner. A BIBLIOGRAPHY OF THE PUBLISHED WORKS OF CHARLES M. RUSSELL. Lincoln, University of Nebraska Press, 1971.

CHAPTER *4*

The Major Illustrators

The number of books and articles dealing with specific illustrators, their lives, and their careers represents an ever-increasing torrent of words. In most cases these are biographies of well-known illustrators, with examples of their artwork to show their styles. Some works provide far more artwork than biography, while too few try to relate illustrators and their artwork to life experiences and approaches to illustration. The uneven quality of much of the material makes it valueless for the comparative study of illustrators and American illustration. At best, we learn more or less about the lives and careers of a large number of individual illustrators.

For that reason I have organized the following material by period and illustrator, which allows for the comparison of various works about given illustrators within a period and a discussion of the utility of material written about them. Given the quantity and uneven quality of the writing, merely surveying the field will be useful. I hope the analysis and criticism will enable the reader to make even better use of the material surveyed. At the same time I have noted illustrators whose biographies are incomplete or nonexistent but who would benefit from a greater exposure of their artwork, illustrators whose biographies would enrich our understanding of American illustration.

THE FIRST ILLUSTRATORS: ANDERSON, DARLEY, AND THE "SPECIAL" ARTISTS

Although Alexander Anderson is considered to be the first American illustrator, little is known about his life and work. The history of Anderson's early career can be read in Frederic M. Burr, LIFE AND WORKS OF ALEXANDER ANDERSON, M.D. (1893), which is based on Anderson's diaries. These entries describe how Anderson combined his interest in art with his father's desire that he be a doctor; he studied medicine, was licensed and did wood engravings, first as a pastime and later to supplement his income. Finally, dispirited from the death of his wife and several members of his immediate family in an influenza epidemic, Alexander devoted more and more time to wood engraving and illustration. Linton's THE HISTORY OF WOOD-ENGRAVING IN AMERICA (1882) and Duyckinck's A BRIEF CATALOGUE OF BOOKS ILLUSTRATED WITH ENGRAVINGS BY DR. ALEXANDER ANDERSON (1885) both make use of the same diaries. It is difficult to trace and analyze Anderson's illustrations since many of the early ones were not signed and it is unclear how many illustrations were done by Anderson during his long career. Georgia S. Haugh (1963) states that Anderson did six hundred or more books, pamphlets, almanacs, and other works during his seventy-year career, but a complete catalog of all his work is not available. Duyckinck catalogs his book illustrations, listing how many and which illustrations in each book were done by Anderson, and Lewis, A GUIDE TO ENGRAVINGS IN AMERICAN MAGAZINES: 1741–1810 (1959), lists Anderson's contributions to fifty-nine American magazines published during the period. Hornung, in HANDBOOK OF EARLY ADVERTISING ART, VOL. I (1947), suggests that many of Anderson's illustrations were used for advertising art and in textbooks and religious tracts; since so many appeared in ephemeral publications and no longer exist, a complete bibliography beyond the Duyckinck and Lewis contributions seems unlikely. Hornung's book is useful for its description of Anderson's advertising illustrations and its brief statement of his role in the development of early American illustration. Linton, after analyzing Anderson's work, describes that of Anderson's pupils—Garrett Lansing, Nathaniel Dearborn, John H. Hall, Elias Whitney, Abel Bowen, William Mason, William Croone, John W. Barber, John Alexander, and Benjamin F. Childs, the last two being judged by Linton as Alexander's best pupils. While little is known about Alexander, virtually nothing is known about his students (except for Linton's book). Anderson's importance as a teacher of wood engraving can be judged by Hornung and Johnson's (1976) estimate that there were no more than twenty professional wood engravers in the United States in 1840. Obviously, Anderson and his students constituted the bulk of those engravers.

Although F.O.C. Darley (1822–1888) drew approximately four thousand designs for books, periodicals, newspapers, and bank notes, very little is known in detail about his life and work. There have been only two major exhibits of his artwork—a 1900 exhibit by the Museum of Modern Art and a 1978 exhibit by the Delaware Art Museum. Two works constitute the primary source materials on Darley's career and artwork: Theodore Bolton's THE BOOK ILLUSTRATIONS OF FELIX OCTAVIUS CARR DARLEY (1952) and Christine Anne Hahler's exhibition catalog, . . . ILLUSTRATED BY DARLEY (1978). Bolton lists all of Darley's major illustrated books and includes an excellent biographical essay detailing his development as an illustrator as well as his role in American illustration. Hahler's exhibition catalog is a useful supplement to the Bolton book; it provides a more extended bibliographic essay analyzing Darley's artwork and 152 examples of Darley's illustrations. A third work on Darley by Ethel King, DARLEY, THE MOST POPULAR ILLUSTRATOR OF HIS TIME (1964) is poorly written, rambling, frequently incorrect, and often irrelevant.

Although there are few biographies of Darley, the outlines of his life and work are reasonably clear. He was born into an artistic family, and during his childhood in Philadelphia he learned how to draw by copying old masters and contemporary illustrations from English books and magazines. In 1840 Darley decided to become an illustrator, and in 1841 he was appointed staff illustrator for GRAHAM'S LADY'S AND GENTLEMAN'S MAGAZINE, where Edgar Allan Poe was an editor. In 1842 Darley completed his first illustrated book, SCENES IN INDIAN LIFE, borrowing from earlier illustrators as to how Indians looked but introducing to American books a linear style of outline drawing reminiscent of European neoclassical art. In 1848 he moved to New York City where he soon did his outline designs for RIP VAN WINKLE (1848) and THE LEGEND OF SLEEPY HOLLOW (1849). These illustrations, combined with those done for Washington Irving, THE SKETCH BOOK OF GEOFFREY CRAYON, ESQ. (1848), A HISTORY OF NEW YORK (1850), THE ALHAMBRA (1851), and THE LIFE OF GEORGE WASHINGTON (1855–1859); Francis Parkman, THE CALIFORNIA AND OREGON TRAILS (1849); James Fenimore Cooper (thirty-two volumes published between 1859 and 1861); and a number of volumes of THE LIBRARY OF HUMOROUS AMERICAN WORKS (1846–1869), were the basis for Darley's reputation and place in the history of American illustration. Darley's "nativist" style fit well with the emerging nationalist fiction of Irving and Cooper. Equally important was Darley's ability to illustrate the dramatic high points in a story, frequently focusing on the confrontations and physical conflict that were part of frontier American life. By the mid-1850s Darley began engraving bank notes, and after the Civil War he did very little work that was ground breaking.

Few writers have critiqued Darley's artwork. Henry Pitz (1977) questions the extent to which Darley was a nativist illustrator. Pitz recognizes that Darley illustrated a number of American novels but suggests that Darley's artistic impetus came from the British school of illustration. As evidence Pitz notes that concurrent with his illustration of American novels Darley was also successfully illustrating novels by Sir Walter Scott, Charles Dickens, Laurence Sterne, and Alfred Tennyson. Budd L. Gambee (1963) notes that Darley worked in two different styles— a "bank note" or chiaroscuro style and an "outline" style—both derived from European sources. But Darley's nativism comes not from his artistic style, but from the application of the style to American subject matter. It is not Darley's illustrations of Scott and Dickens but of Irving and Cooper which make him an important American illustrator.

The "special" artists of the Civil War have also received some attention from writers. Two books in particular, Phillip Van Doren Stern's THEY WERE THERE (1959) and W. Fletcher Thompson, Jr.'s, THE IMAGE OF WAR (1959), provide comprehensive coverage of the role of the "special" artists and give examples of their artwork. Stern focuses more attention on individual illustrators, North and South, while Thompson concentrates more attention on "special" artists as a group and the Northern newspapers for which they worked. Both authors agree that the Civil War created an unprecedented demand for illustrations, which was resolved by using illustrators, cartoonists, commercial artists, fine artists, or artists imported from abroad. In fact, the demand for artwork was so great, Stern notes, that artwork done by amateurs, frequently soldiers in the field, was published. Thompson suggests that whatever their training, "special" artists entered the war with a romantic image of war, of battles being decided by titanic struggles of heroic men—an image of war that was quickly altered by reality and that was reflected in their illustration artwork. Thus, the growing grimness of newspaper illustrations about the war during the period 1861–1863 reflected not only the course of the war for the North but the disillusionment of many "special" artists.

When Southern states began to secede, FRANK LESLIE'S ILLUSTRATED NEWSPAPER (better known as LESLIE'S), HARPER'S WEEKLY, and the NEW YORK ILLUSTRATED NEWS organized to cover the impending war. According to Thompson, HARPER'S WEEKLY and LESLIE'S each had a half-dozen artists assigned full-time to Northern armies by the end of 1861. Among these were Winslow Homer, Thomas Nast, and Alfred and William Waud. Stern notes there were fewer illustrators covering the war for the South, but the best were Conrad Wise Chapman, John Adalbert Volck, and Frank Vizetelly, the last an English illustrator whose artwork appeared mostly in the ILLUSTRATED LONDON NEWS and created favorable English sentiment for the South. W. Stanley Hoole's book, VIZETELLY COVERS THE CONFEDERACY (1957), discusses Vizetelly's operations in the South, including numerous woodcuts, organized by time period, but it is the only work that deals with the activities and artwork of Southern special artists.

For Thompson, special artists needed three qualities—ability to sketch rapidly and accurately, ability to see battle scenes pictorially, and bravery. The last quality, while important, was not crucial since newspapers preferred panoramic battles scenes depicting the clash of opposing forces, scenes that could be drawn from a safe distance after the battle was over. Stern suggests that the most common subject in published Civil War art was the naval battle, but the enormous number of illustrations published makes it difficult to confirm that judgment. It can be said with reasonable certainty, however, that panoramic battle scenes, on land or water, were favorite subjects for illustrators.

How good were the Civil War artists? Thompson states that the illustrators' most frequent critics were the soldiers themselves. Good, accurate illustrators who "paid their dues" in the trenches with the troops were accepted by soldiers as equals who shared common risks. Pratt's analysis in CIVIL WAR IN PICTURES (1957) of how special artists handled various battles generally gives the artists good marks for faithful rendering of what happened. Given the time and battlefield pressures under which they worked that judgment must be the equivalent of a standing ovation. One way of judging the quality of the Civil War special artists is to compare them with their contemporaries covering other battles. Hodgson, in THE WAR ILLUSTRATORS (1977), reviews the war illustrators of the nineteenth century, British and American, and concludes that the British special artists during the last third of the century were the best, partly because changes in technology meant that illustrators no longer had to rely on engravers. Hodgson's most insightful comment is that the war illustrators rarely achieved lasting popularity; the skills necessary for the special artist were not easily transferable into professional skills applicable in a peacetime market. This was true of Civil War special artists—after the war many of them disappeared from view. Several books focus on individual special artists, namely, Ray, in ALFRED R. WAUD: CIVIL

WAR ARTIST (1974) and Grossman, in ECHOES OF A DISTANT DRUM: WINSLOW HOMER AND THE CIVIL WAR (1974). Ray's book, while focusing on Alfred Waud, also discusses the work of his brother William, since both worked for HARPER'S WEEKLY during the war. After a brief biography Ray focuses on Waud's career as a special artist, describing in excellent detail the dangers and boredom of the job, as well as giving insights into the background, training, and operations of special artists in the field and how their sketches were translated by engravers into front-page illustrations. Ray suggests that the demythologizing of the romance of war suggested by Thompson began with the battle of Antietam, where the special artists were appalled at the carnage they saw. After that, their artwork increasingly reflected the realities of the war. Ray's book is also useful in showing the relationship between some of Waud's battlefield sketches and how they were translated by engravers into newspaper images. As special artists grew to trust the judgement of engravers, their artwork became increasingly sketchy because illustrators could rely on engravers to fill in the details.

Grossman's book is the first effort to bring together Homer's Civil War artwork into one volume. Unfortunately Grossman frequently is caught in the dilemma of defending Homer from critics of his war illustrations and then admitting the validity of the criticism. Responding to the criticism that Homer (and Nast as well) spent very little time at the front, Grossman asserts that Homer "must have been" witness to many engagements, but later acknowledges that Homer probably drew mass battle scenes from imagination rather than observation. Grossman suggests that Homer must have been repelled by the horror of battle—as Thompson and Ray suggest special artists were—but he is forced to conclude that Homer was primarily interested in creating a romantic visual image of the war rather than factually reporting it. As such, many of his war illustrations represent excellent propaganda. Gordon Hendricks's THE LIFE AND WORK OF WINSLOW HOMER (1979) questions many of Grossman's conclusions, providing documentary evidence that Homer could not have been at the front doing some of the illustrations attributed to him. Under the circumstances there is the question of which of his war illustrations he drew and, of those, which were witnessed in person and which were the result of his rich romantic imagination. Beam's excellent book, WINSLOW HOMER'S MAGAZINE ENGRAVINGS (1979), spends little time analyzing Homer's Civil War illustrations, aside from concluding that Homer objectively reported what he saw, a conclusion even Grossman could not accept. Beam's checklist of Homer's magazine engravings does show Homer's dependence on HARPER'S WEEKLY for the publication of his Civil War art; during the war HARPER'S WEEKLY published thirty-three of his Civil War drawings.

Although the published engravings of the special artists still exist (both HARPER'S WEEKLY and LESLIE'S republished their Civil War art in commemorative publications during the 1890s), Stern notes that field sketches were often discarded by publishers after publication, so much of the original artwork has been lost. In 1974, however, AMERICAN HERITAGE published the artwork used by CENTURY MAGAZINE in their four-volume work, BATTLES AND

LEADERS OF THE CIVIL WAR (1884–1887). The CENTURY COLLECTION OF CIVIL WAR ART (1974), edited by Sears, presents a great deal of battlefield artwork done by Walton Taber and Theodore Davis, among others, although some of the artwork was done after the war from memory. Nonetheless, it is a rich source of primary material for the study of the sketches of special artists.

THE FIRST PROFESSIONALS: CHARLES PARSONS AND THE STAFF AT HARPER'S

Illustration as a profession, that is, a full-time, adequately compensated occupation producing high-quality work, did not begin until the House of Harper hired Charles Parsons, a lithographer and watercolorist, to head its art department in 1863. Parsons believed that publishing firms like Harper's had an important function in training illustrators and, in return for their training and experience, the illustrators should work exclusively for the firm. Harper's gave Parsons and his staff work space and Parsons supervised and critiqued the efforts of his staff, who in turn were guaranteed publication of their artwork.

Unfortunately, there has been little written about Parsons's tenure at Harper's, even though it lasted twenty-six years. In THE HOUSE OF HARPER (1912), J. Henry Harper devotes one chapter to Parsons and his early staff: C. S. Reinhart, Edwin Austin Abbey, J. W. Alexander, A. B. Frost, and Frank V. DuMond. Later, Howard Pyle was added to the staff and Parsons was responsible for much of the illustration work done for Harper's by Thomas Nast, Winslow Homer, and Frederic Remington. In Harper's book, the characterization of these artists and their relationship with Parsons is very sketchy, so it is difficult to understand Parsons's special role in the history of American illustration. More recently, the Montclair, New Jersey, Art Museum held an exhibit of Parsons's artwork and that of his staff—who presented a portfolio of their artwork to him when he retired in 1890. CHARLES PARSONS AND HIS DOMAIN (1958) remains the only work devoted to Parsons and his career as an art editor. Kathryn Gamble writes in the introduction that Parsons faced a curious problem—the young staff members were talented and eager to make names for themselves but they frequently needed the sympathetic discipline that Parsons provided. Indeed, Parsons's ability to spot talent from the often crude drawings that were submitted to him and to nurture that talent until it bloomed enabled Harper's to maintain its preeminence in illustration until the end of the century.

If there is little written about Parsons, there is even less written about many of those on his early staff. Charles Reinhart, senior man on the staff, is largely forgotten today; his work is discussed in Smith, AMERICAN ILLUSTRATORS (1893) and Smith's article in ILLUSTRATORS MONTHLY (1893), reprinted in DISCUSSIONS ON AMERICAN ART AND ARTISTS (1896).

Three of the most widely recognized and written about members of the Harper's staff were Edwin Austin Abbey, A. B. Frost, and Howard Pyle. Abbey is memorialized in a two-volume biography by E. V. Lucas, EDWIN AUSTIN ABBEY: ROYAL ACADEMICIAN (1921). Volume I covers Abbey's early art education with the Pre-Raphaelites at the Pennsylvania Academy of Fine Arts, his beginning work at Harper's in 1871 at age 18, until his decision in 1878 to live in Great Britain, although still working for Harper's. In addition to detailing Abbey's illustration career Volume I provides an excellent description of the operation of Harper's art department, including Abbey's illustration pay rates at various points in his career.

Although living in England and painting oils and watercolors, Abbey had an exclusive contract with Harper's for his illustrations, and Volume II traces Abbey's pursuit of both careers. When his exclusive contract with Harper's ended in the late 1890s, Abbey was able to devote his attention more fully to his fine art and to fulfilling illustration commissions from other sources. In 1901 he signed a contract with Harper's to do seventy drawings for William Shakespeare's plays, to appear in HARPER'S MONTHLY, and thirty for Oliver Goldsmith's DESERTED VILLAGE. Both commissions fitted nicely into Abbey's pen-and-ink style and his love of the Elizabethan period, upon which his earlier reputation had been founded. These commissions, along with the sale of his fine art, provided him with the financial security he needed until his death in 1911. The Lucas volumes, particularly Volume II, give the reader a sense of how Abbey was accepted by British society and artistic circles. Indeed, by the time of his death, he was looked upon more as a British artist than as an American illustrator. And that is one flaw in the Lucas biography—the emphasis is more on Abbey as British Royal Academician than as American illustrator for Harper's.

That flaw is remedied in EDWIN AUSTIN ABBEY (1974), an exhibition catalog for the Yale University Art Gallery. The analysis focuses on Abbey's style in illustration and fine art, concluding that Abbey remained an illustrator throughout his whole career; in both his illustrations and fine art one can see his concern for concrete expression of a text or scene. For Abbey, technique was always subordinate to content. It was this commitment to realism and Abbey's virtuosity in pen and ink that led Ernest Knauft to label him as the "foremost" pen-and-ink illustrator in America (MODERN PEN DRAWINGS: EUROPEAN AND AMERICAN [1901]).

The material on A. B. Frost is scarce, which is surprising since he was active as an illustrator for over fifty years. Henry Reed's THE A. B. FROST BOOK (1967) is the only full biography of Frost, and it emphasizes Frost's ability to depict rural and sporting scenes, including his illustrations for Harris's Uncle Remus books. The book includes an excellent critique of Frost's illustration style, suggesting that Frost's A BOOK OF DRAWINGS (1904) is typical of his rural style. By the turn of the century Frost was at the peak of his career, and shortly thereafter, like many illustrators who aspired to be fine artists, he went to Europe to study painting. He returned to the United States in 1914 and continued to work intermittently as an illustrator until blindness and death put an end to his career in 1926.

Given the length and diversity of Frost's career it is not surprising that the Reed biography has shortcomings. F. Hopkinson Smith, one of Frost's contemporaries,

writes that a central facet of Frost's work is his humor (AMERICAN ILLUS-
TRATORS [1893]), and one of the most unique expressions of that humor can
be seen in the hundreds of comic-book-style illustrations that Frost did for SCRIB-
NER'S and HARPER'S MONTHLY magazines. Comparatively little attention
is paid to them in the Reed book. Much the same can be said for Frost's sport
illustrations; his golf illustrations during the golfing craze at the turn of the century
are pointed but sympathetic. Sadly, Reed did not have access to the Scribner's
company files when he wrote his book. That material, located at Princeton University, traces Frost's personal history through the eyes of his correspondence
with that company. Most touching are the letters Frost wrote to Joseph Chapin,
a long-time friend and art editor at SCRIBNER'S, asking for more illustration
commissions as his eyesight began to fail him. This correspondence would add
another dimension to the "usual" artistic biography and no one deserves that
recognition more than Frost.

Homer's post-Civil War magazine illustrations, many of them done for Harper's, are discussed in Beam's WINSLOW HOMER'S MAGAZINE ENGRAV-
INGS. Beam notes that the period 1867–1875 produced the largest group of
magazine illustrations done by Homer, nearly one hundred. These illustrations
frequently involved young men and women in the diversions of contemporary
life—picnicking, bathing, playing sports. He also paid tribute to attractive women,
serving as the Charles Dana Gibson of his day. But there is also a touch of
melancholy in his engravings, a yearning for a more rural, bygone era. Beam's
book is unusual because he devotes the bulk of the book to the composition,
design, and aesthetic content of Homer's magazine illustrations; his artistic style
in terms of process and techniques; his development as a professional illustrator
(a role in which he was not comfortable); and the economics of magazine illustration during that period. The placement of Homer and his illustration artwork
within a larger context of magazine illustration enriches our understanding of
Homer and his sudden decision to quit as an illustrator in the 1880s, as well as
our understanding of illustration as a profession. Given the amount of work Homer
did for Harper's it is surprising that Beam makes no mention of Charles Parsons
and his role in Homer's artistic development.

A number of writers have examined the totality of Homer's art, including his
illustrations. Albert Ten Eyck Gardner's WINSLOW HOMER (1961) is a comprehensive volume that suggests his illustration career had an important influence
on his subsequent development, but does not devote much space to analyzing the
relationship between his illustrations and fine art. On the other hand, Gordon
Hendricks's book, THE LIFE AND WORK OF WINSLOW HOMER (1979),
provides an excellent detailed biography of Homer and devotes more time and
space than virtually any other biographer to Homer's magazine artwork, beginning
with his lithographer's apprenticeship in Boston. Using private correspondence
and artwork previously unavailable, Hendricks analyzes a number of Homer's
illustrations and questions many of those attributed to him by other biographers.
Indeed, Hendricks is generally quite critical of earlier Homer biographers, sug-

gesting they have borrowed from one another without reappraisal. Subsequently, some of Hendricks's conclusions, for example, that there is no evidence that Homer visited the troops or the front after returning home in July 1862, are not shared by others, particularly Beam. But Hendricks's intensive analysis of Homer's artwork and correspondence makes his conclusions difficult to refute. This excellent book concludes with a chronology of Homer's life; a checklist of works by Homer in public collections, cataloged by state and city; a checklist of published graphics, listed by year; and an extensive bibliography of books and articles written about Homer, many by his contemporaries.

The literature on Howard Pyle, unlike that of other illustrators, is extensive, if highly repetitive. Pyle's stature stems from the recognition by his contemporaries that he was the leading dramatic illustrator during the last twenty years of the nineteenth century (Ernest Knauft, in MODERN PEN DRAWINGS: EUROPEAN AND AMERICAN [1901]) and his success in making the transition from pen-and-ink to four-color work, while maintaining his preeminence in both (Frank Weitenkampf, THE ILLUSTRATED BOOK [1938]). Harold Von Schmidt labels Pyle as the greatest illustrator America has ever produced (Walt Reed, ed., THE ILLUSTRATOR IN AMERICA: 1900–1960 [1966]). The verdict was not unanimous, however. F. Hopkinson Smith's AMERICAN ILLUSTRATORS pays little attention to Pyle, given his preeminence in the field. Joseph Pennell, in THE GRAPHIC ARTS (1920), suggests that Pyle's early work, particularly ROBIN HOOD, was very good but over time the quality of his work declined.

Pyle's importance stems from his role as teacher as well as that of illustrator. There is very little disagreement that Pyle's influence as a teacher was felt in his lifetime, as his students made their mark on American illustration, and with succeeding generations who studied Pyle's work or studied with some of Pyle's students who became teachers.

If one were to choose a biographer of Howard Pyle it would have to be Henry C. Pitz, whose books HOWARD PYLE (1975) and THE BRANDYWINE TRADITION (1968) constitute the most comprehensive examinations of his life and works. Charles Abbott's HOWARD PYLE: A CHRONICLE (1925) is less biographical than Pitz's books but makes good use of some of Pyle's correspondence, giving the reader some insight into Pyle's thoughts regarding illustration as a profession and what he was striving to do in his teaching. Susan Meyer's chapter on Pyle in AMERICA'S GREAT ILLUSTRATORS (1978) adds some fresh analytic insights into Pyle's artistic development and his contributions to American illustration. In addition, the Brandywine River Museum and the Delaware Art Museum, both repositories of Pyle's artwork, have held major exhibits of Pyle's work and that of his students; their exhibition catalogs constitute an important and continuing source of information.

The outlines of Pyle's career are clear. He was raised in Wilmington, Delaware, studied art for a year in Philadelphia, and then moved to New York. Despite an uneven early publication record Pyle's artistic qualities were recognized by Charles Parsons at Harper's who hired Pyle as a copyist until he could develop his own illustration skills sufficiently. Pyle worked for Harper's for several years, attending classes at the Art Students League in his spare time. By 1879 he felt confident enough of his ability to quit Harper's and return to Wilmington, confident that he could make a living free-lancing. His first successful book was THE MERRY ADVENTURES OF ROBIN HOOD (1883), which was followed by three additional children's books, PEPPER AND SALT (1886), THE WONDER CLOCK (1888), and OTTO OF THE SILVER HAND (1888), during the next five years. These four books established Pyle's reputation as a fine pen-and-ink artist and established his popularity as an illustrator. Pyle continued his pen-and-ink drawing after 1900 in his King Arthur quartet—THE STORY OF KING ARTHUR AND HIS KNIGHTS (1903), THE STORY OF THE CHAMPIONS OF THE ROUND TABLE (1905), THE STORY OF SIR LANCELOT AND HIS COMPANIONS (1907), and THE STORY OF THE GRAIL AND THE PASSING OF ARTHUR (1910)—although his illustration style changed. After 1900 Pyle concentrated more heavily on painted illustrations for halftone and color reproduction, producing a series of historical romances, pirate stories, and medieval tales.

Analyses of Pyle's illustrations have produced occasionally conflicting results. Focusing on the subject matter of his illustration, Pitz (1975) notes that the adult magazine illustrations were almost exclusively devoted to the American scene, while his book illustrations frequently had fantasy or European historical themes. Roland Elzea's analysis of Pyle's artistic content (HOWARD PYLE: DIVERSITY IN DEPTH [1973]) finds that approximately the same percentage (one-third) was devoted to colonial and revolutionary war illustrations and to illustrations for children's works. Although Pyle's pirate illustrations are widely recognized they constitute only 3 percent of his output, far less than his mystical and allegorical illustrations (15 percent), which are not well known or remembered.

The inspirational sources for many of Pyle's illustrations are easy to identify. Pitz, in THE BRANDYWINE TRADITION (1968), suggests it was the history and countryside of the Brandywine River valley, while Susan Meyer (AMERICA'S GREAT ILLUSTRATORS [1978]) adds that the Civil War, his Quaker heritage (although Pitz suggests that his làter Swedenborgian religion played a role), and his childhood literature were influential. Meyer points out that Pyle's illustrations are expressions of two sides of his character—his love for his American roots and the legends and fables that he read as a child.

The sources of Pyle's artistic style are less clear-cut. Pitz (1975) suggests that Pyle's pen-and-ink style was derived from Albrecht Durer, particularly in ROBIN HOOD, but his other children's books of the period show a lighter touch than Durer's work. The influences on Pyle's color work are more controversial. Pitz changes his analysis in the seven years between his two books; in THE BRAN-DYWINE TRADITION (1968) he suggests that Pyle was influenced by French Impressionism but that he did not become a slave to it—light was a means to an end, not an end in itself. Seven years later, in HOWARD PYLE (1975), Pitz argues that Pyle was untouched by Impressionism; Pyle was not interested in a wide range of colors but in a range of tones. This latter interpretation makes sense in terms of Pyle's sensitivity to the needs of halftone reproduction, which favored an illustrator with a limited range of colors but control of those color hues. On the other hand, Pyle's color artwork does show an awareness of light, particularly in some of his pirate pictures. Whether this was a self-conscious adaptation of French Impressionism is difficult to determine; Pyle's unwillingness to acknowledge the value of non-American sources of inspiration suggest that his use of light was his own way of dealing with an illustration problem rather than a conscious aping of an artistic movement. Susan Meyer, in AMERICA'S GREAT ILLUSTRATORS (1978), argues that Pyle's illustrative style reflected two different trends—a traditional decorative approach and the concern with light and shadow typical of the Impressionists. Thus, she sees nothing contradictory in Pitz's two assessments of Pyle's style.

In his introduction to THE BRANDYWINE HERITAGE (1971), Richard McLanathan suggests there is evidence in Pyle's work of his interest in the work of the Pre-Raphaelites in England and America. His ROBIN HOOD certainly contains decorative motifs that could have been influenced by the Pre-Raphaelites or the Arts and Crafts movement in England. But overall, Pyle's artwork is more dramatic than decorative, so the influence was minimal and episodic at best. McLanathan's analysis also suggests that Pyle's artwork contains a darker side, a suggestion of the sinister, the use of the sea as a primal force, and a very personal relationship with nature. Pitz (1975) suggests that this "dark" side of Pyle's artwork comes from his Swedenborgian religion, with its attendant mysticism.

The best description of Pyle's style would be that used by Pitz—a Romantic Realist. His artwork is historically accurate but his scenes and figures fit within a Romantic tradition of American art and literature that eulogized the American past. According to Pitz (1968), the Brandywine River valley of Pennsylvania and Delaware, where Pyle grew up and later painted and taught, was steeped in historical tradition dating to the pre–revolutionary war period, and that tradition had its impact on Pyle's work more than anything else.

Pyle's teaching has been the subject of much analysis. Most illustrators who studied with Pyle acknowledge their debt to him, and their biographies are replete with references to Pyle's teaching style or the organization of his school. The number of students who studied with Pyle is open to some speculation. How long and in what way did someone have to study with Pyle to be listed as one of his students? Maxfield Parrish, for example, spent a very short time studying with Pyle at the Drexel Institute when Pyle began teaching illustration, and he is usually listed as one of Pyle's students. After Pyle's school had received some recognition a number of practicing illustrators brought their specific technical problems to Pyle for help—these people were probably the bulk of his instruction between 1904 and 1910–but they are normally not listed as his students. Pitz (1975) lists 110 students who studied with Pyle while Elzea and Hawkes, in A SMALL SCHOOL OF ART (1980), list 167. Regardless of the total number of students, it is apparent that Pyle taught few students at any one time. Beginning with his first illustration classes at Drexel Institute in Philadelphia in 1894, Pyle rarely had more than thirty students in any class; one reason he quit teaching at Drexel and opened his own school was that he could then control the number and quality of students. A SMALL SCHOOL OF ART gives the reader a good idea of the range of people who studied with Pyle, the quality of their artwork, and their success; the brief biographies and examples of illustration artwork are particularly useful for Pyle's students who are less well known than Wyeth, Parrish, Schoonover, and the like.

A number of writers have described Pyle's teaching style. Perhaps the best short description of Pyle's teaching style is Ann Barton Brown's HOWARD PYLE, A TEACHER (1980). Students interested in studying with Pyle had to submit portfolios of their artwork, and Pyle frequently interviewed them before admitting them. In some years there were more than fifty applicants for every vacancy. Once admitted, students shared the work of maintaining the studio and the cost of materials; Pyle's income came from his illustration artwork. Admitted students were placed on a probationary status and their work closely supervised by Pyle and his two assistants, Stanley Arthurs and Frank Schoonover. Once past this probationary period, students were expected to be at their easels in the morning working on assignments, while afternoons and evenings were devoted to critiques of artwork submitted in response to one of Pyle's assignments. From N. C. Wyeth's letters to his mother during his training (Betsy James Wyeth, THE WYETHS [1971]), one gets some insight into the intensity of the experience. The notes from Pyle's Monday night lectures in 1904 that appear in Rowland Elzea, ed., HOWARD PYLE: DIVERSITY IN DEPTH (1973) give a brief statement of Pyle's philosophy of illustration. But perhaps the most comprehensive description of Pyle's teaching style and content can be found in Pitz (1975), which outlines the basic tenets of Pyle's approach to illustration and describes in graphic detail his teaching style. Central to all these descriptions is the recognition that Pyle seldom spoke of painting technique to his students—he was more interested in teaching an approach to illustration, regardless of technique, an approach that emphasized the need for illustrators to use their imaginations and to immerse themselves in the story they were illustrating. Their artwork was to focus on the dramatic highlights of the story and to draw the viewer into the emotional vortex of the artwork. Pyle's class critiques provided students with evaluations of how well they had internalized Pyle's message and with stimuli to do better in the future. Pyle's ability to see the crux of the problem in a student's work and explain how to deal with that problem made his teaching invaluable and effective.

As students became more accomplished Pyle frequently gave them illustration commissions that he could not finish or sought commissions specifically for them. A letter, quoted in Abbott's HOWARD PYLE: A CHRONICLE (1925), from Pyle to Edward Penfield, then art editor at Harper's, suggests that Pyle sought commissions for his students as a way of determining how effective his teaching had been; if his good students could have their artwork published in magazines and books then he was doing a good job. At the same time, art editors would give commissions to Pyle's students with the understanding that Pyle would supervise them to completion. As a result Pyle's best students frequently had their illustrations published before they had completed their studies. Pyle's relations with HARPER'S MONTHLY, for example, were so good that Best (1980) concludes from an analysis of the artwork published between 1906 and 1910 that the magazine had become an "art gallery" for Pyle and his students.

Pitz is ambivalent about the impact of Pyle on his students. In his 1968 book Pitz argues that since many of Pyle's students adopted his manner, it was easy to identify a "Pyle look" in many magazines. A few pages later he concedes that the work of Pyle's students is markedly individual; their illustrations are the expression of their interests and talents operating within the Pyle approach to illustration. Both these evaluations have legitimacy. Because Pyle was a Romantic Realist, so were many of his students, and this approach to illustration stamps their illustration artwork with basic similarities. Even the women who studied with Pyle shared some commonalities, although they worked within a more decorative style.

In AMERICA'S GREAT ILLUSTRATORS (1978), Susan Meyer provides an interesting analysis of the later years of Pyle's career, suggesting that the professional revolution that Pyle had started and helped foster soon left him behind. As evidence she cites his short-lived career as part-time art editor for McCLURE'S magazine, his growing dissatisfaction with his artwork, his interest in mural artwork, and his decision to go to Italy in 1910 to seek artistic renewal. Her description of Pyle in late middle age, suffering from artistic self-doubt, is not consistent with Pitz's description but is nonetheless an intriguing explanation for some facets of Pyle's last five years as an illustrator.

Pyle's impact on American illustration is quite clear. Ruth Patterson (1954) sees Pyle as pivotal in the development of American illustration—turning illustration from "an inferior and unrecognized art typified by the insipid drawings of the late Victorian era, to an acknowledged artistic medium worthy of consideration as great art, and of serious attention to aspiring artists" (p. 1). Susan Meyer (1978) labels Pyle the father of American illustration—a title that few would dispute, given his impact as illustrator and teacher.

Although Pyle and the Harper's art department were influential in the devel opment of illustration as a profession there were other illustrators of this period who merit recognition. In AMERICAN ILLUSTRATORS (1893), F. Hopkinson Smith discusses Abbey, Reinhart, Frost, and Pyle, as well as Elihu Vedder, Will Low, E. W. Kemble, and Harry Fenn, the last group being illustrators little heard of today. Elihu Vedder has become more visible recently due to the publication of Regina Soria's book, ELIHU VEDDER (1970), and PERCEPTIONS AND EVOCATIONS: THE ART OF ELIHU VEDDER (1979), a catalog of his exhibit at the National Collection of Fine Arts. Soria's book interweaves Vedder's development as a fine artist with his career as an illustrator; from his correspondence she concludes that illustration never appealed to him as a profession, except for the illustration of his own books. Jane Dillenberger has a nice discussion of Vedder's themes for THE RUBAIYAT OF OMAR KHAYYAM in her essay in

PERCEPTIONS AND EVOCATIONS. To her, Vedder was an artist-illustrator: an artist first and an illustrator only when he needed money to live on. The same can be said for Will Low, although his autobiography, A CHRONICLE OF FRIENDSHIP (1908), provides some interesting thoughts on illustration. Unfortunately, a host of talented illustrators from this early period have not received the attention and research they so richly deserve. Edward Blum, Otto Bacher, Harry Fenn, Ernest Peixotto, Reginald Birch, Edward Kemble, and William Drake are discussed in Ernest Knauft's essay in MODERN PEN DRAWINGS: EUROPEAN AND AMERICAN (1901), but almost nowhere else. Even the initial illustrators of the West are largely ignored, except for Robert Taft's excellent book, ARTISTS AND ILLUSTRATORS OF THE OLD WEST, 1850–1900 (1953), which details who the early artists and illustrators were and why they went west. Taft also provides excellent critiques of their artwork, frequently picture by picture, noting, for example, that Alfred Mathews's book, PENCIL SKETCHES OF COLORADO, while important, suffers from Mathews's poor sense of perspective and stiffness in drawing buildings. In this book we discover what happened to Alfred Waud and Theodore Davis—special artists during the Civil War; they went west and did illustrations. Ninety black-and-white plates give a good sense of the major works of each artist, and the footnotes are lengthy and detailed. Unfortunately, there is no bibliography so one must read the text and footnotes to determine where some of the illustrations were published.

THE GOLDEN AGE OF AMERICAN ILLUSTRATION: 1890–1920

Although Howard Pyle was a leading figure during this period the earlier analysis will not be repeated; instead we will focus on Pyle's students and others who made this period one of the most colorful in the history of American illustration. The attention is selective, however. There are excellent works on many illustrators during this twenty-five-year period but others are virtually ignored. This is true for Pyle's students as well; there are works dealing with Frank Schoonover, N. C. Wyeth, Maxfield Parrish, and Jessie Wilcox Smith but virtually nothing regarding their talented contemporaries Thornton Oakley and Sarah Stillwell. We begin with Pyle's students, since much of the writing on illustrators of this period deals with them. Subsequently we will examine the "American Beauty" illustrators, the western illustrators, and others.

Two of Pyle's most talented students—N. C. Wyeth and Maxfield Parrish—have received the greatest attention. Virtually every book dealing with Pyle or the Golden Age of American illustration devotes some space to Wyeth and Parrish. Susan Meyer (AMERICA'S GREAT ILLUSTRATORS [1978]) includes them in her pantheon as two of America's greatest illustrators. There are several outstanding books on N. C. Wyeth: Douglas Allen and Douglas Allen, Jr.'s N. C. WYETH (1972) and Betsy James Wyeth's THE WYETHS (1971). The Allens' book is undoubtedly the most comprehensive book by any researcher to date. It has a good solid biography but much of the space is devoted to analyzing various facets of his artwork, his book illustrations in the Scribner's ILLUSTRATED

CLASSICS series, his advertising art, and his murals, presenting examples of each in color and black and white. Equally important, the book provides the most comprehensive bibliography of his published illustrations currently available. For the collector of Wyeth's illustration artwork the bibliography is sufficient reason to purchase this excellent work. Betsy James Wyeth, Andrew Wyeth's wife and N. C. Wyeth's daughter-in-law, has done the important job of pulling together Wyeth's letters to his family in THE WYETHS (1971). These letters give a firsthand view of Wyeth's development as an illustrator, his reactions to studying with Pyle, and his increasing ambivalence about the value of what Pyle taught him. It is clear from this correspondence that Wyeth always wanted the recognition accorded a fine artist but liked the financial security that accrued from his illustration artwork. Wyeth's correspondence also gives occasional insights into his business dealings with various publishers—questions of how much he should be paid for his artwork, his dependence on Scribner's, and his fear of being stereotyped as doing only one kind of illustration. Wyeth's correspondence in the Scribner's Collection at Princeton adds to this book, and the Wyeth and Scribner's Collection letters, in toto, provide a unique perspective on Wyeth's business relations. The later correspondence in the Wyeth book shows a maturing Wyeth, raising a family and training his son Andrew to be an artist. Betsy James Wyeth's book is valuable because it allows the reader to see his world and his work through Wyeth's eyes, and his letters, intended for his family, are refreshingly honest.

A number of others have written about N. C. Wyeth or some part of his career. The Allens' bibliography lists books and articles dealing with Wyeth and is a good starting point. The bibliography of material written on Wyeth included in Jeff Dykes's FIFTY GREAT WESTERN ILLUSTRATORS (1975) is also helpful. The Pitz article on Wyeth for AMERICAN HERITAGE (1965) is too short to be anything more than an introduction to Wyeth's western art. Susan Meyer's February 1975 issue of AMERICAN ARTIST presents a fascinating artistic genealogy of the Wyeth family, tracing the careers and development of N. C. Wyeth, his children, and his grandchildren. It is, indeed, an artistic dynasty. Her article on N. C. Wyeth in this issue provides an insightful, succinct analysis of his artwork. She pinpoints the conflict between his easel painting and illustration and his debt to Pyle. Indeed, Richard McLanathan's comparison of Pyle and Wyeth in THE BRANDYWINE HERITAGE (1971) makes clear that, while their styles were different, there were many similarities, particularly a preoccupation with the past and a felt need to recreate that past artistically as accurately as possible. Susan Meyer's chapter on Wyeth in AMERICA'S GREAT ILLUSTRATORS (1978) amplifies this point, noting Wyeth's love of nature as well. Meyer emphasizes Wyeth's idea that experience gives one the emotional depth necessary to effectively portray a scene. To paint a western scene one must have lived it or have the necessary experience and imagination to recreate it, a point that Pyle frequently made to his students.

Fortunately, Maxfield Parrish has a biographer as competent as the Allens were in dealing with Wyeth. The result is Coy Ludwig's book, MAXFIELD PARRISH

(1973). After a brief biographical essay, Ludwig analyzes in detail the various facets of Parrish's career: book and magazine illustrations, posters and advertisements, color art prints, murals and paintings, landscapes, and calendar art. The book concludes with a chapter detailing his various artistic techniques, particularly Parrish's glazing, which gave much of his artwork its luminescent quality. There are numerous black-and-white and color plates of Parrish's illustrations, so the reader develops a real sense of the breadth of his skill, as well as the repetition of certain motifs in various media. A compositional device, dynamic symmetry, is apparent in many of Parrish's pieces—one side of the illustration is a mirror image of the other, and Ludwig provides many examples of Parrish's use of this technique.

Although Ludwig's book gives an excellent cross section of Parrish's artwork, Paul W. Skeeters's MAXFIELD PARRISH: THE EARLY YEARS (1973) reproduces in folio size complete sets of illustrations that Parrish used for his early book illustrations. More than two hundred illustrations, many in color, organized chronologically by book, give the reader a sense of how Parrish dealt with various illustration and design problems, the unity of his artwork within a given book, and the development of his illustration skills over time. Unfortunately, little space is devoted to this type of analysis, for this book is truly a lavish "picture book" for the Maxfield Parrish fan.

Susan Meyer's chapter on Parrish in AMERICA'S GREAT ILLUSTRATORS (1978) focuses on his design and technical qualities, suggesting that the compositional balance derived from his long-standing interest in architecture and his adherence to a theory of dynamic symmetry. She marvels at the range of his interests as well as his skills, concluding, "Poster artist, children's book illustrator, humorist, landscape painter, designer, architect, craftsman, and muralist: a more-than-sixty-year career in which none of his creative powers ever diminished" (p. 128). While the last assessment is debatable there is no doubt that Parrish's artistic career was almost da Vincian in scope. A major driving force behind that career, recognized by Ludwig and Meyer, was the quest to make money, to live comfortably. To that end Parrish used his talent in as many money-making ways as possible, leading Meyer to label him as "the businessman with a brush." Both Meyer and Ludwig devote space to Parrish's business relations, particularly with publishing houses and art reproduction firms which were the major sources of his income.

Avis Berman's article in ARTS AND ANTIQUES (1980) notes several characteristics of his artwork other than those mentioned by Ludwig and Meyer—his flair for portraying festive occasions (although these constitute a very small proportion of his output) and, more important, his careful detailing of costume. One has only to study the costumes in THE KNAVE OF HEARTS (1925), a book lavishly designed and illustrated by Parrish, to realize the design skill and detail that went into his costume illustrations. In addition, food, cooks, and eating are recurrent themes in Parrish's artwork; it is little wonder that THE KNAVE OF

HEARTS deals with these themes or that Jell-O hired Parrish for their advertising art.

Given Parrish's interest in architecture, the dynamic symmetry of his design, and his attention to costume, it is useful to view many of his illustrations as stage designs in illustration format. Combining his color sense and glazing techniques, the resulting artwork became "set pieces" of lasting appeal.

Few of Pyle's students have had biographers like the Allens or Ludwig. Frank Schoonover's son, Cortland Schoonover, using his father's artistic production day books and correspondence, has written FRANK SCHOONOVER: ILLUS-TRATOR OF THE NORTH AMERICAN FRONTIER (1976). Schoonover's importance stems from the quantity of artwork produced over his career (over four thousand pictures), his position as Pyle's assistant, the quality of his artwork, and the popular appeal of his books. But Cortland Schoonover relies too heavily on his father's words and there is too little analysis of Schoonover's artwork, compared with that of his contemporaries. What emerges is a fragmented picture of Schoonover's career, work habits, illustration techniques, and publications. Together with Schoonover's reprints of his father's articles about the Canadian North Woods, THE EDGE OF THE WILDERNESS (1974), Frank Apgar's brief biography and reasonably complete bibliography of Schoonover's book illustrations in FRANK SCHOONOVER, PAINTER-ILLUSTRATOR: A BIBLIOG-RAPHY (1969) and the Henry Pitz article in AMERICAN ARTIST (1964), one gets a good sense of the range, quality, and appeal of his artwork. Following Pyle's advice that illustrators must experience what they illustrate, Schoonover spent several years in the Canadian wilderness, even taking his new bride with him on one trip. That intimate knowledge of the wilderness makes his pictures ring true as honest depictions.

Robert Karolevitz's books on Harvey Dunn, THE PRAIRIE IS MY GARDEN (1969) and WHERE YOUR HEART IS: THE STORY OF HARVEY DUNN, ARTIST (1970)—essentially the same book with two titles—describe the career of one of Pyle's few midwestern students, the son of a sod farmer who never forgot his South Dakota roots, who felt most comfortable illustrating that land and its people. It was Dunn's ability to portray "normal" people, even ugly ones, that helped earn him his reputation (see the portfolio of his illustrations in WHERE YOUR HEART IS). After World War I, however, Dunn gave up his illustration career and began to teach illustration, trying to promulgate the tenets of Howard Pyle's approach to illustration and emulate his teaching style. He was far less successful, although Dean Cornwell, one of his pupils, was a leading illustrator of the next generation. Ernest Watson's article in AMERICAN ARTIST (1942) describes the operation of Dunn's art school and its impact. The Delaware Art Museum exhibition catalog, STANLEY ARTHURS (1974), provides a starting point for that illustrator. Arthurs is important because in his artwork one can see most clearly the impact of Pyle's teaching and because Arthurs, along with Schoonover, served as an assistant to Pyle in his school. This catalog focuses on

Arthurs's approach to illustration and contains a number of his illustrations. WHALERS, WHARVES, AND WATERWAYS (1973) may be the only biography and bibliography of Pyle's seafaring student, Clifford Ashley. In addition, the sixty-nine black-and-white and color reproductions of his artwork demonstrate his knowledge of knots and his love of the sea.

W.H.D. Koerner is one of those illustrators difficult to classify as a student of Pyle. Koerner studied at the Art Institute of Chicago and the Art Student's League, and had done extensive advertising illustration before beginning his studies with Pyle in 1907. As W. H. Hutchinson notes in his book, THE WORLD, THE WORK, AND THE WEST OF W.H.D. KOERNER (1978), Koerner's study with Pyle was pivotal in his career development. During the time he spent in Wilmington he was influenced not only by Pyle but by Harvey Dunn, Stanley Arthurs, and Frank Schoonover as well. W.H.D. KOERNER (1977) emphasizes his Wilmington experience but is not as long nor as complete as the Hutchinson book. After leaving Pyle, Koerner devoted himself to western illustration, following a tradition established by Frederic Remington. Interestingly, Koerner was one of the very few Pyle students who became a true "western" illustrator.

The writing on Pyle's women students is modest, and limited to Jessie Wilcox Smith and her two compatriots in their studio at Cogslea, Elizabeth Shippen Green and Violet Oakley. Two works stand as the primary source material: S. Michael Schnessel's JESSIE WILCOX SMITH (1973) and Cathryn Connell Stryker's exhibition catalog, THE STUDIOS AT COGSLEA (1976). The Schnessel book, drawn from the Smith papers at the Archives of American Art and a small number of interviews, ostensibly deals with Jessie Wilcox Smith, but in the process of describing her life story and analyzing her artwork discusses eighteen other women who studied with Pyle. The discussion and the list of illustrators in A SMALL SCHOOL OF ART by Elzea and Hawkes make clear that Jessie Trimble's judgment (THE OUTLOOK [1907]) that Pyle did not encourage women students is incorrect. In fact, Pyle worked to get Jessie Wilcox Smith and Elizabeth Shippen Green their first commission.

In 1901, after studying with Pyle for several years, Smith, Green and Violet Oakley—who achieved success as a muralist—established a joint studio in Bryn Mawr, Pennsylvania. Later they moved their studio to a nearby house, which they called Cogslea. Cathryn Connell Stryker analyzes the three women at Cogslea, but within the framework of a larger set of questions about women in illustration: What attracted women to illustration? Why were they successful? And why were they limited to illustrating only certain subjects, primarily women and children? The careers of the women at Cogslea provide answers to these questions. Women illustrators were limited to drawing or painting women and children because it was assumed that the large female readership of magazines wanted to see illustrations of this type done by other women. The descriptions of the careers of the three women are too brief to be very insightful, and Schnessel's book is more comprehensive in coverage, so the more general discussion of the role of women in illustration provides a useful backdrop for the material in Schnessel's book.

Gene Mitchell's THE SUBJECT WAS CHILDREN (1979) provides a brief biographical sketch of Smith and some useful insights into the appeal of her work; according to Mitchell, Smith was able to show a child's world from a child's perspective in ways that adults could understand, and to transmit her love of motherhood and childhood to her viewers. Indeed, the bulk of the book is devoted to Smith's artwork, showing clearly her talent in dealing with mothers and children. Ruth Freeman's book, JESSIE WILCOX SMITH: CHILDHOOD'S GREAT ILLUSTRATOR (1977), is a brief, breezy, and occasionally incorrect look at the life and career of Jessie Wilcox Smith. It tells nothing new and the bibliography of Smith's illustrations is incomplete—it covers none of her magazine illustrations and fails to list all of her book illustrations.

It is sad that the bulk of attention paid to Pyle's women students has been devoted to these three women. A number of others deserve attention, for example, a more thorough study of Sarah Stillwell. The Delaware Art Museum is doing a good job of publicizing the works of Pyle's lesser-known students, and the catalog by Elzea and Hawkes, A SMALL SCHOOL OF ART, tells us much of what we know about Pyle's women students, combined with the material in the Brandywine River Museum catalog, WOMEN ARTISTS IN THE HOWARD PYLE TRA-DITION (1975). Hawkes's BERTHA CORSON DAY BATES (1978) is a very brief review of her career and introduction to her illustration artwork. Nonetheless, there is an obvious vacuum in our knowledge about women illustrators in general and those who studied with Howard Pyle, in particular.

There were other illustrators besides Howard Pyle and his students who made important contributions to the Golden Age of illustration. One group, the western illustrators, established a tradition and reputation of excellence. The two major western illustrators of this period were Frederic Remington and Charles M. Russell, whose illustration artwork dominated the field between 1890 and 1910.

More has been written about Remington than Russell because Remington was more prolific and because Remington's depiction of the West is more controversial than that of his contemporary. Harold McCracken's book FREDERIC REMING-TON: ARTIST OF THE OLD WEST (1947) was the first comprehensive biography of Remington and established many of the themes subsequent writers have accepted. According to McCracken, Remington's appeal stems from his pictorial story-telling ability, the authenticity of his artwork, and his drawing ability. McCracken does suggest one weakness in Remington's artwork: he was an incurable romantic. For Remington, the story of the West was that of men and horses against near overwhelming odds and this theme dominates his illustrations. As a consequence there a very few women in his artwork and horses play a predominant role. A major contribution of McCracken's book is the bibliographical checklist of 2,739 pieces of Remington's work that appeared in print, as well as 32 color and 8 black-and-white plates of his artwork, thereby documenting the breadth of Remington's artwork. Remington's background—born in the East, studying at Yale, occasional trips to the West in the 1880s and 1890s, and returning to New York to do his finished artwork—allowed Remington a unique perspective on the western experience. This perspective is analyzed by McCracken in one of his later books, THE FREDERIC REMINGTON BOOK (1966), in which he defines Remington's artistic credo as "truthful Realism," and delineates thirteen themes that are prominent in Remington's artwork. Unfortunately, there is substantially more illustration artwork than analysis, and the thematic presentation raises questions about Remington's credo of truthful Realism. For example, Remington did a number of illustrations of early explorers and pioneers of the West who had disappeared by the time Remington made his first trip there. Perhaps McCracken's most critical error was in suggesting that Remington "had a sympathetic attitude toward the Indians, gained from personal friendships with many of the tribesmen and an understanding of them as people" (p. 89). Little of this sympathy comes through in his artwork, where Indians are most frequently portrayed as opponents of the white man.

Susan Meyer's chapter on Remington in AMERICA'S GREAT ILLUSTRA-TORS (1978) accepts McCracken's uncritical stance toward Remington, suggesting that Remington's artwork had only one purpose—to objectively record and document the changing West. Since Remington approached his artwork journalistically, Meyer argues he avoided any temptation to romanticize the West he was depicting (except for his later fine art). Surprisingly, Meyer seems unaware of much of the criticism of Remington's work noted below.

Peter Hassrick's biography, FREDERIC REMINGTON (1973), takes a somewhat different perspective, although still accepting the basic thrust of McCracken's analysis. For Hassrick, Remington was a narrative painter, and in his artistic stories the people and the part they played in history were of primary importance. Given this interest it was only natural that Remington should look to the West and its emphasis on frontier individualism as the source for many of his stories. Remington also liked the West because it was a man's world, a place where a man could prove himself—something Remington was constantly trying to do in his personal life, from playing football at Yale to travelling with the western cavalry. With this emphasis on men proving themselves, conflict became central to much of his artwork, and the western backgrounds of his work diminished into insignificance. It was not the setting but the conflict that was important. One point on which Hassrick and McCracken do disagree is Remington's treatment of Indians. Hassrick disagrees that Remington portrayed Indians truthfully because of his firsthand knowledge of them; he suggests that Remington's inability to understand Indian thought led him to treat them emotionally and romantically, rather than objectively.

In an article for AMERICAN HERITAGE (1975) Brian Dippie is highly critical of McCracken's analysis. He suggests that Remington never really understood the West he sought to portray, that he was always the easterner, the "outsider." To Dippie, Remington's western excursions were merely a seeking out of rigorous adventure, a way of "testing" himself, of demonstrating he had the "right stuff" (to paraphrase a contemporary author). This quest was similar to those undertaken by other upper-class easterners, who bemoaned the loss of opportunity to prove themselves as their pioneering antecedents had. The West thus became a last great arena for testing a man's mettle and building character, an argument made and developed by G. Edward White in THE EASTERN ESTABLISHMENT AND THE WESTERN EXPERIENCE (1968), an effort to understand Remington's preoccupation with the West, as well as that of Owen Wister and Teddy Roosevelt. From this perspective Remington's artwork takes on a different character—it is the projection of Remington's romantic fantasies of the conflict between the white man (settler, explorer, trapper, or soldier) and his opponents, most frequently the Indian. The Indian, according to Dippie, is understood by Remington in only a very narrow sense, and most frequently as the white man's enemy. For these reasons it is difficult to know where reality and romanticism begin and end in Remington's artwork; Dippie suggests that he did much to create the romantic mythology of the American cowboy but that he had no peer as artist-historian for the Indian-fighting army.

Dippie also notes that the quality of Remington's artwork changed through the years, reflecting his maturing proficiency and a swing toward fine art, even in his illustrations. The early artwork was realistic, frequently with exacting detail, giving way during the last ten years of his life to a more Impressionist approach to subject matter, in which backgrounds became even more indistinct and the narrative thrust of the artwork yielded to the use of color for feeling and mood.

Ben Vorpahl, in FREDERIC REMINGTON AND THE WEST (1978), continues much the same line of criticism as Dippie—that Remington used the West as a way of defining himself, so that Remington's western artwork is more a reflection of his response to the West than an accurate depiction of the West. Like Dippie, Vorpahl suggests that Remington was fascinated with the West as a backdrop for conflict; during his lifetime Remington drew and painted more than seven hundred pictures explicitly concerned with war or violent conflict. Both Dippie and Vorpahl disagree with McCracken that Remington was an objective artist. Vorpahl argues that Remington went West with a set of expectations and interpreted his experiences within the context of that set of expectations. Where Remington expected conflict and violence, he "saw" conflict and violence and this was reflected in his artwork. At the same time, Remington was a product of the expectations of editors, publishers, and the public—who saw the West as the last frontier and expected Remington's artwork to confirm those expectations. To the extent that he did his work was popular and sold very well.

Probably the most comprehensive biography to date has been Peggy and Harold Samuels's FREDERIC REMINGTON: A BIOGRAPHY (1982). This book differs from most of the foregoing in that it devotes less time to Remington's artwork and more to his life-style. In the process the Samuelses conclude that Remington liked illustration as a career because of the immediate public acclaim and easy money, which enabled him to take periodic western trips. Remington's affinity for the West was part fact and part myth. The Samuelses accept White's thesis of the parallels between Teddy Roosevelt and Remington and his reasons for loving the West. At the same time, the picture of Remington as a rough and tumble westerner was fostered by a massive promotional campaign by Harper's in 1900, designed to link Remington and his artwork in the public's mind.

Interestingly, only one author, Douglas Allen in FREDERIC REMINGTON AND THE SPANISH–AMERICAN WAR (1971), has dealt with Remington's nonwestern artwork. The book is interesting because it deals with Remington as a "special" artist, covering the Spanish-American War for the New York JOURNAL, a role that required him to write as well as draw, to create news as well as report it. Allen suggests, although not as critically as Vorpahl and Dippie would have, that in this situation Remington also wrote and drew what he expected to see rather than what he did see; in one instance, for example, he wrote a story (which he illustrated) of Spanish inspectors strip-searching three American women on the open deck of an American ship. In fact, the search had been done decorously below decks by women inspectors, who were within their legal rights to engage in such a search. It was some time, however, before the truth caught up with Remington's depiction.

Allen's book contains reprints of a number of Remington's stories and illustrations about the war, and it is apparent that Remington was unhappy with the pace of the war: there wasn't enough action. In this sense Remington shared a desire for action and excitement with Teddy Roosevelt, whom he met during the war and with whom he developed a lifelong friendship. After the war Remington illustrated a number of Roosevelt's books about the West, which both visited but never really understood.

A quite different case is Charles M. Russell, the cowboy artist. Harold McCracken, in THE CHARLES M. RUSSELL BOOK (1957), points out that Russell, while raised in the East, moved West to Montana when he was fifteen and never returned, except periodically to meet with publishers and to sell his artwork. Initially, Russell's goal was to be a cattle wrangler. He did some painting but had no serious ambition to be an artist and, as a result, his reputation was largely local. Occasionally he would pay his bar bills with paintings he had done of scenes that were locally recognizable and appreciated. However, by the late 1880s his work was being published in national magazines, and by the early 1890s he was making his living painting the West. In 1895 he married and his wife served as his business manager, organizing the financial side of his life. By 1896, McCracken suggests, Russell and Remington were the leading western illustrators in America, although their circumstances were wildly different: Remington was living as a "gentleman illustrator" on his estate in New Rochelle, New York, while Russell was working in a shack in Montana. As the years went on Remington saw less of the West he illustrated and Russell saw more. And what Russell saw saddened him, for it was the passing of a West that he knew and loved. The Indians with whom he had lived and whom he painted with understanding were placed on reservations and acclimated to a white man's culture. Even the range country of the Judith Basin of Montana changed, and Russell's artwork drew more and more on his memories of the West and reflected a melancholy that he felt.

Brian Dippie, writing in AMERICAN HERITAGE (1973), suggests that Russell's artwork represents his attempt to retain his ties to a past he loved. Thus, Russell did not objectively portray the West as it was in the 1890s, but Russell's ideas about the West as it once was. His romanticization of the West was not for the recreation of an "ideal" West where good conquered evil, white men overcame red, but the idealization of a West that had once been. Symbolic of the difference between Russell and Remington is the way they treated the Indian. Remington never understood the Indian and sentimentalized him or portrayed him as the white man's protagonist, while Russell treated him sympathetically and as the victim of "progress."

Dippie subsequently published a book of Russell's correspondence, "PAPER TALK": CHARLIE RUSSELL'S AMERICAN WEST (1979), which gives an interesting perspective on Russell's ephemeral artwork and reveals insights into his business dealings. Perhaps the most telling sign of Russell's growing popularity was the increase in prices for his artwork; in 1897 three black-and-white illustrations for a book brought only $30, in 1907 he received $350 for each painting, and by 1919 he received $600 to $2,000 for an oil, a figure that ultimately reached $10,000 per painting—figures that Russell called "dead man's prices."

Although Remington and Russell were the dominant western illustrators of the period there were others who were also successful in the genre. D. Duane Cummins, in WILLIAM ROBINSON LEIGH: WESTERN ARTIST (1980), suggests that Leigh, along with Russell and Remington, formed a triumvirate of western artists during the Golden Age of illustration. The inclusion of Leigh with the other two is interesting in light of the fact that he never met them, often criticized their work, painted the West at a later period, concentrated on a different geographic area, and had far better formal art training than either of them. Cummins's biography shows an illustrator-artist trained to be a fine artist but who could not establish himself as the portrait artist he wishèd to be. After his first trip to the Southwest in 1906 Leigh discovered the area and the mode in which he wanted to work. Since Leigh and Remington focused on many of the same topics, albeit in different locales, Cummins provides an interesting comparison between the two artists. He argues that one major difference was in the subject matter on which they focused; Remington's artwork was often filled with white men dominating less civilized people Remington disliked, while Leigh's bias was in the opposite direction. His artwork focused on members of primitive tribes sympathetically treated, with nary a white man to be seen. Cummins's book on Leigh is more useful than that of June DuBois, W. R. LEIGH (1977), which concentrates more on Leigh's fine art than his illustration. She does suggest, however, that Leigh's fascination with the West represented his feeling that the West represented "authentic" America, a feeling he shared with Remington.

Another successful western illustrator was Harold Borein. Harold Davidson's biography, HAROLD BOREIN: COWBOY ARTIST (1974), discusses Borein's career, placing special emphasis on his illustration career in New York from 1907 to 1919. As a boy Borein admired Remington, but his illustrations of cowboy life reflect his life experiences and contact with Russell, who encouraged him in his work. After World War I, however, Borein moved to California and made his living from his etchings and watercolors, for which he is better known today.

Of the ten illustrators analyzed by Susan Meyer in AMERICA'S GREAT IL-LUSTRATORS (1978), three—Charles Dana Gibson, James Montgomery Flagg and Howard Chandler Christy—are what I have called "American Beauty" il-lustrators, that is, they specialized in depicting the ideal of American womanhood around the turn of the century. First and foremost among this group is Charles Dana Gibson, whose career spanned the Golden Age of illustration. Fairfax Downey, in PORTRAIT OF AN ERA AS DRAWN BY C. D. GIBSON (1936), has written the most comprehensive biography. Gibson's career began in 1885, and by 1890 he was earning $600 to $800 per month from his artwork. It was during this time that he began to draw the Gibson Girl, which became his trademark. The Gibson Girl was appealing because she was not the "typical" American girl but was American womanhood idealized; she was not the "average" but the ul-timate. Gibson's rendering of face and fashion struck a responsive chord in Amer-ican society, and his drawings were watched by women to see how they should look and dress. Soon he was pursued by women who wanted to pose as Gibson Girls. There was another side to Gibson's pen-and-ink work. He had a keen eye for the foibles of Society and took real delight in caricaturing them in such a way that Society could laugh at itself.

By 1904 Gibson had become one of the most popular and recognized illustrators in America, so it was no surprise that he signed a contract with COLLIER'S magazine to do one hundred double-page illustrations over a four-year period for a fee of $100,000. This fee was to guarantee COLLIER'S that Gibson would work exclusively for them (although they acknowledged he could continue to work for LIFE magazine) but Nick Meglin, in AMERICAN ARTIST (1975), suggests that Gibson's "exclusive" contract with COLLIER'S was not as exclusive as they might have wished.

Despite his success as a pen-and-ink artist—and he was ranked as one of the best in the world—Gibson decided to work in oils and went to Europe to study painting. Downey states that Gibson gave up a $65,000 per year income because he felt that he was at the limit of his talents in pen and ink, and that color work was the logical next step. His oil painting career was curtailed, however, by the panic of 1907, which wiped out much of his money, so he returned to the United States and began working again in pen and ink. During World War I Gibson was actively involved in the drive to create effective poster art for the war effort. At the end of the war Gibson and a syndicate of investors purchased LIFE magazine and Gibson took over as editor. But Gibson was not an effective editor and the Gibson Girl did not make the transition into the postwar period very well. According to Downey, "When (John) Held drew the girl of the period, it was youth drawing youth. When Gibson's pen outlined her, there was apparent more than a trace of the wonder, the incomprehension, and dismay of the older generation beholding a rather alarming phenomenon" (p. 348). Downey's book is a sympathetic treatment of its subject, but its strength comes from the attempt to relate Gibson and his popularity to the culture of which it was a part—not a common approach among illustrators' biographers. If the book has a weakness it is its lack of effort to unravel a fairly complex person; it is more descriptive than analytical.

Susan Meyer's biography, JAMES MONTGOMERY FLAGG (1974), her chapter on Flagg in AMERICA'S GREAT ILLUSTRATORS (1978), and Flagg's acerbic autobiography, ROSES AND BUCKSHOT (1946) are the primary source materials on James Montgomery Flagg. Flagg's career began at age ten when he sold his first illustration, and by age fourteen he was a regular staff member of LIFE magazine. He and Gibson were similar in a number of ways: both were unrivalled as pen-and-ink artists and both concentrated on drawing pretty women. But the Flagg Girl was different; over time she adapted to a changing society, becoming more modern and liberated, while retaining her feminine charm and allure. In many ways Flagg was the antithesis of Gibson. While Gibson became a part of the Society he drew, Flagg became a "bohemian" who lived outside Society and made fun of it. Where Gibson was conservative in opinion, dress, and action, Flagg was liberal, even libertine. Artistically, Flagg was able to develop his talents outside of pen and ink; Susan Meyer (1978) notes his skill in opaque and transparent watercolors and oils, charcoal and pencil, and even as a sculptor. His closest friends came from the movies rather than the art community. As Flagg moved through the 1920s and 1930s he became increasingly unhappy. The world changed but he found it increasingly difficult to understand and appreciate the change. Meyer notes that in his later years he found himself in two hostile worlds—an art world he did not comprehend and the world of old age, which he deplored and feared. If Remington can be accused of using the West as a vehicle for "proving" his masculinity, Flagg can be said to have used women, in art and in person, for the same purpose.

Several of the American Beauty illustrators have had little or nothing written about them. Susan Meyer's chapter on Howard Chandler Christy in AMERICA'S GREAT ILLUSTRATORS (1978) is one of the few pieces on that noted illustrator. The lack of writing is surprising since the Christy Girl was certainly as famous and as popular as the Flagg and Gibson Girls, starring in such favorite books as THE AMERICAN GIRL (1906), THE CHRISTY GIRL (1906), and LIBERTY BELLES (1912). Christy lived much of his early career in Ohio and New York City, spending time in New York trying to break in as an illustrator and returning home when his money was exhausted. By 1915, however, he had established his reputation and moved to New York City, but in 1921 he announced his retirement from magazine illustration to devote himself to portrait painting. Thus, it is the decade 1910–1920 that established Christy's reputation, and his posters during

World War I that helped substantiate it. The comparative brevity of Christy's career and the lack of biographical material make Meyer's chapter on him one of the weakest in an otherwise excellent book.

Amazingly, no book has been written about one of the most prolific and financially successful of the American Beauty illustrators, Harrison Fisher. Certainly, the Fisher Girl was an artistic rival to the Girls drawn by Gibson, Flagg, and Christy. Despite his artistic and financial success there are no biographies or major analyses of his work yet written. Perhaps the magnitude of his output has deterred writers; his initial artwork was frequently reprinted in a number of formats, from which Fisher profited with each reprinting.

One American Beauty illustrator, widely recognized and acclaimed by his contemporaries but then forgotten, was Coles Phillips. In her time the Phillips Girl was as recognizable as the Christy Girl, the Flagg Girl, and the Gibson Girl. Fortunately, Michael Schau's biography, ALL-AMERICAN GIRL: THE ART OF COLES PHILLIPS (1975), has rescued him from obscurity. The Phillips Girl was more easily identifiable than those done by Christy, Flagg, and Gibson because of the color and graphic designs used by Phillips. The Phillips Girl was known as the "fadeaway" girl because Phillips would use the same color in dress and background, thereby emphasizing the dominant color and the contrasting beauty of face, hands, and feet. Schau argues that the Phillips Girls were less elegant but more saucy and sexy than those of his artistic contemporaries. This may have been the reason why Phillips was hired to do a great deal of advertising art for hosiery and ladies' undergarments.

Schau's book gives a brief biography of Phillips, but it is devoted mainly to an analysis of his artwork and a presentation of a number of his more popular illustrations. One drawback of the book is its concentration on his magazine and advertising artwork, which is different from his book illustrations. Being tied to the text in a book Phillips was less free to do only pretty girls in "fadeaway" outfits. For this reason the book illustrations also demonstrate Phillips's versatility as an illustrator and his command of color and graphic design.

Another group of illustrators of the period would be unhappy about their inclusion in this book. These artist-illustrators viewed themselves as fine artists doing illustrations only as a way of earning a living until their fine art reputations had been established. The best known of these were the illustrators who were part of the Ash Can school of American art, part of the artistic circle of Robert Henri in New York. While they may have been uncomfortable being labelled as illustrators, these artist-illustrators nonetheless made important contributions to the development of American illustration, particularly during the first decade of the twentieth century. Perhaps the best picture of this group can be derived from Bruce St. John's editing of John Sloan's diaries in JOHN SLOAN'S NEW YORK SCENE (1965), which covers Sloan's art career from 1906–1913. These day-by-day entries give an interesting perspective on the "struggling artist," doing illustrations during the day and easel art at night. From these entries the conflict between the two roles is quite apparent—in 1907 Sloan was elected to the Society of Illustrators, an honor that he accepted but without relish. Edith Deshazo's biography, EVERETT SHINN (1974), suggests a similar conflict between the roles of artist and illustrator for Shinn. Indeed, she concludes that it was Shinn's magazine illustrations that ruined his fine art. This book, along with St. John's on Sloan, are useful in tracing the relationships between Shinn, William Glackens, George Luks, and Sloan, which began in Philadelphia where they started as newspaper artists and developed when they moved to New York City and came under the influence of Robert Henri. But overall, Deshazo's book tells us very little about his illustration career, which continued until the early 1950s. Nonetheless, the book does contain a nice and seemingly complete bibliography of Shinn's book and magazine illustrations.

Shinn, in turn, wrote one of the few pieces analyzing his good friend William Glackens, which appeared in AMERICAN ARTIST (1945). In this piece Shinn claims that Glackens was the leading "urban" illustrator, a claim subsequently supported by the Delaware Art Museum in CITY LIFE ILLUSTRATED, 1890–1940 (1980). In his piece Shinn discusses several of Glacken's city scenes.

Arthur Dove was another artist-illustrator who attempted to fulfill both roles. Sasha Newman, in ARTHUR DOVE AND DUNCAN PHILLIPS: ARTIST AND PATRON (1981), focuses much of her attention on the former, although she does include a discussion of how his illustration style influenced his fine art, particularly the design elements of his illustrations. And the book does contain a selected bibliography of his work. Barbara Gallati (ARCHIVES OF AMERICAN ART JOURNAL [1981]), on the other hand, focuses on Dove as an illustrator. She divides his illustration career into two periods, broken by a trip to Europe to study painting and a commitment to fine art when he returned. In 1919, after almost ten years of trying, he realized the need to do illustration to make a living, although it was not until the mid-1920s that he became committed to illustration and developed a more mature style. Shortly thereafter, however, the demand for illustrations declined and Dove resumed his fine art career once again. The Gallati article is useful for the insight it provides on Dove's relations with other artist-illustrators in New York City and the relationship between his illustration and fine art careers and their respective styles. Gail Levin's EDWARD HOPPER AS ILLUSTRATOR (1979) fills an important gap in our knowledge of Hopper's artistic career and shows the conflicts—financial and artistic—between the role of illustrator and fine artist. It is interesting to compare Hopper's business and restaurant illustrations with the stark Urban Realism of his later fine art—making it easy to see the thread that ties his fine art and illustration artwork together.

A number of other illustrators of the period have written about their work or have been written about. Joseph Pennell and his wife wrote a number of biographical and autobiographical works on Pennell's life and career, notably Elizabeth Robins Pennell, in THE LIFE AND LETTERS OF JOSEPH PENNELL, VOLS. I AND II (1929) and Joseph Pennell's MODERN ILLUSTRATION (1905) and THE ILLUSTRATION OF BOOKS (1896). Elizabeth Pennell's biography of her husband is understandably laudatory, and critical of anyone who disagreed with him, leaving one with the impression that Pennell was misunderstood and abused, particularly by publishers. Correspondence in the Pennell Collection at the Library of Congress, however, indicates that editors and publishers were more likely to be abused by the Pennells. Nonetheless, the Pennells' books describe the life-style of a successful authoress and illustrator as they scrambled for commissions and status in a highly competitive market. Pennell's artistic talent is clearly evident in his artwork and his success, and his acerbic wit is also evident in his evaluation of other illustrators in MODERN ILLUSTRATION.

Leading magazines of the day also did biographies and analyses of illustrators during this period, which are frequently helpful in finding information on then-popular illustrators who have since been forgotten. For example, an article by Ernest Dressel North in THE OUTLOOK (1899) discusses F. C. Yohn, Walter Appleton Clark, Ernest Peixotto, and Ernest Haskell, as well as the still-renowned Maxfield Parrish and Howard Chandler Christy. Nonetheless, a number of important illustrators have had very little written about them; in this group are Jules Guerin, May Wilson Preston, F. W. Taylor, Frederic Dorr Steele, Andre Castaigne, George Wright, Jay Hambridge, Harry Fenn, Leon Guipon, Sigismund Ivanowski, Hans Hermann, William Stevens and Louis Hitchcock, all of them mentioned by Best in the JOURNAL OF AMERICAN CULTURE (1980) as being leading magazine illustrators during the period 1906–1910. Even some of the illustrators mentioned by Walt Reed in THE ILLUSTRATOR IN AMERICA: 1900–1960 (1966) as important during the first twenty years of the century are today biographical unknowns. The QUARTERLY ILLUSTRATOR (1893–1894) contains a number of articles dealing with contemporary illustrators, as well as describing the artistic content of most of the leading illustrated magazines of the day. For some illustrators, the QUARTERLY ILLUSTRATOR articles provide our major source of information about their lives and careers.

Aside from Pyle's students who illustrated juveniles, children's book illustrators have received little attention. Only recently has a biography been written of one of the most popular children's book illustrators at the turn of the century, W. W. Denslow, who did the illustrations for the original WIZARD OF OZ (1900). Douglas Greene and Michael Hearn, in W. W. DENSLOW (1976), and Douglas Green, in THE JOURNAL OF POPULAR CULTURE (1973), provide a comprehensive and critical analysis of this complex man's life and career. They trace the variety of influences that changed Denslow from a successful San Francisco newspaper artist to an important book illustrator: his discovery of oriental art, which resulted in his later use of Japanese wood-block techniques in his illustrations (black outline, large areas of solid color, and an absence of modeling), his learning to design pictures rather than merely draw them, and the influence of Elbert Hubbard and Denslow's work with the Roycroft Press. Greene and Hearn do an excellent analysis of the development, and later decay, of Denslow's illustrations, tracing part of the decay to his fight with L. Frank Baum after the success of THE WIZARD OF OZ, his bohemian life style, his attempts to write some of his subsequent books as well as illustrate them, and his drinking. The book contains an excellent bibliography of Denslow's published illustrations for books, book covers, magazines, newspapers, posters, and prints, and a good bibliography of works written about Denslow, particularly his relations with Hubbard and Baum.

The illustrator of another set of children's favorites has received even less attention than Denslow. J. Allen St. John, who did much to create the public image of Tarzan through his illustrations of the Edgar Rice Burroughs books, has received attention in an article by Darrell Richardson that appeared in THE EDGAR RICE BURROUGHS LIBRARY OF ILLUSTRATION: VOL. I (1976). This article contains a brief biography of St. John and an analysis of his artwork for Tarzan; the larger book reproduces all of the artwork for Burroughs's books, showing how it appeared on the printed page. It is interesting to note in passing that both N. C. Wyeth and Frank Schoonover published their own renditions of Tarzan, but neither captured the spirit of Burroughs's concept as well as St. John.

THE TRANSITION PERIOD: 1920–1945 ·

In the return to "normalcy" after World War I, the nature of American illustration changed. The demand for large, lavishly illustrated books and magazines declined and, as a result, fewer illustrators than ever before were able to make names for themselves. Many illustrators, who had established successful careers in the years before World War I, were unable to sustain those careers as society and the economics of illustration changed. Some illustrators, who had begun their careers during the Golden Age of illustration, found the 1920s and 1930s to be peak periods for their artwork. Others began their careers during the interwar period. Many illustrators were unable to make the transition and disappeared from the traditional illustration media.

Two of the most prolific illustrators of the transition period, J. C. Leyendecker and Norman Rockwell, began their careers before World War I but it was the interwar period that was most productive for them. Leyendecker had a lengthy career spanning over forty years, as noted by Michael Schau in J. C. LEYENDECKER (1976). Although he did his first cover for THE SATURDAY EVENING POST in 1899, it was during the 1920s and 1930s that he and Norman Rockwell dominated the cover art of that magazine. Schau's book, one of the few works written about this complex individual, includes a solid biography of Leyendecker's early career, including his poster art, and his relationship with his brother Frank, a talented illustrator who committed suicide in his twenties. Schau notes, quite correctly, that Leyendecker, through his Arrow Shirt advertisements and many of his illustrations, did for the American male what Charles Dana Gibson had done for the American female—established a standard of the "ideal." This standard can be seen in the examples of his illustrations, posters, advertisements, and magazine covers that are included in the Schau book. The lack of a complete bibliography mars this otherwise excellent book.

Although Leyendecker and Norman Rockwell did almost the same number of covers for THE SATURDAY EVENING POST, there are far more books on Rockwell and his artwork. Rockwell began his illustration career in 1912 at age eighteen, and within a year he was art editor for BOY'S LIFE, the Boy Scout magazine. He did his first POST cover in 1916 and by the 1920s he had established himself as one of America's leading illustrators. His career was not always a smooth one—he had three wives, frequently had difficulty getting ideas for illustration (subsequently, the same idea would occasionally appear in various guises), and was insecure about his success, going to Europe in the 1930s to "learn how to paint."

There are a number of biographies of Rockwell, as well as two autobiographical "fragments." Donald Walton's book, A ROCKWELL PORTRAIT (1978), probably spends more time than the others dealing with Rockwell's personal life and contains some material not available elsewhere. The book is interesting in its analysis of what Rockwell learned while studying at the Art Students League in New York City, his life in New Rochelle, New York, with his first wife, and his relations with other major illustrators—Gibson, Flagg, Christy, and the Leyendeckers—who lived in the community. The book has a number of factual errors, however, and given Rockwell's penchant for obfuscation on personal matters, one should read the material on his early life and career with some skepticism. Susan Meyer's book, NORMAN ROCKWELL'S PEOPLE (1981), ostensibly not a biography, does contain some excellent biographical material, gleaned from interviews with Rockwell's family, friends, and acquaintances, as well as Rockwell's two books, ROCKWELL ON ROCKWELL (1979) and MY ADVENTURES AS AN ILLUSTRATOR (1960). She questions the accuracy of some of Rockwell's writings, suggesting either forgetfulness or a deliberate desire to mislead or misdirect the reader. This is particularly true in Rockwell's discussion of his first wife and the reasons for their divorce.

There is less controversy surrounding Rockwell's professional career, and a number of books do an excellent job analyzing his professional and artistic development. Christopher Finch, for example, has analyzed Rockwell's life and art from two different perspectives; in NORMAN ROCKWELL'S AMERICA (1975) he does a thematic analysis of Rockwell's work, while in NORMAN ROCKWELL: 332 MAGAZINE COVERS (1979) he does a historical and developmental analysis of Rockwell's POST covers. In the first book he describes Rockwell's art as "common sense" Realism, fusing with myth around a variety of themes—growing up in America, young love, home and family, growing old in America, American history, democracy, presidential portraits, America in uniform, Americans at work, and the sporting life. These themes convey the breadth of Rockwell's interest and his concern for things truly "American." Within these themes Finch discusses some of the changes that have occurred over the years in their treatment. In his later book Finch covers much of the same artwork but from a different perspective, one that focuses on Rockwell and his artwork as a product of his culture and his development as an illustrator within that cultural context. He suggests that Rockwell was a product of the Victorian era and embodied many of its values; as society changed, Rockwell adapted but did not change his basic values. According to Finch, Rockwell's most deep-seated value was a belief in the fundamental decency of the vast majority of mankind. It was this fundamental value, expressed artistically in a variety of settings over a number of years, that forms the basis for much of Rockwell's enduring appeal. The 1979 book is organized by time period, containing a complete survey of his magazine covers during the period, frequently related to Rockwell's life and times. Rockwell's covers are seen as part of a massive developmental body of work that did not mature until the late 1930s, and the covers painted between 1943 and 1962, for Finch, represent the "mature" Rockwell art.

Donald and Marshall Stoltz cover much the same territory—Rockwell's covers for THE SATURDAY EVENING POST—in their three volumes of NORMAN ROCKWELL AND THE SATURDAY EVENING POST (1976), but are less successful. There is a brief description and analysis of each cover as well as attempts to relate one cover with others dealing with the same theme, or to relate covers to events in Rockwell's private life. This is not done in sufficient depth to make these three volumes more than coffee table art books of his covers.

Susan Meyer, in NORMAN ROCKWELL'S PEOPLE (1981), provides a different perspective by analyzing Rockwell's artwork in terms of the people used as models and what Rockwell was striving to achieve. Thus, Meyer sees Rockwell's artistic development in terms of the people he could use as models; in Vermont, Rockwell found a work environment in which he could concentrate totally and where people were "typical" of the people he wished to paint. The maturity Finch finds in his artwork of the 1940s and 1950s is due, according to Meyer, to his move to Vermont. Whether the maturity of Rockwell's artwork stemmed from his experience or from his move to another environment may be an impossible question to answer. His move to Vermont corresponded with a period of artistic growth and undoubtedly played a role in that growth; whether it "caused" that artistic growth is impossible to tell.

Meyer's book is important because of its insights into his work habits, showing the importance he placed on finding the right models, his increased reliance on photography as a tool, and her analysis of the development of his artwork, from rough sketch to finished oil painting. A very substantial segment of the book deals with Meyer's discussion of the models Rockwell used (most were friends and neighbors), showing their appearances and reappearances in his artwork. Unfortunately no bibliography is provided to trace his models as they appear in various works at various times.

Arthur Guptill, in NORMAN ROCKWELL, ILLUSTRATOR (1970) and Rockwell, in THE NORMAN ROCKWELL ALBUM (1961) discuss Rockwell's work habits and approach to illustration. Guptill's book, based on his long friendship with Rockwell, is a reasonably frank discussion of how and why Rockwell painted, including detailed discussion of his illustration techniques. His chapter, "How Rockwell Paints a Post Cover," is an excellent description of how Rockwell approached an illustration problem and can be profitably read in conjunction with Meyer's description of his work habits. Rockwell's discussion of his own artwork provides interesting insights into why he approached some illustration assignments as he did—some of the POST covers are accompanied by little vignettes describing or explaining the cover. In this book Rockwell describes what he considers his major artistic weakness, a tendency toward caricature, even when caricature is inappropriate.

Western illustration continued to be a major market during this transitional period. Will James and Harold Von Schmidt were among those who followed in the artistic footsteps of Remington and Russell. Will James was probably the best known and most popular of the group; his illustrated books, SMOKY (1928) and THE LONE COWBOY (1930) became children's classics. His stories and artwork reflect a West that became increasingly romanticized by writers and artists as it disappeared. There is an interesting congruence between his western stories of the 1930s and the western movies of the same period. Like Remington, James saw the West as the place where men (and boys) could be (or become) men. Anthony Amaral's book, WILL JAMES, THE LAST COWBOY LEGEND (1980), documents the gap between the James who appeared in print and the private James, who was not raised in the West, was convicted of cattle rustling, and had drinking and marital problems. According to Amaral, the West depicted by James in words and pictures was a fairy-tale land into which he escaped as a way of dealing with personal problems. Amaral's approach is an interesting one because it is one of the few biographies that suggests that an illustrator's artwork may be a way of compensating for personal inadequacies.

Harold Von Schmidt was one of the most successful and prolific western illustrators of the transitional period, and he made the transition to the 1950s and 1960s. Walt Reed's biography, HAROLD VON SCHMIDT (1972), begins with a nice autobiographical piece by Von Schmidt, in which he outlines the salient features of his professional career—he studied with Harvey Dunn and was very much influenced by Dunn (and indirectly by Pyle)—and his personal life. Reed's book includes a discussion of his illustration techniques and an analysis of a number of his illustrations. John M. Carroll's VON SCHMIDT: THE COMPLETE ILLUSTRATOR (1973) is an excellent companion to the Reed book. It contains very little biographical material, showing instead examples of his advertising art, historical characters, cowboys and cattle, wartime, sea tales, animal studies, calendar art, the army on the frontier, Indians, Tugboat Annie, and western scenes, as well as containing an extensive bibliography of his illustrations in books, book dust jackets, pamphlets, bulletins, newspapers, catalogs, advertising art, and magazines. The bibliography is a must for anyone collecting Von Schmidt materials.

Walt Reed's JOHN CLYMER: AN ARTIST'S RENDEZVOUS WITH THE FRONTIER WEST (1976) is an extensive examination of the life and artwork (with more emphasis on the latter) of an active but not well known western illustrator. This book, like Reed's book on Joseph Clement Coll (1978), reminds us that there are many illustrators whose work deserves broader exposure and wider recognition.

Another illustrator influenced indirectly by Pyle, through his study with Harvey

Dunn, was Dean Cornwell. Cornwell was a Romantic Realist in the Pyle, Dunn, Wyeth, and Schoonover tradition and his work was immensely popular; from 1914 to the late 1950s he completed over one thousand illustrations. During much of this period he was known as the "dean" of illustrators, although his artwork did not dominate the profession as Pyle's once had. His popularity can be seen in the prices of his artwork; according to Patricia Janis Broder, in DEAN CORN-WELL: DEAN OF ILLUSTRATORS (1978), Cornwell signed a contract with Hearst publications that paid $2,500 for each square or double-spread oil illustration and half that for crayon illustrations. The Depression cut deeply into his illustration income and during the 1930s he broadened his base, teaching illustration and doing murals. Broder's book gives examples of his artwork and contains a bibliography of his book and magazine illustrations.

The 1920s and 1930s saw an increase in the numbers of people doing political illustrations (as opposed to editorial cartoons). The Russian Revolution, World War I, and the global economic depression of the 1930s provided these people with ample impetus for their work, and several magazines, most notably MASSES and LIBERATOR, served as vehicles for their artwork. A number of artists led dual lives, doing illustrations for commercial publishing firms and then contributing artwork to political publications. Art Young, Robert Minor, John Sloan, K. R. Chamberlin, Maurice Becker, Boardman Robinson, and George Grosz were among them. Richard Fitzgerald, in ART AND POLITICS: CARTOONISTS OF THE MASSES AND LIBERATOR (1973), discusses political art in general and analyzes the works of Young, Minor, Sloan, Chamberlin, and Becker that appeared in MASSES and LIBERATOR, while commenting on the contributions of Robinson and Grosz. But there is very little analysis of the specifically political illustrations of any of these people. Albert Christ-Janer's biography, BOARD-MAN ROBINSON (1946), analyzes Robinson's commercial and political illustrations; since Robinson contributed to MASSES for only seven years, little space is devoted to this period of his career. Nonetheless, the book does contain a chronology and bibliography of his illustrations, as well as a catalog of his major book illustration artwork.

An exhibition catalog by the Delaware Art Museum, CITY LIFE ILLUS-TRATED, 1890–1940 (1980), suggests another group of illustrators survived by focusing on city life and the contemporary scene. Foremost among this group were William Glackens, George Luks, Everett Shinn, and John Sloan and their relatives and friends. These "Urban Realists" brought to the illustration of urban American a compassion and empathy. The catalog contains biographies of twenty-seven illustrators as well as a bibliography of their major works. One can argue with some of the artists included as Urban Realists—May Wilson Preston was more a comic illustrator, Art Young and Boardman Robinson were more political than urban, and Rockwell Kent was more interested in the Arctic than in urban America—and some of those excluded—Edward Hopper, for one—but this catalog does focus attention on an important segment of American illustration during the transitional period between the two wars.

The biographies of some of these Urban Realists give a better picture of the quality of their illustrations. Edward Laning's book, THE SKETCHBOOKS OF REGINALD MARSH (1973), provides a brief biography interwoven with an analysis of Marsh's artwork. The bulk of the book is devoted to a presentation of his sketches and watercolors, some of which provided the basis for his urban illustrations. Laning makes an interesting comparison between the Urban Realism of Edward Hopper and Marsh, in which he concludes that Marsh gives a better sense of the teeming quality of urban life, while Hopper focuses on its loneliness.

Gail Levin's analysis of Hopper's illustration career, EDWARD HOPPER AS ILLUSTRATOR (1979), notes that Hopper began his career as an illustrator but after meeting John Sloan he became more interested in fine art. He was unable to sell his paintings, however, and returned to illustration as a way of supporting himself. Hopper's attitude toward his illustration career therefore reflects the ambivalence of an artist-illustrator who wished to be the former but must be the latter. While Hopper was ambivalent about his illustration career (he would work no more than three days a week on illustration commission) he was very successful in doing illustrations of "places without people"—offices, ships, railroads, hotels, and restaurants—the same sources of inspiration for many of his urban paintings. Levin suggests that one can see Hopper's illustrations as an important formative contribution to his more mature oils—they established a style and tone and defined a world that he explored through much of his artistic life. Levin's book concludes with a useful bibliography of Hopper's magazine illustrations.

The several books by and about Rockwell Kent would challenge his classification as an Urban Realist. Very few of his book illustrations dealt with urban topics and Fridolph Johnson's book, THE ILLUSTRATIONS OF ROCKWELL KENT: 231 EXAMPLES FROM BOOKS, MAGAZINES AND ADVERTISING ART (1976), provides very little visual evidence in support of that definition. Johnson's book, in addition to presenting examples of his artwork, provides an excellent analysis of the major components of the Kent style—dramatic figures that dominate their surroundings, firmly outlined figures in heroic stances, solid areas of black and white used for stark contrast. Also included is a chronological list of his illustrated books. In ROCKWELLKENTIANA (1933), Kent presents a series of articles on various topics and a bibliography of his writings and illustrations to that date. Since he continued writing and illustrating after 1933, the list is obviously dated. The best information on his life and career can be gleaned from Rockwell's autobiography, IT'S ME O LORD: THE AUTOBIOGRAPHY OF ROCKWELL KENT (1955) and David Traxel's biography, AN AMERICAN SAGA: THE LIFE AND TIMES OF ROCKWELL KENT (1980), a not always affectionate look at its subject. Kent's book is an attempt to explain and defend his life and art against those whom he sees as his critics; he is not very successful, particularly in dealing with his various wives and lovers. Traxel's book is somewhat more successful, particularly when it examines the influences on Kent's artistic career, especially Robert Henri and Gerald Thayer. There is also a very good discussion of Kent's experiences in Newfoundland and Alaska and their impact on his life and art.

Another illustrator working in the same woodcut style as Kent was Lynd Ward, whose books without words traced their artistic heritage to Franz Masereel rather than Rockwell Kent. Ward's book STORYTELLER WITHOUT WORDS (1974) is both a biography and an analysis of his artwork. In the latter Ward details, for each book, his techniques and how the subject matter was influenced by the cultural context in which the book was executed. Thus we have the illustrator's statement of how and why he chose the approach he did. In the process we also see how an illustrator with a social conscience and political concerns weaves those into the substance of his illustrations. Unfortunately, Ward's book deals solely with his books without words, for Ward made the transition in substance to a children's book illustrator in the 1930s and that aspect of his career still awaits analysis.

The decline in the appeal of American Beauty illustrators and their art can be seen in the dearth of illustrators working in this genre during the interwar period. It is interesting to compare John Held's artwork in Carl Weinhardt's THE MOST OF JOHN HELD, JR. (1972) with that of Gibson, Christy, Flagg, Fisher, and Phillips. This comparison makes it clear why the last illustrators were not as successful during the transitional period as they had been earlier. Susan Meyer's chapter on Held in AMERICA'S GREAT ILLUSTRATORS makes clear that Held was an oddball whose work, while popular, had no stylistic resemblance to any other illustrator before him. His ability to capture and caricature the mood and morals of the 1920s made him successful. But Meyer correctly warns against regarding Held solely for his flapper-period illustrations; his skills as a draftsman and designer of illustrations transcend his period and mark him as one of America's greats.

Even some of the more obscure illustrators of this period have received attention. The Bowers's biography, ROBERT ROBINSON: AMERICAN ILLUSTRATOR (1981), provides a brief life history and artwork examples of an illustrator known for his covers for AMERICAN DRUGGIST and MOTORING magazines. Artists who did cover illustrations for science fiction pulps are covered in Anthony Frewin's ONE HUNDRED YEARS OF SCIENCE FICTION ILLUSTRATION: 1840–1940 (1974) and Ian Summers's TOMORROW AND BEYOND: MASTERPIECES OF SCIENCE FICTION ART (1978).

THE ILLUSTRATION RENAISSANCE: 1945–PRESENT

Although American illustration flourished anew in the wake of World War II, changes in the nature of the profession made it difficult for one or a small group of illustrators to capture and command the public's attention. Book illustration disappeared except for children's books. Mass market magazines disappeared and specialty magazines appealing to a specific segment of the market replaced them; illustrators working for these magazines became known to only one segment of the public. The development of illustration studios to handle assignments guaranteed work and incomes but increased the anonymity of the individual illustrator. While more illustrators than ever were working, fewer than ever were widely known. As a consequence, less has been written about recent illustrators than about those in any other period heretofore analyzed. In addition, a maxim from art history is undoubtedly true—an artist should be dead before his or her life and works can receive adequate attention.

It is not surprising that children's book illustrators have continued to receive attention from writers. Some attention has been self-serving; Addison-Wesley has published several "self-portraits" of illustrators working for the firm, that is, Erik Blegved, in SELF-PORTRAIT: ERIK BLEGVED (1979), and Trina Schart Hyman, in SELF-PORTRAIT: TRINA SCHART HYMAN (1981). These short autobiographical "scraps" serve as useful introductions to the illustrator and his or her artwork, but the book on Hyman should be read in conjunction with Michael Hearn's analysis of her artwork in AMERICAN ARTIST (1979) to capture a more fully rounded picture of the illustrator and her work.

Nancy Eckholm Burkert, whose illustration artwork has some of the flavor of Andrew Wyeth, has been the subject of one of many books edited by David Larkin, THE ART OF NANCY ECKHOLM BURKERT (1977), and while the brief biography and analysis in this book are helpful for understanding her artwork, she still remains as enigmatic a figure as much of her artwork. Her ability to combine the natural and the supernatural in a way that is appealing to both children and adults makes her the illustration world's counterpart to Steven Spielberg and rivals that of her contemporary Maurice Sendak. Unfortunately, the Larkin book is too brief to provide much more than an introduction to Burkert and her artwork.

Selma Lanes's biography and analysis of Maurice Sendak, THE ART OF MAURICE SENDAK (1980), is an excellent book on one of America's most interesting and appealing children's book illustrators. Lanes's book accomplishes a number of things: it is a comprehensive biography of Sendak, in which she ties events from his childhood into the content and style of his illustrations; it is a book-by-book analysis of Sendak's illustrated works, focusing on WHERE THE WILD THINGS ARE and IN THE NIGHT KITCHEN, two of his most important books; and it concludes with an interview with Sendak in which he discusses some of the themes that appear in his book and his plans for the future. Her analysis of Sendak's appeal is insightful. She argues that Sendak shows pictorially the dark side of children's psyches in ways that children can understand and appreciate but their parents cannot. Sendak's ability to move between fantasy and reality ties together his artwork and his childhood experiences. As Anthony Amaral does with Will James (1980), Lanes relates Sendak's development as an artist to his childhood.

Several other children's book illustrators have had books written about them or their work. Helen Jones's ROBERT LAWSON: ILLUSTRATOR (1972) contains a brief, two-page biography and then concentrates on his illustrations organized by subject matter, with a concluding chapter on his vital statistics and artistic techniques. Bethany Tudor's biography of her mother, Tasha Tudor,

DRAWN FROM NEW ENGLAND (1979), is a strange book that is really more autobiographical than biographical; there is little discussion or analysis of Tasha Tudor's artwork, although there are examples, many in color, throughout the book. Marguerite Henry's book, THE ILLUSTRATED MARGUERITE HENRY (1980), takes a different approach. In this book, a popular children's book author discusses the illustrators who have worked with her on her books—there are chapters on Wesley Dennis, Robert Lougheed, Lynd Ward, and Rich Reedish. These chapters give a fascinating (and well written) picture of the interaction between author and illustrators; since she did most of her work with Wesley Dennis, the bulk of the analysis concerns their collaboration. Finally, for those seeking to find brief biographical information about contemporary illustrators, a short pithy statement from each, representative books they have illustrated, and a few illustrations by each, Phillip Dennis Cate's exhibition catalog, CONTEM-PORARY AMERICAN ILLUSTRATORS OF CHILDREN'S BOOKS (1974), is good. Thirty-two illustrators and 155 pieces of artwork are included; one can always quibble about those whose work was left out—Nancy Eckholm Burkert, for one.

Western illustration has remained a strong market, although western illustrators are now called "cowboy artists." Don Hedgpeth's biography, COWBOY ARTIST: THE JOE BEELER STORY (1979), describes the struggles of a cowboy to establish a reputation as a painter and earn a living working his own small ranch. In many ways there are interesting parallels between Beeler and Charles Russell, although Hedgpeth does not raise them. Finally, the umbrella organization for cowboy artists cooperated in the publication by James K. Howard of TEN YEARS WITH THE COWBOY ARTISTS OF AMERICA (1976), which provides, high school yearbook style, an overview of the development of western art over time, a ten-year history of the organization, the Cowboy Artists of America, and brief biographies and examples of artwork for thirty-one cowboy artists. Only members of the Cowboy Artists of America are included, so there is nothing on James Bama, for example.

While science fiction art has moved from the covers of pulps into renewed respectability, there has been surprisingly little written about the major "sci-fi" illustrators. The histories of the genre frequently do a reasonable job of analyzing the major contributors, but they tend to focus on the older, Golden Age of science fiction illustration. Subsequently, more contemporary illustrators have received little attention. Frank Kelly Freas's artistic autobiography, THE ART OF SCI-ENCE FICTION (1977), provides an interesting perspective of one man's artwork as it has developed over a twenty-five-year career. It is interesting to see Freas's style change through time, as events changed his knowledge and perceptions of the subject matter he dealt with. Equally interesting is his technique of providing commentaries about each picture in the book, commentaries that show the thought process involved in dealing with the illustration problem rather than the methods used. Frank Frazetta, whose career has been shorter than that of Freas, has none-theless been the subject of far more ink, ranging from Donald Newlove's worshipful piece in ESQUIRE (1977) to Nick Meglin's more traditional analysis in AMERICAN ARTIST (1976). These two pieces form an interesting set; both authors interviewed Frazetta and analyze the hypermuscular figures in his artwork, but have quite different reactions. Newlove's article has a "gee whiz" quality about it because the author is obviously impressed with the dimensions of the "Frazetta Woman" and the machismo of the artist. Meglin is impressed with the quality of the artwork but not the character of the artist, whose artwork he views as being sexually exploitive and whose work procedures are completely without discipline.

Two other contemporary illustrators have been the subject of books. Murray Tinkelman has been the subject of a book edited by Daniel Kagan, THE ILLUS-TRATIONS OF MURRAY TINKELMAN (1980) and an article by Nick Meglin in AMERICAN ARTIST (1979). Kagan's book contains a very brief but good analysis of Tinkelman's style, suggesting that he has moved from the decorative illustrations of the past to a more fine-arts approach today, in which, like the Impressionists, Tinkelman uses an abstract pattern of crosshatches to create Realist images. The book concludes with examples of five types of artwork—bestiary, landscape, op-ed, mechanicals, and fiction—that demonstrate Tinkelman's artistic breadth and control of his medium. Meglin's article focuses on Tinkelman as he works in his studio, particularly his approach to his illustrations for Giovanni Boccaccio's DECAMERON. This piece focuses more on Tinkelman's statement of his approach, including an interesting discussion of the use of the camera to record visual images, and the need for the illustrator to act as a "director" for this image recording.

Steve Dohanos, one of the first photo-Realist illustrators and still one of the most popular and successful, has written an autobiographical and analytic book about his work, AMERICAN REALIST (1980). After a brief autobiographical statement he discusses those artists who influenced his work and how he perceives his own work. It is not surprising to find that he was inspired by the Realist painters Charles Burchfield, Grant Wood, and Edward Hopper, but it is surprising to find Dohanos identifying himself as the artistic stepchild of the Ash Can school of painting, not because of technique but because of his focus on depicting beauty in ordinary things. The bulk of the book is devoted to showing examples of his illustration artwork in a number of sources and covering a variety of subjects, showing the breadth and range of his artwork. Unhappily, the quality of the color reproductions is not very good (a shame given the quality of Dohanos's color work) and there is no bibliography of his published artwork. Another contemporary Realist, James McMullan, has written an excellent book, REVEALING ILLUS-TRATIONS (1981), that is partly autobiographical, partly analytical. The auto-biographical segment, based on an interview with Milton Glazer, gives a splendid insight into how and why McMullan began his illustration career and the basis for his unique approach to illustration assignments. In the analytical part of his book, McMullan describes how and why he approached a number of illustration assignments, showing his artwork at various stages. "Realism in Illustration" (1978) is devoted to a look at contemporary Realist illustrators like Dohanos and McMullan.

Biographical information on other contemporary illustrators is sadly lacking. Some information can be gleaned from review articles that appeared in PRINT, GRAPHIS, U&LC and other specialized professional magazines. But this coverage is spotty, incomplete, and not necessarily representative of the totality of contemporary American illustration. In some ways it may be easier to determine who the "best" contemporary illustrators are by looking at the ILLUSTRATORS annual of the Society of Illustrators, than to find biographical information about them.

There is obviously a very substantial amount of biographical information on selected individual illustrators. It is equally obvious that a number of excellent illustrators, from various historical periods, have remained virtual unknowns, biographically and artistically. More important, there is very little written that seeks to synthesize the information in these biographies in a way that says something important about illustration and illustrators in general. If we continue writing individual biographies the ever-increasing number of contemporary illustrators ensures that the task of adequately covering everyone will never be completed. As a result, we may never be able to answer a number of important questions about illustrators and illustration in the past and present, questions that may provide useful insights into the future.

Among the questions awaiting answers, even from the available bibliographical material, are the following: What has motivated illustrators to become and stay illustrators? How have they viewed their roles as professionals and to what extent have they aspired to be fine artists as well or instead? To what extent have motivations, roles, and aspirations changed through time? What factors have accounted for some of these changes? Many biographers have argued that their subject's artwork was a response to the subject matter to be illustrated or a reflection of the cultural values of the time. To what extent can we view illustration artwork, as Lanes, Vorpahl, and Amaral have suggested, as an expression of how illustrators seek to deal with themselves in relation to their psychic and physical environment? Would psychohistory provide us with insights into illustrators and their artwork? Certainly, the Wyeth correspondence in Betsy James Wyeth's THE WYETHS (1971) contains some psychologically suggestive material.

Nor has there been any research comparing the lives and artwork of American illustrators with their contemporaries living and working abroad. Given the differential development of European and American illustration during the Golden Age of American illustration it would be interesting to know why the impact of that Golden Age was geographically isolated. To what extent, for example, were American and European illustrators aware of each others' work—and influenced by it? Elsewhere I have suggested that Americans were aware of European illustration but generally were not heavily influenced by it. Why not?

It is hoped that the wealth of biographical material now available, particularly regarding many of the most important early illustrators, will provide us with materials to answer some of the foregoing questions. But first, we must be aware that these questions must be asked before they can be answered.

BIBLIOGRAPHY

EDWIN AUSTIN ABBEY. New Haven, Yale University Art Gallery, 1974.

Abbott, Charles D. HOWARD PYLE: A CHRONICLE. New York, Harper and Bros., 1925.

Allen, Douglas. FREDERIC REMINGTON AND THE SPANISH–AMERICAN WAR. New York, Crown Publishers, 1971.

Allen, Douglas, and Douglas Allen, Jr. N. C. WYETH. New York, Bonanza Books, 1972.

Amaral, Anthony. WILL JAMES: THE LAST COWBOY LEGEND. Reno, University of Nevada Press, 1980.

Apgar, Frank P. FRANK SCHOONOVER, PAINTER-ILLUSTRATOR: A BIBLIOG-RAPHY. Morristown, N.J., published by author, 1969.

STANLEY ARTHURS. Wilmington, Delaware Art Museum, 1974.

Baigell, Matthew. THE WESTERN ART OF FREDERIC REMINGTON. New York, Ballantine Books, 1976.

Baker, Douglas. "Al Parker, Founder of the Modern School of Glamour Illustration." AMERICAN ARTIST, September 1946, 25–29.

Beam, Phillip C. WINSLOW HOMER'S MAGAZINE ENGRAVINGS. New York, Harper and Row, 1979.

Berman, Avis. "Maxfield Parrish." ARTS AND ANTIQUES, January/February 1980, 86–93.

Best, James J. "The Brandywine School and Magazine Illustration, HARPER'S, SCRIB-NER'S and CENTURY, 1906–1910." JOURNAL OF AMERICAN CULTURE, no. 3 (1980), 128–44.

Blegved, Erik. SELF-PORTRAIT: ERIK BLEGVED. Reading, Mass., Addison-Wessley, 1979.

Bolton, Theodore. THE BOOK ILLUSTRATIONS OF FELIX OCTAVIUS CARR DAR-LEY. Worchester, Mass., American Antiquarian Society, 1952.

Bowers, Q. David, and Christine Bowers. ROBERT ROBINSON: AMERICAN IL-LUSTRATOR. Vestal, N.Y., Vestal Press, 1981.

THE BRANDYWINE HERITAGE. Chadds Ford, Pa., Brandywine River Museum, 1971.

Broder, Patricia Janis. DEAN CORNWELL: DEAN OF ILLUSTRATORS. New York, Watson-Guptill, 1978.

Brown, Ann Barton. HOWARD PYLE, A TEACHER. Chadds Ford, Pa., Brandywine River Museum, 1980.

Brown, Arthur. "Howard Chandler Christy." AMERICAN ARTIST, January 1952, 50–51, 68.

Buechner, Thomas. NORMAN ROCKWELL: A SIXTY-YEAR PERSPECTIVE. New York, Henry Abrams, 1972.

Burr, Frederic M. LIFE AND WORKS OF ALEXANDER ANDERSON, M. D. New York, Burr Bros., 1893.

THE EDGAR RICE BURROUGHS LIBRARY OF ILLUSTRATION: VOL. I. West Plains, Mo., Russ Cochran, Publisher, 1976.

Carroll, John M. VON SCHMIDT: THE COMPLETE ILLUSTRATOR. Fort Collins, Colo., Old Army Press, 1973.

Cate, Phillip Dennis, ed. CONTEMPORARY AMERICAN ILLUSTRATORS OF CHILDREN'S BOOKS. New Brunswick, N.J., Rutgers University, 1974.

Christ-Janer, Albert. BOARDMAN ROBINSON. Chicago, University of Chicago Press, 1946.

CITY LIFE ILLUSTRATED, 1890–1940. Wilmington, Delaware Art Museum, 1980.

Cummins, D. Duane. WILLIAM ROBINSON LEIGH: WESTERN ARTIST. Norman, University of Oklahoma Press, 1980.

Davidson, Harold G. HAROLD BOREIN: COWBOY ARTIST. Garden City, N.Y., Doubleday, 1974.

Deshazo, Edith. EVERETT SHINN. New York, Clarkson N. Potter, 1974.

Dippie, Brian. "Charlie Russell's Lost West." AMERICAN HERITAGE, April 1973, 5–21, 89.

——— "Frederic Remington's Wild West." AMERICAN HERITAGE, April 1975, 6–24, 76–79.

——— "PAPER TALK": CHARLIE RUSSELL'S AMERICAN WEST. New York, Knopf, 1979.

DISCUSSIONS ON AMERICAN ART AND ARTISTS. New York, American Art League, 1896.

Dodd, Loring H. A GENERATION OF ILLUSTRATORS AND ETCHERS. Boston, Chapman and Grimes, 1960.

Dohanos, Steve. AMERICAN REALIST. Westport, Conn., Northern Lights Publishing Co., 1980.

Downey, Fairfax. PORTRAIT OF AN ERA AS DRAWN BY C. D. GIBSON. New York, Scribner's, 1936.

DuBois, June. W. R. LEIGH. Kansas City, Lowell Press, 1977.

DOUGLAS DUER. Wilmington, Delaware Art Museum, 1976.

Duyckinck, Everett A. A BRIEF CATALOGUE OF BOOKS ILLUSTRATED WITH ENGRAVINGS BY DR. ALEXANDER ANDERSON. New York, Thompson and Moreau, 1885.

Dykes, Jeff. FIFTY GREAT WESTERN ILLUSTRATORS: A BIBLIOGRAPHIC CHECKLIST. Flagstaff, Ariz., Northland Press, 1975.

Eastman, Max. JOURNALISM VERSUS ART. New York, Alfred Knopf, 1916.

Elzea, Rowland, ed. HOWARD PYLE: DIVERSITY IN DEPTH. Wilmington, Delaware Art Museum, 1973.

Elzea, Rowland, and Elizabeth H. Hawkes. A SMALL SCHOOL OF ART: THE STUDENTS OF HOWARD PYLE. Wilmington, Delaware Art Museum, 1980.

Ewer, J. E. "Not Quite Redmen: The Plains Indian Illustrations of Felix O. C. Darley." AMERICAN ART JOURNAL, no. 3 (1971), 88–98.

Finch, Christopher. NORMAN ROCKWELL'S AMERICA. New York, Henry Abrams, 1975.

——— NORMAN ROCKWELL: 332 MAGAZINE COVERS. New York, Random House, Abbeyville Press, 1979.

Fitzgerald, Richard. ART AND POLITICS: CARTOONISTS OF THE MASSES AND LIBERATOR. Westport, Conn., Greenwood Press, 1973.

Flagg, James Montgomery. CELEBRITIES. Watkins Glen, N.Y., Century House, 1951.

——— ROSES AND BUCKSHOT. New York, Putnam's, 1946.

Freas, Frank Kelly. THE ART OF SCIENCE FICTION. Norfolk, Va., Donning, 1977.

Freeman, Ruth S. JESSIE WILCOX SMITH: CHILDHOOD'S GREAT ILLUSTRATOR. Watkins Glen, N.Y., Century House, 1977.

Frewin, Anthony. ONE HUNDRED YEARS OF SCIENCE FICTION ILLUSTRATION: 1840–1940. London, Jupiter Books, 1974.

Gallati, Barbara D. "Arthur Dove as Illustrator." ARCHIVES OF AMERICAN ART JOURNAL, no. 21 (1981), 13–22.

Gambee, Budd L. "American Book and Magazine Illustration of the Late Nineteenth Century." In Francis J. Brewer, ed., BOOK ILLUSTRATION: PAPERS PRESENTED AT THE THIRD RARE BOOK CONFERENCE OF THE AMERICAN LIBRARY ASSOCIATION IN 1962. Berlin, Gebr. Verlag, 1963, pp. 45–55.

Gardner, Albert Ten Eyck. WINSLOW HOMER. New York, Bramhall House, 1961.

Greene, Douglas G. "W. W. Denslow, Illustrator." THE JOURNAL OF POPULAR CULTURE, no. 7 (1973), 87–96.

Green, Douglas G., and Michael Patrick Hearn. W. W. DENSLOW. Mt. Pleasant, Clarke Historical Library, Central Michigan University, 1976.

Grossman, Julian. ECHOES OF A DISTANT DRUM: WINSLOW HOMER AND THE CIVIL WAR. New York, Henry Abrams, 1974.

Guptill, Arthur L. NORMAN ROCKWELL, ILLUSTRATOR. New York, Watson-Guptill, 1970.

Hahler, Christine Anne, ed. . . . ILLUSTRATED BY DARLEY. Wilmington, Delaware Art Museum, 1978.

Harper, J. Henry. THE HOUSE OF HARPER. New York, Harper's, 1912.

Hassrick, Peter. FREDERIC REMINGTON. New York, Henry Abrams in association with the Amon Carter Museum of Western Art, 1973.

Hassrick, Royal B. WESTERN PAINTING TODAY. New York, Watson-Guptill, 1975.

Haugh, Georgia S. "The Beginnings of American Book Illustration." In Francis J. Brewer, ed., BOOK ILLUSTRATION: PAPERS PRESENTED AT THE THIRD RARE BOOK CONFERENCE OF THE AMERICAN LIBRARY ASSOCIATION IN 1962. Berlin, Gebr. Verlag, 1963, pp. 34–41.

Hawkes, Elizabeth H. BERTHA CORSON DAY BATES: ILLUSTRATOR IN THE HOWARD PYLE TRADITION. Wilmington, Delaware Art Museum, 1978.

Hearn, Michael Patrick. THE ANNOTATED WIZARD OF OZ. New York, Clarkson N. Potter, 1973.

————"The 'Ubiquitous' Trina Schart Hyman." AMERICAN ARTIST, May 1979, 36–43, 96–97.

Hedgpeth, Don. COWBOY ARTIST: THE JOE BEELER STORY. Flagstaff, Ariz., Northland Press, 1979.

Hendricks, Gordon. THE LIFE AND WORK OF WINSLOW HOMER. New York, Henry Abrams, 1979.

Henry, Marguerite. THE ILLUSTRATED MARGUERITE HENRY. Chicago, Rand McNally, 1980.

Hodgson, Pat. THE WAR ILLUSTRATORS. New York, Macmillan, 1977.

Hoole, W. Stanley. VIZETELLY COVERS THE CONFEDERACY. Tuscaloosa, Ala., Confederate Publishing Co., 1957.

Hornung, Clarence P. HANDBOOK OF EARLY ADVERTISING ART, VOLS. I, II. New York, Dover Publications, 1947.

Howard, James K. TEN YEARS WITH THE COWBOY ARTISTS OF AMERICA. Flagstaff, Ariz., Northland Press, 1976.

Hutchinson, W. H. THE WORLD, THE WORK, AND THE WEST OF W.H.D. KOERNER. Norman, University of Oklahoma Press, 1978.

Hyman, Trina Schart. SELF-PORTRAIT: TRINA SCHART HYMAN. Reading, Mass., Addison-Wessley, 1981.

Johnson, Fridolph, ed. THE ILLUSTRATIONS OF ROCKWELL KENT: 231 EXAMPLES FROM BOOKS, MAGAZINES AND ADVERTISING ART. New York, Dover Publications, 1976.

Jones, Helen. ROBERT LAWSON: ILLUSTRATOR. Boston, Little Brown, 1972.

Kagan, Daniel, ed. THE ILLUSTRATIONS OF MURRAY TINKELMAN. New York, Art Directors Book Co., 1980.

Karolevitz, Robert. THE PRAIRIE IS MY GARDEN. Aberdeen, S.D., North Plains Press, 1969.

——— WHERE YOUR HEART IS: THE STORY OF HARVEY DUNN, ARTIST. Aberdeen, S.D., North Plains Press, 1970.

Kent, Norman. "Harry Beckhoff, Illustrator." AMERICAN ARTIST, January 1947, 19–21, 42.

——— "Paul Bramson." AMERICAN ARTIST, April 1947, 19–23.

——— "C. B. Falls, 1874–1960: A Career in Retrospect." AMERICAN ARTIST, February 1962, 24–41.

Kent, Rockwell. IT'S ME O LORD: THE AUTOBIOGRAPHY OF ROCKWELL KENT. New York, Dodd, Mead, 1955.

——— ROCKWELLKENTIANA. New York, Harcourt Brace, 1933.

King, Ethel. DARLEY, THE MOST POPULAR ILLUSTRATOR OF HIS TIME. Brooklyn, N.Y., Gaus's, 1964.

Knauft, Ernest. "American Pen Drawings." In Charles Holme, ed., MODERN PEN DRAWINGS: EUROPEAN AND AMERICAN. New York, Special Winter Number of THE STUDIO: 1900–1901, 1901.

W.H.D. KOERNER. Wilmington, Delaware Art Museum, 1977.

Lanes, Selma G. THE ART OF MAURICE SENDAK. New York, Henry Abrams, 1980.

Laning, Edward. THE SKETCHBOOKS OF REGINALD MARSH. Greenwich, Conn., New York Graphic Society, Ltd., 1973.

Larkin, David, ed. THE ART OF NANCY ECKHOLM BURKERT. New York, Peacock Press, 1977.

Levin, Gail. EDWARD HOPPER AS ILLUSTRATOR. New York, W. W. Norton, 1979.

Lewis, Benjamin M. A GUIDE TO ENGRAVINGS IN AMERICAN MAGAZINES: 1741–1810. New York, New York Public Library, 1959.

Linton, W. J. THE HISTORY OF WOOD-ENGRAVING IN AMERICA. Boston, Estes and Laureate, 1882.

Low, Will. A CHRONICLE OF FRIENDSHIP. New York, Charles Scribner's Sons, 1908.

Lucas, E. V. EDWIN AUSTIN ABBEY: ROYAL ACADEMICIAN. 2 vols. New York, Charles Scribner's Sons, 1921.

Ludwig, Coy. MAXFIELD PARRISH. New York, Watson-Guptill, 1973.

McCracken, Harold. FREDERIC REMINGTON: ARTIST OF THE OLD WEST. New York, J. B. Lippincott, 1947.

———— THE FREDERIC REMINGTON BOOK. Garden City, N.Y., Doubleday, 1966.

———— THE CHARLES M. RUSSELL BOOK. Garden City, N.Y., Doubleday, 1957.

McMullan, James. REVEALING ILLUSTRATIONS. New York, Watson-Guptill, 1981.

Maxwell, John. "Henry C. Pitz: Picture Maker," AMERICAN ARTIST, May 1977, 58–65, 93–98.

Meglin, Nick. "Frank Frazetta at Bat." AMERICAN ARTIST, May 1976, 38–45, 77.

———— "Charles Dana Gibson and the Age of Exclusivity." AMERICAN ARTIST, March 1975, 62–63, 69.

———— "Murray Tinkelman: My Studio Has No Time Clock." AMERICAN ARTIST, January 1979, 70–75, 95–96.

Meyer, Susan E. AMERICA'S GREAT ILLUSTRATORS. New York, Henry Abrams, 1978.

———— JAMES MONTGOMERY FLAGG. New York, Watson-Guptill, 1974.

———— NORMAN ROCKWELL'S PEOPLE. New York, Henry Abrams, 1981.

———— ed. "Three Generations of the Wyeth Family." AMERICAN ARTIST, February 1975.

Mitchell, Gene. THE SUBJECT WAS CHILDREN: THE ART OF JESSIE WILCOX SMITH. New York, E. P. Dutton, 1979.

Newlove, Donald. "The Incredible Paintings of Frank Fazetta." ESQUIRE, June 1977, 86–94, 149–54.

Newman, Sasha. ARTHUR DOVE AND DUNCAN PHILLIPS: ARTIST AND PATRON. New York, George Braziller and the Phillips Collection, 1981.

North, Ernest Dressel. "A Group of Young Illustrators." THE OUTLOOK, December 2, 1899, 791–97.

Parry, E. C., and M. Chamberlin-Hellman. "Thomas Eakins as an Illustrator, 1878–81." AMERICAN ART JOURNAL, May 1973, 20–45.

CHARLES PARSONS AND HIS DOMAIN. Montclair, N.J., Montclair Art Museum, 1958.

Patterson, Ruth G. "The Influence of Howard Pyle on American Illustration." M.A. thesis. Cleveland, Ohio, Department of Library Science, Western Reserve University, 1954.

Pennell, Elizabeth Robins. THE LIFE AND LETTERS OF JOSEPH PENNELL, VOLS. I AND II. Boston, Little Brown, 1929.

Pennell, Joseph. THE GRAPHIC ARTS. Chicago, University of Chicago Press, 1920.

———— THE ILLUSTRATION OF BOOKS. New York, Century Co., 1896.

———— MODERN ILLUSTRATION. London, George Bell and Sons, 1905.

PERCEPTIONS AND EVOCATIONS: THE ART OF ELIHU VEDDER. Washington, D.C., National Collection of Fine Arts, Smithsonian Institution Press, 1979.

Perlman, Bernard B. THE GOLDEN AGE OF AMERICAN ILLUSTRATION: F. R. GRUGER AND HIS CIRCLE. Westport, Conn., Northern Lights Publishers, 1978.

Pitz, Henry C. THE BRANDYWINE TRADITION. New York, Weathervane Books, 1968.

———— HOWARD PYLE. New York, Clarkson N. Potter, 1975.

———— "Frank Schoonover: An Example of the Pyle Tradition." AMERICAN ARTIST, November 1964, 64–68, 83.

———— 200 YEARS OF AMERICAN ILLUSTRATION. New York, Random House and the Society of Illustrators, 1977.

—— "N. C. Wyeth." AMERICAN HERITAGE, October 1965, 36–41, 82–84.

Pratt, Fletcher. CIVIL WAR IN PICTURES. Garden City, N.Y., Garden City Books, 1957.

Ray, Frederic E. ALFRED R. WAUD: CIVIL WAR ARTIST. New York, Viking, 1974.

"Realism in Illustration." PRINT, January/February 1978.

Reed, Henry. THE A. B. FROST BOOK. Rutland, Vt., Charles E. Tuttle, 1967.

Reed, Walt. JOHN CLYMER: AN ARTIST'S RENDEZVOUS WITH THE FRONTIER WEST. Flagstaff, Ariz., Northland Press, 1976.

—— GREAT AMERICAN ILLUSTRATORS. New York, Abbeyville Press, 1979.

—— HAROLD VON SCHMIDT. Flagstaff, Ariz., Northland Press, Press, 1972.

—— ed. THE ILLUSTRATOR IN AMERICA: 1900–1960. New York, Reinhold Publishing Co., 1966.

—— comp. THE MAGIC PEN OF JOSEPH CLEMENT COLL. West Kingston, R.I., Donald M. Grant, 1978.

Renwick, Stephen Lee. "Walter Biggs." AMERICAN ARTIST, May 1945, 19–24.

—— "F. R. Gruger." AMERICAN ARTIST, October 1943, 14–17, 32b.

Rockwell, Norman. MY ADVENTURES AS AN ILLUSTRATOR. New York, Doubleday, 1960.

—— THE NORMAN ROCKWELL ALBUM. New York, Doubleday, 1961.

—— ROCKWELL ON ROCKWELL. New York, Watson-Guptill, 1979.

St. John, Bruce, ed. JOHN SLOAN'S NEW YORK SCENE. New York, Harper and Row, 1965.

Samuels, Peggy and Harold. FREDERICK REMINGTON: A BIOGRAPHY. Garden City, N.Y., Doubleday and Co., 1982.

Schau, Michael. ALL-AMERICAN GIRL: THE ART OF COLES PHILLIPS. New York, Watson-Guptill, 1975.

—— J. C. LEYENDECKER. New York, Watson-Guptill, 1976.

Schnessel, S. Michael. JESSIE WILCOX SMITH. New York, Thomas Y. Crowell, 1973.

Schoonover, Cortland. FRANK SCHOONOVER: ILLUSTRATOR OF THE NORTH AMERICAN FRONTIER. New York, Watson-Guptill, 1976.

—— ed. THE EDGE OF THE WILDERNESS. Toronto, Methuen, 1974.

Sears, Stephen, ed. CENTURY COLLECTION OF CIVIL WAR ART. New York, American Heritage, 1974.

Shinn, Everett. "William Glackens as an Illustrator." AMERICAN ARTIST, November 1945, 22–27, 37.

Skeeters, Paul. MAXFIELD PARRISH: THE EARLY YEARS. Secaucus, N.J., Chartwell Books, 1973.

Smedley, W. T. LIFE AND CHARACTER. New York, Harper's, 1899.

Smith, F. Hopkinson. AMERICAN ILLUSTRATORS. New York, Charles Scribner, 1893.

Soria, Regina. ELIHU VEDDER. Rutherford, N.J., Fairleigh Dickinson University Press, 1970.

Stern, Phillip Van Doren. THEY WERE THERE. New York, Crown Publishers, 1959.

Stoltz, Donald R. NORMAN ROCKWELL AND THE SATURDAY EVENING POST, VOL. I. New York, Four S Corp., 1976.

Stoltz, Donald R., and Marshall L. Stoltz. NORMAN ROCKWELL AND THE SATURDAY EVENING POST, THE LATER YEARS, 1943–1971. New York, Four S Corp., 1976.

────── NORMAN ROCKWELL AND THE SATURDAY EVENING POST, THE MID-
DLE YEARS, 1928–1943. New York, Four S Corp., 1976.
Stryker, Cathryn Connell. THE STUDIOS AT COGSLEA. Wilmington, Delaware Art
Museum, 1976.
Summers, Ian. THE ART OF THE BROTHERS HILDEBRANDT. New York, Ballantine
Books, 1979.
────── ed. TOMORROW AND BEYOND: MASTERPIECES OF SCIENCE FICTION
ART. New York, Workman Publishing Co., 1978.
Taft, Robert. ARTISTS AND ILLUSTRATORS OF THE OLD WEST, 1850–1900. New
York, Charles Scribner's Sons, 1953.
"Telephone Poles and Fire Plugs." AMERICAN ARTIST, January 1941, 16–20.
Thompson, W. Fletcher, Jr. THE IMAGE OF WAR. New York, Thomas Yoseloff, 1959.
Traxel, David. AN AMERICAN SAGA: THE LIFE AND TIMES OF ROCKWELL
KENT. New York, Harper and Row, 1980.
Trimble, Jessie. "The Founder of an American School of Art." THE OUTLOOK, February
23, 1907, 453–60.
Tudor, Bethany. DRAWN FROM NEW ENGLAND. Boston, William Collins, 1979.
Vorpahl, Ben Marchant. FREDERIC REMINGTON AND THE WEST. Austin, Uni-
versity of Texas, 1978.
Walton, Donald. A ROCKWELL PORTRAIT. Kansas City, Mo., Sheed, Andrews and
McNell, 1978.
Ward, Lynd. STORYTELLER WITHOUT WORDS. New York, Henry Abrams, 1974.
Watson, Ernest W. "Harrison Cady." AMERICAN ARTIST, April 1945, 11–15, 34.
────── "Albert Dorne, An 'Horatio Alger' Story." AMERICAN ARTIST, May 1943,
13–17, 30.
────── "Harvey Dunn: Milestone in the Tradition of American Illustration." AMERICAN
ARTIST, June 1942, 16–20, 31.
────── "Glamor Is His Business and His Art." AMERICAN ARTIST, February 1945,
24–27, 34.
────── "An Interview with Dean Cornwell." AMERICAN ARTIST, April 1942, 23–
28.
────── "Fred Ludekins." AMERICAN ARTIST, October 1946, 25–29, 40.
────── "Martha Sawyers: Illustrator of Oriental Lore." AMERICAN ARTIST, April
1944, 22–25, 30.
────── "Donald Teague, Illustrator of Frontier and Sea." AMERICAN ARTIST, Sep-
tember 1944, 25–30.
Weinhardt, Carl J. THE MOST OF JOHN HELD, JR. Brattleboro, Vt., Stephen Green
Press, 1972.
Weitenkampf, Frank. THE ILLUSTRATED BOOK. Cambridge, Mass., Harvard Uni-
versity Press, 1938.
WHALERS, WHARVES, AND WATERWAYS: AN EXHIBITION OF PAINTINGS
BY CLIFFORD W. ASHLEY. Chadds Ford, Pa., Brandywine River Museum,
1973.
White, G. Edward. THE EASTERN ESTABLISHMENT AND THE WESTERN EX-
PERIENCE. New Haven, Conn., Yale University Press, 1968.
WOMEN ARTISTS IN THE HOWARD PYLE TRADITION. Chadds Ford, Pa., Bran-
dywine River Museum, 1975.
Wyeth, Betsy James, ed. THE WYETHS. Boston, Gambit Press, 1971.

CHAPTER 5

The Social and Artistic Context
of Illustration

A complete understanding of American illustration would be impossible without a discussion of the various social and artistic factors that influenced the development of American illustration. In this chapter I shall examine two: the social milieu of American illustration, particularly the relationships that developed between illustrators and facilitated the growth and development of their artwork, and the impact of various artistic movements from abroad and at home, in other branches and fields of art, on American illustration. In the first instance I will pay particular attention to the network of social and professional organizations that developed as illustration became professionally legitimate and the formal and informal friendship patterns that developed between illustrators and with editors, that influenced their work. In the second I will pay particular attention to schools of art rather than individuals and examine their impact on American illustration as a whole and on particular illustrators as well.

THE SOCIAL MILIEU

The growth of illustration as a profession, particularly in the post-Civil War period, prevented the isolation of illustrators from one another and the publishers for whom they worked. Even Alexander Anderson and F.O.C. Darley, two of the early American illustrators, were readily accepted in the society of their day. Indeed, their professional preeminence ensured they would be important figures in their respective cultural circles. Darley was recognized by the National Academy of Design in 1852—a sign of his importance and legitimacy. But the lack of real peers meant that both men worked in comparative artistic isolation until the Civil War produced a generation of illustrators and created a "critical mass" of artistic talent that fed the demands of the public for illustration artwork.

The creation of a full-time art department at the House of Harper under the direction of Charles Parsons helped create a social and artistic setting within which illustration could flourish, and established New York City as a center of illustration. One has only to read Exman's THE BROTHERS HARPER (1965), J. Henry Harper's THE HOUSE OF HARPER (1912), and the excellent museum catalog, CHARLES PARSONS AND HIS DOMAIN (1958), to understand Parson's role as social as well as artistic leader for the illustration department at Harper's. Within this milieu, illustrators such as Howard Pyle, Edwin Austin Abbey, Edward Kemble, and A. B. Frost learned, developed, and honed their professional skills under the watchful eye of Parsons and with the encouragement of each other. The success of Harper's art department was soon imitated by other firms, and New York became the publishing and illustration center of America. Drake at Century and Chapin at Scribner's were important as art editors for their respective firms, helping each achieve a positon of accomplishment in the field comparable to that of Harper's. However, Joseph Chapin at Scribner's was able to create the camaraderie achieved by Parsons at Harper's. Parsons and Chapin were more than editors: they were talent spotters, talent nurturers, mentors, friends, golf partners, even financial advisors. Best's manuscript on editor-illustrator relations (1982), based on correspondence from the Scribner's company records at Princeton, illustrates the multiple facets of this relationship, which frequently extended beyond artistic or professional questions. In the 1920s, when his eyesight was failing, A. B. Frost appealed to Chapin for illustration assignments and Chapin responded, even though the quality was not as good as Frost's best illustrations and Frost was occasionally unable to meet deadlines. But Chapin was aware of the services that Frost had performed for Scribner's during his career and what those illustration assignments meant for Frost's self-respect. The Scribner's correspondence makes it clear that the shift to a more formal, contractual relationship between illustrator and publisher made it more difficult to sustain warm personal relations. Becoming more "professional" carried with it a very real price.

At the same time the foundation of the Art Students League in New York City in 1875 facilitated the development of illustration and strengthened New York City's claim to preeminence in the field. Marchal Landgren's book, YEARS OF ART (1940), provides a badly needed but not very insightful history of the League. It lists the organization of the League, gives data on enrollment (more than one thousand at its peak), discusses some of its faculty (William Merritt Chase and Kenyon Cox were of importance to illustrators), and lists those illustrators who studied at the League—Robert Blum, Howard Chandler Christy, Thomas Fogarty, Oliver Herford, A. B. Frost, Walter A. Clark, Charles Dana Gibson, Jay Hambridge, Howard Pyle, Albert Sterner, and William Rogers, to name a number from the Golden Age of illustration. Unfortunately, Landgren doesn't explore the League's success in attracting illustrators to its classes or its influence on their development. Did the fact that Howard Pyle attended League classes in 1877, at the recommendation of Charles Parsons, affect his illustration style? Pitz's book, HOWARD PYLE (1975), suggests the answer was no. But the role of the League and its impact on students was probably more complex than Pitz recognized in the case of Pyle. The Art Students League provided a gathering place for illustrators working in New York City who wanted to learn or improve their skills. What they learned from each other may have been more important than what they learned in class (while the League had many illustrators in its classes it was very slow to establish classes in illustration). Few illustrators spent extended periods of time studying at the League; they were more interested in developing their professional careers. In addition, the League provided a common meeting ground for fine artists and illustrators, under the watchful eye of the faculty. In the process many fine artists learned they could earn a decent living as illustrators until they became recognized as fine artists. Illustrators, on the other hand, were exposed to the major art movements of the day and were able to choose those techniques that enabled them to deal with their day-to-day illustration problems. For the illustrator or artist recently arrived in New York City, enrolling at the Art Students League was an important introduction to the artistic scene of the city. The importance of the League to John Sloan and William Glackens can be seen in Bruce St. John's JOHN SLOAN'S NEW YORK SCENE (1965), Sloan's diaries of his early years in New York. Sloan's diaries, as well as Deshazo's biography of Everett Shinn (1974) and Gail Levin's study of Edward Hopper's illustrations (1979), point to the dual nature of the illustration profession in New York at the time. In addition to those illustrators like Pyle, who identified themselves as illustrators, there were a number of artist-illustrators like Sloan, William Glackens, and many of their friends, who worked as illustrators but viewed themselves primarily as fine artists. To them, illustration was merely a means to an end, not an end in itself. As a result, the artist-illustrators tended to socialize with each other and with other fine artists, rather than with their fellow illustrators. Sloan's diaries note, for example, his discomfort at being elected as a member of the Society of Illustrators. Perhaps the most striking example of this duality is Edward Hopper, who began his career unsuccessfully as a fine artist, became a modestly successful illustrator, and then when his fine art began to sell, returned to being a fine artist once again.

Once illustration had been accepted as a legitimate profession—in the early 1890s—illustrators became part of the cultural milieu of New York City, where many of the leading illustrators worked and lived. In 1871 Will Low, F. S. Church, J. Scott Hartley, Joseph Hartley, and W. H. Shelton—successful illustrators but largely outside the group at Harper's—formed the Salmagundi Club in New York. According to Shelton's history of the Club, THE SALMAGUNDI CLUB (1918), membership was initially limited to twenty men who would meet periodically, hang an illustration assignment and do a critique, eat sausages, drink coffee, sing, and occasionally box. By the late 1870s membership in the Club included some of the leading "new" names in American illustration—Howard Pyle, Walter A. Clark, and George McCutcheon. The Club remained a professionally based social organization until 1887, when it became a strictly social organization—according to Shelton—for Bohemians, not stuffed shirts. In a later book (THE HISTORY OF THE SALMAGUNDI CLUB . . . [1927]) Shelton offers an interesting comparison between the world of the Club in the 1870s and that of the 1920s; by the latter date the Club had moved into permanent headquarters that included a lovely rooftop restaurant with superb chef, where "members lingered over their cups of black coffee and glass of mint frappé or ponies of cognac dripped on lumps of sugar suspended over the coffee" (p. 9). Quite a change from those "early" days when coffee and fried sausages were served, but reflective of the changed status of illustrators and the commercial arts in New York during the fifty-year period.

According to Shelton many members of the Salmagundi Club were also members of the Tile Club, an organization for the cultural elite of New York City. A BOOK OF THE TILE CLUB (1886) contains chapters by Edward Strahan—"Their Habitat" and "One of Their Meetings"—and F. Hopkinson Smith—"Shop Talk," "Around Their Wood Fire," and "Club Chestnuts Warmed Over"—that describe the Tile Club house, meetings, and members. According to Strahan, the Club started with painters, added sculptors and musicians and soon everyone wanted in, so they limited membership to an elite of twenty-two, each of whom took a "nom de work." Among the members were August St. Gaudens, A. B. Frost, Alfred Parsons, Elihu Vedder, Stanford White, Napoleon Sarony, and William Gidney Bunce, who adopted such pseudonyms as Polyphemus, The Griffin, Haggis, and The Saint. Strahan describes one of their meetings, which began with predinner festivities, followed by an enormous meal during which "Chestnut" (Edwin Austin Abbey) described life in his new home town of London. After dinner the group sat saround the fire, drinking and talking art. F. Hopkinson Smith's chapter on the Tile Club in AMERICAN ILLUSTRATORS (1893) provides little additional information but is easier to find than the Strahan book.

A BOOK OF THE TILE CLUB and Shelton's two books are the only books that describe these social and cultural organizations in which illustrators played a major role, although illustrators were also involved in a number of other social clubs in New York City. The Century Club, which had a broader base within the business and economic elite as well as within the cultural elite, counted a number of the most widely recognized illustrators as members.

The Society of Illustrators was formed in 1901 by Otto Bacher, Albert Sterner, and Henry Fleming, who were soon joined by Reginald Birch, Louis Loeb, A. B. Wenzell, F. V. DuMond, F. C. Yohn, Henry Hutt, and B. W. Cliendienst. It was initially a professional organization for the purpose of bringing illustrators, editors, and publishers together to discuss common problems. However, Norman Price's HISTORY OF THE SOCIETY OF ILLUSTRATORS (1939) and the earlier history, THE SOCIETY OF ILLUSTRATORS, 1901–1928 (1928), suggest the dinners, art exhibits, and yearly musical reviews came to assume increasing importance for the members, necessitating the purchase of a building in midtown Manhattan. Some illustrators avoided joining the Society of Illustrators because they feared carrying the label of "illustrator" or because they were not happy with the social aspects of the organization's activities. But for many illustrators the Society provided a useful meeting place and social outlet, in much the same way as the Art Students League, and within ten years most of the leading illustrators—Abbey, Pyle, Remington, Gibson, the Leyendeckers, and Penfield, for example—were members. The 1911 ANNUAL lists ninety-six full members (all men) and four associate members—Elizabeth Shippen Green, Violet Oakley, May Wilson Preston, and Jessie Wilcox Smith—all women. The fact that the Society did not become the "union" that some editors and illustrators feared that it might, undoubtedly heightened its appeal to both groups. In the process of their monthly dinners, editors and illustrators often found an informal setting for dealing with their most pressing business problems. The combination of a professional organization with a social function was appealing to many people associated with illustration.

The location of major publishing firms, the Art Students League, the Society of Illustrators, and major cultural clubs in New York City made that locale the center of American illustration during the Golden Age of American illustration. Illustrators had their studios in the city or in nearby suburbs. Another group of illustrators lived and worked in the Philadelphia-Chadds Ford-Wilmington triangle, many of them having studied under Howard Pyle. Some of Pyle's students became so enamored of the area, they lived there for decades; N. C. Wyeth and his family moved to Chadds Ford in 1908, where the family has lived to this day. Jessie Wilcox Smith, Elizabeth Shippen Green, and Violet Oakley established their studio at Cogslea on the Philadelphia Main Line, and Frank Schoonover, Clifford Ashley, Clyde DeLand, and many others who studied with Pyle stayed in the area after becoming successful illustrators. (See Pitz [1975], Schnessel [1973], and Stryker [1976].) When necessary they could travel by train to New York to deal with editors or publishers, or to attend social events, and express service became proficient in shipping crated artwork up and down the Northeast corridor between Wilmington and New York. The camaraderie among Pyle's students existed long after his death, perpetuating the impact of his teaching and style by the intense interaction of his students throughout their professional careers. It was not unusual, for example, for his students to critique each other's artwork before submission or to swap copies of their published works. Thornton Oakley seems to have been a central figure in this network and his correspondence at the Philadelphia Free Library gives an interesting picture of the "Brandywine School alumni association."

Not all illustrators lived in the New York area within easy commuting time of the major publishing houses. Maxfield Parrish moved to New Hampshire in 1898 and became part of the art and cultural community in Cornish. But Parrish was one of the few year-round residents and, as Coy Ludwig notes in MAXFIELD PARRISH (1973), he was unreachable for most of the winter months. This isolation, however, ensured that Parrish could work undisturbed by the time pressures imposed by publishers and could lavish attention on his artwork. Parrish's isolation had other advantages. His artistic isolation allowed him to develop his own style and approach to illustration, without daily comment and criticism from his peers. It also reinforced his perceptions of his unique skills.

Other illustrators lived further afield. Will Bradley began his career in Chicago, as did W. W. Denslow, although both moved to the East Coast at various points in their careers. The further from publishers, the more hazardous the profession was during the early years of the twentieth century. Editors frequently had difficulty with illustrators who went away on story assignments, particularly when working within tight publication deadlines. Dorie Schmidt's collection of Frank Schoonover's correspondence during a western trip in THE AMERICAN MAG-AZINE (1979) demonstrates the editor's dismay at the lack of artwork in the face of publication deadlines. As the West Coast grew in population a number of illustrators lived and worked there. SUNSET MAGAZINE became a major publication source for many West Coast illustrators—Will James, Harold Von Schmidt, and Harold Borein, for example—and even A. B. Frost moved to Pasadena late in his illustration career.

The diffusion of illustration talent into art colonies within commuting distance of New York had a number of consequences: they allowed illustrators to meet one another socially and professionally on a regular basis (and to share the costs of live models, for example), and they were within reasonable commuting distance of their business connections in New York City. The importance of being able to talk with professional peers about one's work can be seen throughout Pitz's discussion of Howard Pyle in HOWARD PYLE (1975). Susan Meyer's book, NORMAN ROCKWELL'S PEOPLE (1981) describes the importance in the case of Mead Schaefer and his family, who served as models for some of Rockwell's illustrations. According to Meyer, Rockwell moved to New England because he felt the people there were more typically "American," and large numbers of his friends and neighbors appeared in his illustrations to prove the point. Meyer's book documents who these people were, their appearances in Rockwell's art, and Rockwell's rationale for using them.

As the publication media for illustrations changed over time—from books and magazines to paperbacks and record albums—the community of professional illustrators became more fragmented. The record industry, for example, is centered on the West Coast, and illustrators who work primarily in that medium tend to congregate there. Increasing specialization in illustration meant that illustrators in one field were less likely to be aware of illustrators in other fields, to interact with them, or to regard them as relevant professional contemporaries. In addition, the dramatic increase in the numbers of illustrators since World War II has made it difficult for them to experience a sense of community. There has been a shift from learning skills on one's own, on the job, or by studying with a "master" teacher; illustrators now are trained in academic environments or schools of art or illustration that are quite different from that established by Howard Pyle at Chadds Ford. As a result today's illustrators are more technically competent than their predecessors, but have a quite different orientation to their profession. Unfortunately, there has been no one who has examined the impact of this change on the quality of American illustration or the meaning of "profession" for contemporary American illustrators.

The tensions that John Sloan and his fellow artist-illustrators felt in their dual roles have been largely abated. The distinction between the studio and commercial arts, at least in terms of academic training, is quite clear, and illustrators are now committed more than ever to being "professionals." The headquarters for the Society of Illustrators still serves as a meeting ground for illustrators who live or work in the city, but its newsletter and annual shows have now become important vehicles for communication between members. The fragmented nature of the profession and the geographic dispersion of its members places more importance on vehicles of professional communication as a means for keeping current. In addition to the Society's activities, publications like PRINT, GRAPHIS, and other illustration-oriented magazines serve as news sources and art galleries for professionals who cannot interact with one another.

As the nature of the profession has changed so have relations with editors and publishing houses. Long-term, exclusive contracts with one publisher are infrequent, with most illustrators now working as free lancers or as part of illustration groups. The former allows the greater artistic freedom but is financially uncertain, while the latter provides a modicum of financial security at the cost of artistic identity. Art editors remain as important as ever, although the quality of their relations with illustrators has changed somewhat. The larger number of illustrators and the smaller number of publication media make it difficult for art editors to provide continuing personal and professional attention to the illustrators who work for them. Certainly, well-recognized illustrators will have friendly and personal relations with their editors, but it is difficult to envision a relationship developing between an editor and an unknown illustrator similar to the one that developed between Parsons and Pyle when Pyle first came to New York (see Pitz [1975]).

THE ARTISTIC MILIEU

From its early years American illustration has been affected, to a greater or lesser extent, by artistic currents in the United States and abroad. There is no question of the debt that early American illustrators like Anderson and Darley owed to their British contemporaries. English illustrated books and magazines, with designs by James Gilray, Thomas Bewick, and Thomas Rowlandson, were widely read and served as models for American craftsmen. Hahler's . . . ILLUSTRATED BY DARLEY (1978) argues that Darley, raised in Philadelphia in the 1830s, must have been aware of the artwork of Jean Grandville, Thomas Rowlandson, George Cruickshank, "Phiz," and William Thackeray, and that his initial linear style was distinctively British in origin. It was only after these early American illustrators had developed their own styles and had a distinctively American genre of literature to illustrate that American illustration freed itself from the influence of British art. After all, which British illustrators could accurately portray the frontier scenes depicted in words by James Fenimore Cooper or Washington Irving?

The outbreak of the Civil War created a demand for illustrators, a demand that could not be satisfied by indigenous artists. European-trained artists, illustrators, and engravers helped fill the void. They brought with them their knowledge of the latest illustration techniques and, in the process, accelerated the development of American illustration. The emigration of William Linton and the diffusion of lithography and chromolithography from Europe were major factors in the development of American popular art in the last half of the nineteenth century.

In the post-Civil War period American illustration continued to develop a more purely "American" character and style, spurred in part by the development of an indigenous literature and the need of illustrated books and magazines for illustrations that appealed to a mass market, an American market. PICTURESQUE AMERICA (1872–1874) was one of the first books to recognize this need and successfully exploit that market. One has only to look at the eighteenth-century illustrations in Pitz's 200 YEARS OF AMERICAN ILLUSTRATION (1977) to see the distinctively American content and style of such artists as A. B. Frost and Edward Kemble. This seems to have been particularly true of illustrators who perceived themselves to be professional illustrators rather than illustrators who aspired to be fine artists (illustrator-artists) or fine artists who did illustrations to earn a living that their fine art did not provide (artist-illustrators). Howard Pyle, the epitome of the professional illustrator, felt no need to look abroad for inspiration in content or style; as noted by Abbott, in HOWARD PYLE: A CHRON-ICLE (1925), Pyle felt that illustration artwork had to flow from the juxtaposition of the author's words and the illustrator's imagination, so the illustrator's style was always subordinate to the subject matter being illustrated. Nonetheless, Henry Pitz (HOWARD PYLE [1975]) argues that Pyle's pen-and-ink style was influenced by the artwork of Albrecht Dürer and the naturalism of the English Arts and Crafts movement, while his later color oil reflected an Impressionist influence. There is little doubt that Pyle was aware of these artistic currents, but it is not to say that he emulated them. As an illustrator he used the techniques that best enabled him to solve an illustration problem. His palette, for example, was more a reflection of his experience as a magazine illustrator—in which he worked in tonal values of gray—rather than the influence of then-current Impressionism.

The artwork of artist-illustrators and illustrator-artists was more responsive to trends in European and American fine art. Which trends is a matter of debate. David Dickason's book, THE DARING YOUNG MEN (1953) argues for an American school of Pre-Raphaelites, whose work mirrored that of their British contemporaries, but there is little in his book to suggest that the Pre-Raphaelites had much impact on American illustration, except insofar as they were a stimulus for the Art Nouveau movement. In HERE THE COUNTRY LIES (1980) Charles Alexander provides an explanation for why the Pre-Raphaelites had little impact; American artists working prior to 1900 did not go to Europe to be exposed to the "avant garde" but to study the Old Masters. The American magazine that stood as the leading proponent of the Genteel Tradition, CENTURY, reflected that commitment to the Old Masters in its illustrations, which were dedicated to the replication of the fine arts. CENTURY was not the only magazine to have a fine art orientation in its artwork. Michael Quick, in his introduction to the exhibition catalog EDWIN AUSTIN ABBEY (1974), argues that HARPER'S MONTHLY was influenced by the "English" school while SCRIBNER'S favored the Spanish–Italian School. Unfortunately, there is no evidence, artistic or otherwise, to substantiate this argument. The fact that Pyle and many of his students had their artwork published in HARPER'S suggests that they were members of or influenced by the "English" school—which is not true. Although each illustrated magazine had its own "look" or "style," that was the result of the art editors' needs for illustration artwork and whom he chose to do it rather than a conscious effort on his part to emulate a particular school of art. Because of its commitment to the values of the Genteel Tradition, American art—and CENTURY MAGAZINE—was criticized for its lack of relevance for contemporary life. Artistically, the Genteel Tradition looked to the past, the European past, rather than the present or the future.

For some artist-illustrators—John Sloan, William Glackens, and Everett Shinn—their fine artwork represented a revolt against the dominant American style. Mellquist, in THE EMERGENCE OF AN AMERICAN ART (1942), suggests that these men, central figures in the Ash Can school of Social Realism, revolted against the formalism of American art, and the revolt was reflected in their illustrations as well and in the artwork of a generation of illustrators (the "Silver Age" of American illustration) who were their peers. According to Mellquist, Boardman Robinson, Arthur Dove, F. R. Gruger, Walter Appleton Clark, F. C. Yohn, Frank DuMond, F. Luis Mora, A. I. Keller, and George Wright, as well as A. B. Frost, Charles Dana Gibson, James Montgomery Flagg, and Howard Chandler Christy were the "Social Realists" of illustration during the period 1905–1915. It is difficult to call the latter group of illustrators "Social Realists" in the same way the artist-illustrators of the Ash Can school were. For the Ash Can school, their artwork—fine or illustration—was a social and political as well as artistic statement about their environment. Those illustrators whom Mellquist labels "Realists" merit that label only because they dealt with their subject matter realistically, and Realism was a necessary motif for the sale of illustration artwork to mass market magazines. And I would strongly disagree that Gibson, Flagg, Christy, and Harrison Fisher—whom I have labelled as leading "American Beauty" illustrators—were Social Realists. If anything, they were "idealists," painting pictures and setting standards to which American women could aspire. Even when their illustrations had the satirical sting of Social Realism, they did not contain the implicit political values one finds in the artwork of the Ash Can school. Alexander goes even further, suggesting that the revolt against the Genteel Tradition produced the Romantic Nationalism of the 1920s, which at its heart was Realistic, and the Modernism of the 1940s, which at its heart was Surrealistic. Thus the Regionalists of the 1920s and 1930s—Charles Burchfield, Edward Hopper, Thomas Hart Benton, John Stewart Curry, and Grant Wood—were the artistic heirs of the revolt against the formalism of the eighteenth century.

Monroe Wheeler's exhibition catalog, MODERN PAINTERS AND SCULPTORS AS ILLUSTRATORS (1936), provides an interesting and inadvertent view of the artist-illustrator conflict. In his catalog Wheeler presents the illustration artwork of a number of artists who also did illustrations during the period 1900–1935. Of the one hundred artists listed in the catalog only Peggy Bacon, George W. Bellows, Thomas Hart Benton, Alexander Calder, Charles Demuth, Wharton Esherick, Hugo Gillert, William Glackens, George Grosz, Edward M. Kauffer, Rockwell Kent, William Littlefield, Boardman Robinson, John Sloan, Max Weber, and Grant Wood are Americans. Within this group are a fascinating mix of people, some of whom were fine artists who only occasionally did illustration artwork—Alexander Calder and Boardman Robinson, for example; some who were primarily illustrators who did some fine artwork—Rockwell Kent; and some who were illustrators at one point in their career and fine artists at another, frequently later, point—such as William Glackens and John Sloan.

A number of illustrator-artists, who aspired to be fine artists, studied abroad and were undoubtedly affected by their experiences. Fairfax Downey (1936) notes that Charles Dana Gibson went to Europe to study painting, to master a technique other than his excellent pen-and-ink illustration style. Financial reality intruded, however, and Gibson had to return to pen-and-ink illustration in order to make a living. Studying fine art at home or abroad became commonplace for those illustrators whose financial success gave them time and money to "retool" artistically. Comparatively few of them made the transition completely away from illustration. Dippie (1975) notes the change in Frederic Remington's illustration artwork through time, becoming more Impressionist in his later years. But Remington could never completely break away from illustration as a career—its financial rewards were too great. At the same time, the mass market standards for illustration meant that his artwork could never become too "avant garde." Somewhat the same phenomenon occurred in the career of Norman Rockwell, who went to Europe in the early 1930s to study contemporary European art; his illustration artwork suffered—he did very few covers for THE SATURDAY EVENING POST during this period—because the illustration market called for Realism, not Modernism. Chastened, Rockwell returned to America, more firmly committed than ever to being an illustrator in his own style.

The need for a revolution in illustration was never imperative. To appeal to a mass market, magazine and book illustrations had to be "realistic," so the formalism of the Genteel Tradition was never a dominant style in American illustration prior to 1900, and Howard Pyle and the "Romantic Realists" in illustration led quite naturally to Norman Rockwell's Realism and the later Photo-Realism of Steve Dohanos. Thus, the dominant development in American illustration in the period prior to World War I was its increasingly realistic style, which was independent of artistic and illustration trends in Europe.

The greatest penetration of American illustration by European art trends occurred in the area of poster and advertising art. European poster art reached its peak in the late 1880s and 1890s in the unique combination of a number of artistic elements that characterized the Art Nouveau movement. According to Larry Freeman (VICTORIAN POSTERS [1969]), Art Nouveau posters were characterized by a naturalistic flowing line, derived from the Pre-Raphaelites, and silhouettes in two-dimensional space, shapes delineated by sharp color contrasts, a restricted range of highly saturated colors, and brush lettering—characteristics of Japanese wood-block prints and art, that had become quite popular in Europe. Continental and British poster artists, notably Henri de Toulouse-Lautrec and Jules Cheret in France and the Beggarstaffs and John Hardy in Great Britain, developed these elements into a unique style that was artistically appealing and set the tone for not only posters but much of the decorative arts of the period. Blanche and

Haywood Cirker (1971), Bevis Hillier (1969), Clarence Hornung and Fridolph Johnson (1976), Clarence Hornung (1974), Diane Johnson (1979), Victor Margolin (1975), and Ervine Metzl (1967) provide excellent analyses of the development of European art and its impact on American poster art. In the United States Will Bradley and Edward Penfield were the two poster artists most immediately and obviously influenced by the Art Nouveau movement. Bradley's covers and posters for THE CHAP BOOK, as well as his bicycle and paper advertisements, and Penfield's monthly posters for HARPER'S MONTHLY are clearly in that tradition. Hornung's book on Bradley (1974) provides a good pictorial statement of his poster style.

Bradley and Penfield carried their poster styles into their book illustrations and decorations—see Penfield's HOLLAND SKETCHES (1907)—but few American illustrators outside of the poster arts were so influenced. Overall, British and European book illustrators had little impact on their American counterparts. While many American illustrators were aware of Arthur Rackham's work, which appeared in American editions of his books and a number of American illustrated magazines, few sought to emulate his style or techniques. The same can be said of Edmund Dulac, W. Heath Robinson, Aubrey Beardsley, Harry Clarke, and Kay Nielsen, who were known but not widely imitated in America. The cool reception for Beardsley, Clarke, and Nielsen, members of the "decadent" school of British illustration, was because their artwork was too erotic for the more puritanical American audience. That Rackham, Dulac, and Robinson had so little influence on American illustration is surprising. They illustrated fairy tales, children's stories, and Shakespearean classics, that traditionally appealed to Americans. Interestingly, the biographers of these three have not noted their lack of impact on American illustration, noting instead their influence on one another.

There are several reasons why British and European illustration had so little influence on American illustration. American illustration during this period was becoming not only increasingly "realistic" but also nationalistic. The ideal prevalent in the 1890s, that an American illustrator had to either imitate his contemporaries or study abroad, had disappeared. Study in Europe was still appealing for artist-illustrators and illustrator-artists, who still harbored at least some aspirations for success in the fine arts. But the success of Howard Pyle and his students provided concrete evidence that study in America with a professional illustrator was very satisfactory. Thus, the influence of European art and illustration had to be indirect, by example rather than by instruction. At the same time the nature of British and European illustration affected its quality, made it different from American illustration, and less appealing for an American mass market. A quite different literary tradition in Europe produced a different type of illustration; European children's stories, for example, were far more grotesque, more frightening, than those in the United States, which were more moralistic and uplifting in tone. As a result there was a macabre element to some illustration which, like the "decadent" art, was far less appealing to an American audience. In addition, the status of illustrators in Europe was different from their counterparts in America.

The distinction between fine artist and illustrator was far more distinct in the United States than abroad—witness the illustrators who aspired to be fine artists and fine artists who did illustrations only to earn a living—which meant that illustration artwork in Europe was designed more for a middle-class rather than a mass audience. The perception of illustration as a "commercial" art rather than a "fine" art meant that aesthetic standards for illustration in Europe and America were quite different.

In the transitional period between the wars there was a convergence to some degree in American and European illustration. The emigration of European illustrators to the United States, particularly those working in children's books, had an homogenizing effect noted by Bader (1976). The Art Deco movement, more angular and utilitarian than Art Nouveau, became popular and was reflected stylistically by J. C. Leyendecker's covers for THE SATURDAY EVENING POST in the 1930s (see Schau, J. C. LEYENDECKER [1976], for examples). Lynd Ward followed the lead of Franz Masereel of Belgium in using woodcuts for his "books without words," while Rockwell Kent's starkly linear black-and-white illustrations contain some of the elements of the Art Deco movement. Nonetheless, the bulk of American illustration was still realistic and nativist in content—mass market and pulp magazine illustrations remained clearly "American."

After World War II there was an even greater convergence between American and European illustration that was less the influence of European art and illustration on America but the reverse. American cultural imperialism extended to illustration as well; as Europe rebuilt after World War II it looked to America for leadership in a variety of areas, including illustration. The impact of television on public taste, and the dominance of world television by American programs, produced the "global village" envisioned by Marshall McCluhan. GRAPHIS, the European illustration magazine, is now as widely read as its American counterpart, PRINT.

While there has been a global homogenization of illustration, some aspects of American illustration have remained the same. The separation between the fine arts and illustration has remained quite clear. Fine artists who have done book illustrations have not been notoriously successful. One type of illustrated book by fine artists—the livre d'artiste—differs from the traditional illustrated book in several important respects: the illustrations are original works of art executed by the artist himself and are designed to stand independent of text, the book is printed under his supervision, and the book is usually published in limited editions of three hundred or less, with the illustration artwork signed in hand by the artist. Breon Mitchell's BEYOND ILLUSTRATION: THE LIVRE D'ARTISTE IN THE TWENTIETH CENTURY (1976) examines this body of illustration artwork and finds the format was most popular in France but several twentieth-century American artists—Robert Andrew Parker, Mary Ellen Solt, and Robert Marx—have worked this way. Almost by definition the livre d'artiste was not meant to be a form of popular illustration, but rather an expression of the artist published in book form.

The post-World War II period of American illustration has been characterized by its eclecticism, its willingness to borrow whatever is necessary from whatever sources to deal with the illustration problems at hand. Materials and techniques have been borrowed from a broad spectrum of sources, from photography, "op" art, television, even the fine arts. While "Realism" is still central to American illustration (see the January/February 1978 issue of PRINT for its discussion of "Realism in Illustration"), illustrators are much more pragmatic in their approach than before, particularly in some of the nontraditional illustration media, such as record album covers and fantasy art. As can be seen in Ian Summers's book THE ART OF THE BROTHERS HILDEBRANDT (1979), at least two contemporary American fantasy illustrators have taken their inspiration from a variety of sources— Howard Pyle, Maxfield Parrish, Steve Dohanos, and René Magritte—combined with their own imaginative style into a unique perspective. At the core of their artwork, nonetheless, they are "Realists," of one sort or another.

Very little attention has been paid to the cultural context of illustration during the past one hundred or more years. The emphasis in much of the writing on individual illustrators has made it difficult to discuss the relationships between illustrators and with other important people in their environment. While much of the information is there, in fragmentary form for much of the Golden Age of illustration, it is difficult to piece together into a richly textured whole. Questions frequently arise that cannot be answered directly. What were the primary factors that determined which illustrators interacted with one another? Was it merely physical propinquity? Or did subject matter play a role—did Remington and Russell, for example, get together during Russell's infrequent visits to New York to talk about western illustration? There is no evidence they did. Were illustrators more willing to talk with peers with whom they didn't compete for commissions?

Given the geographic dispersion of many illustrators today (although New York is still the illustration capital), how do they keep in touch with one another? What standards do they use in judging their artwork? The artwork of others? To what extent do contemporary illustrators experience a community of professional interests, like that felt at the turn of the century that led to the formation of the Society of Illustrators when those interests were challenged.

Aesthetically, where do contemporary illustrators derive their inspiration? Since there are comparatively few academic courses in the history of illustration, it is difficult to see much direct continuity of style in American illustration. While it is clear that Brian Froud in Great Britain was aware of Arthur Rackham's fantasy illustrations, and that Rien Poortvliet's drawings of gnomes are clearly within a European tradition of fantasy illustration, such connections are more difficult to make in America. American illustration has developed pragmatically, independent of major artistic currents in European and American fine arts as well as of its own historical past. As a result, contemporary American illustration is not derived from one or a few sources but many. This has given it a freshness of approach that is appealing, but overall it has a certain rootless quality to it.

BIBLIOGRAPHY

EDWIN AUSTIN ABBEY. New Haven, Conn., Yale University Art Gallery, 1974.

Abbott, Charles D. HOWARD PYLE: A CHRONICLE. New York, Harper and Bros., 1925.

Alexander, Charles. HERE THE COUNTRY LIES: NATIONALISM AND ART IN TWENTIETH CENTURY AMERICA. Bloomington, Indiana University Press, 1980.

Bader, Barbara. AMERICAN PICTURE BOOKS FROM NOAH'S ARK TO THE BEAST WITHIN. New York, Macmillan, 1976.

A BOOK OF THE TILE CLUB. New York, Houghton Mifflin, 1886.

Brooks, V. "Love and Magic: The Naive Style in Illustration." PRINT, May 1974, 33–41.

Cirker, Haywood, and Blanche Cirker. THE GOLDEN AGE OF THE POSTER. New York, Dover Publications, 1971.

Dalley, Terrence, ed. THE COMPLETE GUIDE TO ILLUSTRATION AND DESIGN. London, Chartwell Books, 1980.

Deshazo, Edith. EVERETT SHINN. New York, Clarkson N. Potter, 1974.

Dickason, David Howard. THE DARING YOUNG MEN. Bloomington, Indiana University Press, 1953.

Dippie, Brian. "Frederic Remington's Wild West." AMERICAN HERITAGE, April 1975, 6–24, 76–79.

Downey, Fairfax. PORTRAIT OF AN ERA AS DRAWN BY C. D. GIBSON. New York, Charles Scribner's Sons, 1936.

Exman, Eugene. THE BROTHERS HARPER. New York, Harper and Row, 1965.

Freeman, Larry, comp. VICTORIAN POSTERS. Watkins Glen, N.Y., American Life, 1969.

Hahler, Christine Anne, ed. . . . ILLUSTRATED BY DARLEY. Wilmington, Delaware Art Museum, 1978.

Harper, J. Henry. THE HOUSE OF HARPER. New York, Harper's, 1912.

Hillier, Bevis. POSTERS. New York, Stein and Day, 1969.

Hornung, Clarence P. WILL BRADLEY: HIS GRAPHIC ART. New York, Dover Publications, 1974.

——— HANDBOOK OF EARLY ADVERTISING ART, VOLS. I, II. New York, Dover Publications, 1947.

Hornung, Clarence P., and Fridolph Johnson. 200 YEARS OF AMERICAN GRAPHIC ART. New York, George Brazillier, 1976.

Johnson, Diane Chalmers. AMERICAN ART NOUVEAU. New York, Henry Abrams, 1979.

Landgren, Marchal E. YEARS OF ART. New York, Robert McBride and Co., 1940.

Levin, Gail. EDWARD HOPPER AS ILLUSTRATOR. New York, W. W. Norton, 1979.

Ludwig, Coy. MAXFIELD PARRISH. New York, Watson-Guptill, 1973.

Margolin, Victor. AMERICAN POSTER RENAISSANCE. Secaucus, N.J., Castle Books, 1975.

Margolin, Victor, Ira Brichta, and Vivian Brichta. THE PROMISE AND THE PRODUCT: 200 YEARS OF AMERICAN ADVERTISING POSTERS. New York, Macmillan, 1979.

Meglin, Nick. ON-THE-SPOT DRAWING. New York, Watson-Guptill, 1969.

Mellquist, Jerome. THE EMERGENCE OF AN AMERICAN ART. New York, Charles Scribner's Sons, 1942.

Metzl, Ervine. THE POSTER: ITS HISTORY AND ITS ART. New York, Watson-Guptill, 1967.

Meyer, Susan E. NORMAN ROCKWELL'S PEOPLE. New York, Henry Abrams, 1981.

Mitchell, Breon. BEYOND ILLUSTRATION: THE LIVRE D'ARTISTE IN THE TWEN-TIETH CENTURY. Bloomington, Lilly Library, Indiana University, 1976.

CHARLES PARSONS AND HIS DOMAIN. Montclair, N.J., Montclair Art Museum, 1958.

Pitaja, Emile, comp. and ed. THE HANNAH BOK MEMORIAL SHOWCASE OF FANTASY ART. San Francisco, Sisu Publishers, 1974.

Pitz, Henry C. HOWARD PYLE. New York, Clarkson N. Potter, 1975.

——— 200 YEARS OF AMERICAN ILLUSTRATION. New York, Random House and the Society of Illustrators, 1977.

Price, Norman. HISTORY OF THE SOCIETY OF ILLUSTRATORS. New York, Society of Illustrators, 1939.

"Realism in Illustration." PRINT, January/February 1978.

St. John, Bruce, ed. JOHN SLOAN'S NEW YORK SCENE. New York, Harper and Row, 1965.

Schau, Michael. J. C. LEYENDECKER. New York, Watson-Guptill, 1976.

Schmidt, Dorie, ed. THE AMERICAN MAGAZINE: 1890–1940. Wilmington, Delaware Art Museum, 1979.

Schnessel, S. Michael. JESSIE WILCOX SMITH. New York, Thomas Y. Crowell, 1973.

Shelton, William Henry. THE HISTORY OF THE SALMAGUNDI CLUB AS IT AP-PEARED IN THE NEW YORK HERALD TRIBUNE MAGAZINE ON SUNDAY DECEMBER EIGHTEENTH NINETEEN TWENTY SEVEN. New York, privately printed, 1927.

——— THE SALMAGUNDI CLUB. New York, Houghton Mifflin, 1918.

Smith, F. Hopkinson. AMERICAN ILLUSTRATORS. New York, Charles Scribner's Sons, 1893.

THE SOCIETY OF ILLUSTRATORS, 1901–1928. New York, Society of Illustrators, 1928.

Stryker, Cathryn Connell. THE STUDIOS AT COGSLEA. Wilmington, Delaware Art Museum, 1976.

Summers, Ian. THE ART OF THE BROTHERS HILDEBRANDT. New York, Ballantine Books, 1979.

Wheeler, Monroe, ed. MODERN PAINTERS AND SCULPTORS AS ILLUSTRATORS. New York, Museum of Modern Art, 1936.

CHAPTER 6

Illustration Media

Any discussion of illustration must acknowledge that the processes by which illustrations are executed and reproduced and the sources of publication are important for an understanding of the field. The two are obviously linked. Changes in illustration techniques, from steel and copper engraving to wood engraving, for example, resulted in the possibility of mass reproduction of illustration artwork and permitted the development of illustrated newspapers and magazines. The shift from wood engraving to photographic halftone and four-color reproductions reduced the price of illustration reproduction further, making illustrated magazines even more available to a mass market. At the same time, the competitiveness of various publication media resulted in a demand for technological developments that would permit better quality, lower cost illustrations.

In this chapter we will examine the literature dealing with various illustration techniques, ranging from wood engravings through airbrush. The coverage will be cursory rather than comprehensive, omitting many of the "how to" books. The focus will then shift to writings that have dealt with the various media as publication sources, examining the role that illustration played in the history of American publication. Attention will be paid to histories of various publishing firms, particularly those such as Harper and Brothers and Scribner and Sons, which had an instrumental role in the development of American illustration.

ILLUSTRATION TECHNIQUES

There are a number of excellent books that trace the historical development and evolution of illustration techniques. Frank Weitenkampf's AMERICAN GRAPHIC ART (1912) gives the development of various graphic arts up to 1910; his chapters on wood engraving and wood-block engraving as illustration techniques are excellent. Particularly useful is his discussion of the ramifications flowing from the development of wood engraving; the movement away from steel and copperplate engraving made illustrated books economically viable but also placed increased emphasis on the relationship between the artist and the engraver. In some instances, the two were the same, which ensured that the artist's intent would be faithfully executed. Several books on Civil War "special" artists suggest, however, that artists who worked in the field came to rely on the skills and imagination of their engravers. Finished sketches sent to New York from the front frequently contained little more than instructions as to what should be in the background, with the artist supplying important foreground details. Under those circumstances, the finished illustration was indeed a joint product.

W. J. Linton, a noted English wood engraver who moved to America after the Civil War, wrote THE HISTORY OF WOOD-ENGRAVING IN AMERICA (1882) to trace the development of this art in his adopted land. In addition to his discussion of wood engraving as a technique, Linton traced the evolution of American wood engraving from Alexander Anderson through his students, including an evaluation of their skills. Linton suggests that the development of illustrated newspapers and magazines before and during the Civil War led to an increase in demand for wood engravers and opened the field to new and skilled people. The lack of skilled wood engravers initially made it possible for illustrators to work as their own engravers, and even those who relied on others became sensitive to the demands of the profession. It was the American commitment to wood engraving after the Civil War that induced Linton, then one of Britain's foremost practitioners of the art, to emigrate. Linton was bothered by the English preoccupation with mechanical and photomechanical reproduction of illustrations, that he saw as marking the end of an era. The American commitment to these processes did not take place until nearly a generation later. As a result American wood engraving developed from the point where British engraving ended, producing different and more skilled illustrators and works. In fact, Linton's book contains a lengthy analysis of the two major illustrated works of his day done by American wood engraving—PICTURESQUE AMERICA (1872–1874) and PICTURESQUE EUROPE (1874). Linton regards both these books as prime examples of the excellence of American wood engraving. PICTURESQUE AMERICA certainly represented a major commitment of energy and money, and was designed as a showpiece of American artistry. Only recently, however, have book collectors expressed strong interest in this two-volume set. The companion set, PICTURESQUE EUROPE, printed in response to the success of its predecessor, was not as popular and demand for it today is negligible compared with demand for the former.

While wood engraving became widely used for mass market black-and-white illustration until the 1890s, lithography and chromolithography were popular means of producing color prints. During the early part of the nineteenth century, color illustrations were done first in black-and-white and then hand colored. The development of lithography and chromolithography processes in Europe, their acceptance there and export to the United States, resulted in a richer, more varied form of illustration and introduced color processes to American illustration. Unfortunately, lithographic processes required many separate press runs and thus were not very economical for many forms of book illustration. Nonetheless, lithography and chromolithography became popular for children's book illustrations, album cards, trade cards, greeting cards, advertisements, and a variety of other paper products consumed by a mass market. The technique of chromolithography is described in Katherine Morrison McClinton's THE CHROMOLITHOGRAPHY OF LOUIS PRANG (1973) but a better (albeit rarer) book is

George Ashdown Audsley's THE ART OF CHROMOLITHOGRAPHY (1883), which describes the process and then shows in forty-six plates the additive process by which a twenty-two color chromolithograph is put together. The resultant picture is an impressive testament to the skills of the chromolithographers who used an enormous number of stones and runs to create their finished products. The richness and vibrancy of the finished product ensured their success, however, and it was only the development of photomechanical four-color reproduction in the early twentieth century that spelled the end of this process. Because "chromos" were designed for a mass market and frequently for "disposable" items, little attention has been paid to collecting them and many have disappeared. The recent resurgence of interest in Victorian era collectibles has rekindled interest in "chromos," as witnessed by the publication of Francine Kirsch's CHROMOS: A GUIDE TO PAPER COLLECTIBLES (1981). Colored lithographs were used for mass market illustrations, particularly art prints produced by major publishers. Currier and Ives were probably the best known of the lithograph publishers and their products—with over two thousand available to the American public. While poster art developed as the art form for the masses in Europe it was the colored lithographs of Currier and Ives and their competitors that served to raise American aesthetic standards.

Although wood engraving had died as an illustration technique by the turn of the century, replaced in large measure by photomechanical techniques for halftone black-and-white and four-color reproduction, increased competition and rising production costs after World War I made wood-block reproductions attractive once more. The interest was in the use of woodcuts rather than wood engraving, however. Herbert Furst's book, THE MODERN WOODCUT (1924), differentiates between lithography, wood engraving, and woodcuts as illustration techniques, suggesting that woodcuts require more imagination and are the natural method of the creative artist. Furst then analyzes European, largely British, woodcuts. Unfortunately, woodcuts became popular in America shortly after the publication of Furst's book, as typified by the work of Lynd Ward and Rockwell Kent; a comparison of their woodcuts with those of their European contemporaries, particularly Franz Masereel, would have been instructive. Howard Simon's chapter on U.S. illustration in 500 YEARS OF ART AND ILLUSTRATION (1942) provides that comparison indirectly by giving examples of leading American and European woodcut artists working in the 1930s and 1940s. Unfortunately, there is no direct comparison between the various illustrators and their styles.

The reemergence of pen-and-ink draftsmen is highlighted by Walt Reed's compilation of Joseph Coll's artwork in THE MAGIC PEN OF JOSEPH CLEMENT COLL (1978), which rivals the artwork of his predecessors, like Frederic Richardson's BOOK OF DRAWINGS. . . (1899). The pen-and-ink skills of Coll, Richardson, Howard Pyle, and Charles Dana Gibson make clear the American preeminence in this field of illustration for more than forty years. Although Joseph Pennell might complain about the decline in pen-and-ink artwork (see below) the quality of American work in the media stands out.

A number of books have dealt generally with the craft of illustration, rather than focusing on a specific technique. Joseph Pennell was probably one of the foremost writers and speakers on American illustration during the first thirty years of this century. His writings represent an effort to analyze the state of illustration, teach others what was required for good illustration, and demonstrate various illustration techniques. THE GRAPHIC ARTS (1920), for example, represents an analysis of the leading illustrators and illustration trends in America at that time. Pennell was a merciless critic. He regarded Pyle's ROBIN HOOD as a masterpiece but bemoaned the decline in quality in Pyle's later illustrations, particularly his pen-and-ink work. In fact, Pennell's writings in the 1920s generally decry the decline in quality of illustrations, citing photography and "artless editors" as the chief culprits. In PEN DRAWING AND PEN DRAUGHTSMEN (1920), his comparative analysis of pen drawing in the United States, various countries in Europe, and Japan rues the decline of American illustration, attributing much of it to the growing commercialism of art. Implicitly, Pennell's criticism reflects his regret at the passing of the Golden Age of illustration—the "good old days." In the 1920s there were very few who could carry on as before—Rockwell Kent was one of them. What was to be done? Establish a National School of the Graphic Arts, so that atrophying illustration techniques and skills could be preserved and nourished, Pennell believed. What he failed to realize, of course, was that changes in the nature of illustration were the result of social and economic forces as well as artistic ones. As a result it would be impossible to recapture the glory, or the art, of an earlier period.

Pennell's other books are less caustic in tone. THE ILLUSTRATION OF BOOKS (1896) represents a series of lectures, most of which deal with various illustration techniques—line drawing, wash drawings, wood engraving, lithography, etching, photogravure, and photolithography—and their means of reproduction. Based on his experiences with various illustration media, Pennell was able to give useful technical and practical hints in the use of each technique, for example, in his chapter on drawing for reproduction in line there is an extensive discussion of various brushes and papers that an illustrator can use. This type of knowledge is crucial for Pennell, since two of the four requirements for illustrators are to have sound training in drawing and to understand the use of various mediums, as well as artistic imagination (this is similar to Pyle's argument that the illustrator understand the author's work before he can successfully illustrate it) and education.

Since Pennell, a number of books have been written to deal with illustration in general. For example, Andrew Loomis, in CREATIVE ILLUSTRATION (1947), Steven Spurrier, in BLACK AND WHITE ILLUSTRATION (1958), Robin Jaques, in ILLUSTRATORS AT WORK (1963), Henry Pitz, in ILLUSTRATING CHILDREN'S BOOKS (1963), Diana Klemin, in THE ILLUSTRATED BOOK: ITS ART AND CRAFT (1970), Jan Portenaar, in THE ART OF THE BOOK AND ITS ILLUSTRATION (1935), and Lee Kingman, ed., in THE ILLUSTRATOR'S NOTEBOOK (1978), discuss various illustration techniques. The contemporary illustration student is hardly bereft of advice on techniques.

Although there are continuities in illustration style and techniques, a number of more "modern" illustration techniques have been developed that are part of the arsenal of contemporary illustrators. The airbrush, for example, is now as recognized a tool as the engraver's burin of the last century. There are several excellent books on airbrush techniques—S. Ralph Maurello's THE COMPLETE AIRBRUSH BOOK (1955) and Richard Childer Productions' AIR POWERED: THE ART OF THE AIR BRUSH (1979). The Maurello book is simplistic in its treatment of equipment and materials (or is it because the equipment and materials have become more sophisticated?) but the how-to-do-it section with photographs is helpful. The remainder of the book is devoted to how the airbrush can be used to deal with various illustration problems. To see the impact of the airbrush on contemporary illustration one has AIR POWERED (1979), a lavish art book that demonstrates what can be achieved with an airbrush handled by experts, with a number of excellent examples. For a contemporary body of airbrush artwork one has only to look at record albums; for à good collection of airbrushed album covers see Benedict and Barton's PHONOGRAPHICS (1977). Computer graphics have also become an important tool for the contemporary illustrator, but there has been little written on the subject even though computer-generated graphics have been used with great success in movies and in television advertising. One of the best sources of information on the applications and future of computer graphics has been the series of articles in U&LC, particularly Marion Muller's "Connecting the Dots" (1982), a nonmathematical, nontechnical introduction to the terminology and techniques of computer-generated illustrations and graphics. Of particular interest are the eight pages of "cutting edge" applications in color.

Several books have taken a more "holistic" approach to illustration, arguing that the illustrator must work in conjunction with other artists in the production of their product. A. P. Tedesco, in THE RELATIONSHIP BETWEEN TYPE AND ILLUSTRATION IN BOOKS AND BOOK JACKETS (1948), argues that the typographer and illustrator should work together to create a harmonious whole, both in terms of style and layout. There is a nice analysis of the typefaces, layouts, and distribution of illustration in several books, which substantiates Tedesco's argument. Sid Hydeman's book, HOW TO ILLUSTRATE FOR MONEY (1936), suggests that the art editor is a major creative force with whom the illustrator must deal. Hydeman's common-sense suggestions to the illustrator—don't try to "high pressure" the art editor, be familiar with the artwork published by the firm—combined with his discussion of problems faced by art editors makes this one of the few books that deal with the relationship between illustrator and art editor. Best's manuscript on art editor-illustrator relations during the Golden Age of illustration (1982) provides interesting historical examples of the nature and complexity of that relationship. He notes, for example, the delicate problem art editors faced in retaining favor with noted illustrators while getting them to modify their artwork to meet the needs of the story or the magazine; the correspondence between Henry Burlingame at Scribner's and Howard Pyle regarding Pyle's illustrations of a Rudyard Kipling poem are a case in point. Competent art directors were a boon for both their employers and for the illustrators they employed. Matlack Price's testimonial to Harry Quinan (1945) and the festschrift JOSEPH HAWLEY CHAPIN (1939) attest to the vital importance of these people.

More secondary aspects of illustration techniques have been the subject of two books. Dorothy Abbe's book, STENCILLED ORNAMENT AND ILLUSTRA-TION (1979), discusses W. A. Dwiggins's preliminary writing on the process and art of stenciling, while providing many black-and-white examples of his stencils. However, not many illustrators followed Dwiggins's lead into using stencils for ornamentation, so the book is of largely historical interest. In the days before dust jackets, a book's cover was as important for sales as a magazine's cover. Consequently, during the period 1800–1915 book publishers focused a great deal of artistic effort on book cover design. The article by Charles Gullano and John Esprey in Jean Peters, ed., COLLECTIBLE BOOKS (1979) discusses the major designers of American trade bindings, including Margaret Armstrong and Will Bradley; analyzes their work, giving titles of some of their most important works; and provides insights into how to spot their bindings. This article is a must for anyone interested in Victorian bookbinding.

A surprising amount of space is also devoted to how illustrators should approach their subject. Howard Pyle's advice is still echoed in these pages—directly in Loomis's CREATIVE ILLUSTRATION (1947)—but there is an awareness that not everyone can be a Howard Pyle nor does everyone have to work as he suggested. Diana Klemin, in THE ILLUSTRATED BOOK: ITS ART AND CRAFT (1970), reminds us that the illustrator can assume many roles—he or she can be the principal storyteller in a picture book, a supportive artist where the text must convey the story line, or an instructive artist in those situations where diagrams are designed for instructional purposes. The diversity in roles can be seen in the advice that Fritz Eichenberg, Warren Chappell, Hilda Van Stockum, Barbara Cooney, Marcia Brown, and Lee Kingman convey in their essays for Kingman's excellent book, THE ILLUSTRATOR'S NOTEBOOK (1978). Warren Chappell and Hilda Van Stockum, for example, argue that the illustrator's role is to complement the work of the author; for Van Stockum, the role of the illustrator is to fill in the visual holes left by the author. Barbara Cooney disagrees, arguing that decoration is the first function of the illustrator, while elucidating the text is secondary.

Some books provide more specific advice to illustrators about how to practice their craft. Ernest Thompson Seton's excellent book, STUDIES IN THE ART ANATOMY OF ANIMALS (1896), is a classic in the art of animal anatomy for illustration and is still being reprinted. In it, Seton examines the muscle and skeletal structures of a number of domestic and wild animals and provides drawings of these same animals in motion and at rest. From this work it is easy to understand why Ernest Thompson Seton was the leading naturalist illustrator of his day. More recently, Bob Kuhn, in THE ANIMAL ART OF BOB KUHN (1973), offers advice and suggestions regarding how he draws animals, providing examples from much of his artwork, showing how to incorporate character in one's artwork.

Kuhn also has an interesting discussion of the qualities necessary for a top-flight animal illustrator; in addition to being technically competent an animal illustrator must be an enthusiastic researcher and a bit of a liar—he must be able to recreate from the author's words and enthusiasm scenes that the illustrator has never seen or imagined. There is also an excellent discussion of the role of the art editor in the illustrator's work, including a critical analysis of a number of illustrations Kuhn submitted to art editors and the ones the art editors chose.

For those less interested in how natural history illustration is done but what has been produced, the books by S. Peter Dance, THE ART OF NATURAL HISTORY (1978), and Martyn Rix, THE ART OF THE PLANT WORLD (1980), provide historical overviews that are primarily European in content, although Dance's analysis of John J. Audubon's illustrations, particularly BIRDS OF AMERICA, is excellent. Fashion illustration receives a comprehensive treatment in the recent Sharon Lee Tate and Mona Shafer Edwards's book, THE COMPLETE BOOK OF FASHION ILLUSTRATION (1982), which differentiates fashion illustration from other forms of illustration. According to the authors the goal of fashion illustration is to create a stylized version of reality, so that exaggeration and idealism are the norms rather than reality. The remainder of the book deals with drawing the human figure for fashion illustration (which is different from drawing it for other purposes), drawing clothes, rendering fabrics, drawing men and men's clothing, and even drawing fashion accessories. Sport illustration has been the subject of several pieces. One issue of AMERICAN ARTIST (July 1977), titled "Sports Illustration," was devoted to a discussion of the subject by leading practitioners and included examples of their art. The Ray Didinger and Tex Maule book on pro football, THE PROFESSIONALS (1980), is an interesting combination of biographical sketches of seventy-two pro "all-stars" and portrait illustrations of each one in action.

Several books seek to teach illustration by example, by showing examples of successful illustrators and analyzing their styles and work habits. Ashby Halsey's book, ILLUSTRATING FOR THE SATURDAY EVENING POST (1951) discusses the needs of magazine illustration and then analyzes a number of POST covers, from preliminary sketches to finished products. Arthur Guptill has followed Meade Schaefer through the painting of one SATURDAY EVENING POST cover (1945). Ernest Watson's FORTY ILLUSTRATORS AND HOW THEY WORK (1946) represents Watson's interviews with forty leading illustrators and discussions of how each one approaches his craft. Unfortunately, Watson does little to tie the interviews together, so we know very little about how illustrators, in general, practice their craft. For example, how do illustrators feel about using photographs rather than live models? Perhaps the best of these "technique" books is James McMullan's REVEALING ILLUSTRATIONS (1981), in which McMullan goes through the process by which he researched, rough sketched, and did the final artwork for a series of his most successful illustrations. McMullan reveals the painfulness and wheel spinning of much illustration work as he struggles to come up with a saleable concept for an assignment with which he can be happy as well. From his examples one can see a lively and creative mind at work, stymied, struggling, and finally realizing the "best" way to approach the assignment.

A number of illustrator's biographies have also discussed how they worked, either in general or using specific techniques and approaches. For example, in Coy Ludwig's MAXFIELD PARRISH (1973) there is an excellent and detailed discussion of how Parrish used dynamic symmetry as a structural principle for many of his illustrations and how Parrish developed glazing techniques to achieve the luminescent quality of much of his illustration artwork. The discussion of Pyle's teaching philosophy in Pitz's HOWARD PYLE (1975) and Elzea's HOWARD PYLE: DIVERSITY IN DEPTH (1973) provides an excellent picture of his approach to illustration. Susan Meyer's NORMAN ROCKWELL'S PEOPLE (1981) provides interesting insights into how Rockwell "staged" his illustrations—with live models initially and then for the camera. His trick of paying his child models from stacks of nickels kept plainly visible during the modeling session would scarcely work today: the model's agent would probably object.

Finally, one of the few books that attempts to bring much of this material together in an annotated bibliography is that compiled by Vito J. Brenni, BOOK ILLUSTRATION AND DECORATION (1980), which cites two thousand published books, pamphlets, essays in books, periodical articles and theses, and categorizes them as book decoration, manuals for illustration and other writings on technique, history of methods of illustration, history of book illustration organized by century and by country, and various types of illustration—children's books, science and technology, medicine, music, geography, and history. In addition, author and subject indexes make this book even more valuable. The book has several faults, however. It focuses very heavily on contemporary works, overlooking a number of the "classics," particularly those dealing with older illustration techniques. And there are few citations of work on American book illustration and decoration; while the British have been concerned with these topics more than Americans, the imbalance is curious and limits the utility of this book for students of American illustration. Equally curious, although more understandable, is a lack of reference to writings on individual illustrators. An inclusion of such references would have made this a truly valuable work but far too large and costly to produce.

PUBLICATION MEDIA

The history of early American illustration is inextricably tied to the development of the publishing industry, particularly of books and magazines. There are two historians of publishing whose works dominate this field: Frank Luther Mott, whose series A HISTORY OF AMERICAN MAGAZINES (1938–1968) is the standard for the field and John Tebbel, whose work on magazines, THE AMERICAN MAGAZINE: A COMPACT HISTORY (1969), supplements that of Mott and whose volume on book publishing, A HISTORY OF BOOK PUBLISHING

IN THE UNITED STATES (1972), is an interesting counterpart to Mott's series on magazines.

Mott's series on magazine publishing is a monumental work and an intellectual tour de force. The five volumes cover the periods 1776–1850, 1850–1865, 1865–1885, 1885–1905, and 1905-1930. The format for the first four volumes is the same; an overview of trends in magazine publishing during the specific period and a long concluding section analyzing the more important magazines published during the period. The last volume contains only the historical sketches.

Volumes I, II, and III contain material on the economics, politics, and socio-cultural bases of magazine publishing during the first one hundred years of American life. The time periods dealt with represent important "turning points" in magazine publication history, that is, Volume II begins with the year 1850 because the decade of the 1850s represents the emergence of illustrated magazines like HARPER'S WEEKLY, HARPER'S MONTHLY, and LESLIE'S ILLUS-TRATED. According to Mott, the founding of HARPER'S MONTHLY in 1852 marked the end of an era and the beginning of the "illustrated" era of American magazine publishing. In like manner the year 1865 marked the end of "wartime" magazine publishing. These first three volumes spend some time discussing the role of illustration in the history of magazines, but the treatment is uneven. In Volume II, for example, there is a discussion of the importance of illustration to the growth of HARPER'S WEEKLY and MONTHLY magazines but there is virtually no space devoted to the phenomenon of "special" artists used by illus-trated magazines and newspapers for their Civil War coverage. Volume IV (1885–1905) is particularly useful for understanding the rise of illustrated magazines and the preeminence in this field of HARPER'S, CENTURY, and SCRIBNER'S. Mott notes that one reason for the rise of mass market illustrated magazines was the development of halftones for illustration; woodcuts cost $300 per page and halftones were less than $20, so the price of illustrated magazines, led by this technological development but spurred by competition, dropped to ten cents for all but the three "quality" magazines, which were priced at twenty-five or thirty-five cents. The last volume of the series, covering the period 1905–1930, could have been one of the best. Unfortunately, its utility is limited. Instead of providing an overview of magazine publishing during this period and analyzing the changes that occurred, Mott provides only sketches of twenty-one magazines that were important during the period. The magazines are an interesting and diverse col-lection so that their histories provide, inadvertently, some real insights into mag-azine publishing during the period, but a more comprehensive overview would have been helpful. Such an overview was probably planned but the author's death necessitated the publication of the volume as he had written it. John Tebbel's single-volume history is, in some ways, more useful. By concentrating on the major magazines, Tebbel is forced to examine trends and provide reasons for those trends. One of the factors Tebbel acknowledges as important is the role of editors and publishers. He suggests, for example, that the content of HARPER'S magazine changed after Henry Aldren retired in 1919 after fifty years as editor; after 1925 it became primarily a journal of opinion rather than an illustrated magazine. As we shall see shortly, however, there were other factors in that content shift besides Aldren's retirement. Tebbel also notes the importance of advertising during the period 1885–1892 in the transformation of American magazines, providing the money for magazines to hire illustrators and using illustration in their magazine advertisements. As a result magazines went from drab black-and-white productions to lavish four-color works of art in the space of one generation.

Both Mott and Tebbel focus on magazine publishing in general, with a discussion of illustration only incidental to their main themes. The Delaware Art Museum exhibition catalog, THE AMERICAN MAGAZINE, 1890–1940 (1979), edited by Dorrie Schmidt, redresses that imbalance and provides some interesting insights regarding the period covered by Mott's weakest volume, 1905–1930. Elizabeth Hawkes's article, "Magazines and Their Illustrators," provides an overview of the role of illustration in magazine publishing during the period, suggesting that each magazine had its own "look," which reflected the artwork it contained. Rowland Elzea, "That Was 'Life' (and Its Artists)," provides empirical evidence regarding the few illustrators who did the bulk of the illustrations for LIFE magazine; Elzea's findings are similar to those of Best (1980) with regard to HARPER'S, CENTURY, and SCRIBNER'S. Margaret Cohen's article, "Telling a Magazine by Its Cover," describes the importance of cover art to a magazine and the relationship between art editor and illustrator in the design of cover art.

John Tebbel's projected three-volume history of American book publishing fills an important void. Volume I (1972) provides a very nice survey of early American book illustration (up to 1850), including some of the work published before that of Alexander Anderson. Indeed, Tebbel suggests that book illustration was common in America during the last decade of the eighteenth century, much of it imitative or derivative. Anderson's importance stems from the quality of his work and his increasing originality in execution.

In addition to these comprehensive publishing histories there are a number of histories of different publishing firms or editors and their relationships with illustrators and illustration. Roger Burlingame's OF MAKING MANY BOOKS (1946) is a history of Scribner's publishing company; J. Henry Harper's THE HOUSE OF HARPER (1912) and Eugene Exman's THE BROTHERS HARPER (1965) are histories of the Harper and Bros. publishing firm; Arthur John's THE BEST YEARS OF THE "CENTURY" (1981) is a history of that firm; Peter Lyon's SUCCESS STORY: THE LIFE AND TIMES OF S. S. McCLURE (1963) provides interesting insight into that magazine; and John Tebbel's GEORGE HORACE LATIMER AND THE SATURDAY EVENING POST (1948) is the biography of the POST's most influential editor. Given the importance of these magazines and publishing houses in the history of American illustration it is nice to have well-written histories. Not all of these books are equally useful, however. Roger Burlingame's history of Scribner's devotes a large amount of space to discussing the impact of illustration on SCRIBNER'S magazine and, as an important adjunct, the relationship between art editors and illustrators. In fact, his discussion of Joseph Chapin as Scribner's art editor provides much of the information we have on this important man, stressing Chapin's role in selecting artwork for the firm and in encouraging illustration in general. Chapin's role at Scribner's was crucial because of Burlingame's judgment that it was illustration as much as text that made Scribner's reputation during the late 1800s. Burlingame's knowledge of the firm, gained from his experience as an editor there and his access to company records, correspondence, letter books, and Chapin's diary make his analysis especially insightful. Many of Burlingame's judgments regarding Chapin's talents as art editor are substantiated by the testimonials of Chapin's illustrators in JOSEPH HAWLEY CHAPIN (1939). Andrew S. Berg's MAX PERKINS (1978) is one of the few books that deal with the efforts and impact of a publishing house editor on Scribner's product and reputation. This excellent biography provides an "insider's" perspective on one of the two family owned and operated publishing firms in New York and discusses the day-to-day operation of the firm. Using Scribner's company records and interviews, Berg provides an excellent picture of how Perkins managed to keep some of the twentieth century's most influential writers—Thomas Wolfe, Ernest Hemingway, and F. Scott Fitzgerald—in line and on schedule. Unfortunately, the emphasis of the book is on the literary side of the publishing trade and little attention is paid to Perkin's counterpart Joe Chapin or his illustrators.

J. Henry Harper's history (1912), written by one of the co-owners of the firm at the time, provides an interesting insider's perspective on the development of the Harper's empire during the last half of the nineteenth century. One chapter is devoted to the role of illustration at Harper's, including their use of "special" artists during the Civil War and the hiring of Charles Parsons and his role in the development of Harper's art department. The chapter reads like a WHO'S WHO of early American illustration and it is interesting to see Harper's thumbnail descriptions of the original staff artists. Unfortunately, the book was written at the height of the Golden Age of American illustration and is incomplete. Exman's book was written long after that of Harper's and his focus on the early years of the firm is far more critical. In fact, Exman accuses J. Henry Harper of overlooking many of Harper's errors in judgment; especially telling is his discussion of their treatment of Herman Melville. Unfortunately, he has very little to say about the illustrators who worked for Harper's during these early years—his concern is more directly with the firm's literary publishing history.

Arthur John's history of CENTURY magazine focuses on the editorial role of Richard Watson Gilder with SCRIBNER'S and CENTURY magazines from 1870 to 1909. One chapter is devoted to CENTURY's illustrations, focusing primarily on the role of the art editor, Arthur Drake. Equally important, John attributes much of CENTURY's artistic success to the printer and engravers and Drake's supervision of them. John argues that Gilder made the magazine a spokesman for the arts and their illustrations as an exemplar of good taste. This was particularly important for Gilder, labelled by Tomsich in A GENTEEL ENDEAVOR (1971) as one of the defenders of the Genteel Tradition against encroachment by the "popular" arts.

We can be thankful that the three most important illustrated magazines during the Golden Age have had histories written about them, histories that pay attention to the role of illustration in their development. Interestingly, all three books point to the importance of the various art editors—Charles Parsons at HARPER'S, Joe Chapin at SCRIBNER'S, and Alexander Drake at CENTURY—in their respective magazine's rise to preeminence. This should serve to remind us that the development of American illustration depended not only on the skill of illustrators and the technologies that reproduced their artwork but also on the talents of men who decided which illustrators would do which illustrations for which story, and using what media. There is only one study that examines the role of art editors across several publishing firms. Best's unpublished manuscript (1982) uses Scribner's company records as a base for examining the relationship between Joe Chapin and the illustrators used by SCRIBNER'S, but then compares his results with relationships discussed by John, Burlingame, and others. He finds that art editors played important roles in assigning stories to illustrators, deciding pay rates for artwork, negotiating control over subsidiary rights, and serving as friends as well as employers.

The Lyon (1963) and Tebbel (1948) histories are less useful in their explanation of the role of illustration in the development of their respective magazines. Lyon, for example, attributes the rise of magazine illustration to photoengraving, which made illustration less expensive and inexpensive magazines possible and which increased advertising revenues, making magazines more profitable. As a result more money could be spent on illustrations, which could be reproduced more inexpensively. There is virtually no discussion of the role of McCLURE'S art editors, except when Howard Pyle assumed that role for a mercifully short period. There is no discussion of why it was important to have Pyle in that role, what impact he had (although other sources indicate neither he nor the other illustrators were particularly happy), or why he left. Tebbel's history of THE SATURDAY EVENING POST focuses on the career of George H. Latimer from 1898 to 1936. Unfortunately, only three pages of this well-written book deal with illustrations at the POST—unfortunate because doing a cover for the POST during the interwar period was a sure sign of recognition. Apparently, the main criterion used by Latimer was that the covers and interior illustrations be realistic so that "average" Americans could understand and enjoy them. This "explanation" may help explain why Norman Rockwell did so many covers for the POST, but it doesn't provide much insight into the popularity of J. C. Leyendecker's Art Deco covers.

Books and magazines have not been the only publication media for illustrations. Advertisements, since the early 1800s, have used illustrations of one sort or another to sell their products. Clarence Hornung's HANDBOOK OF EARLY ADVERTISING ART (1947) provides a useful introduction to the early American wood engravers who did advertising art, discussing the process by which wood engravings were cast into type metal, reproduced by type foundries, and subsequently sold to printers. THE PROMISE AND THE PRODUCT: 200 YEARS OF AMERICAN ADVERTISING POSTERS (1979), by Margolin, Brichta, and Brichta, is a visual history of advertisements through American history, highlighting changes in products and their presentation. The Atwar, McQuade, and Wright book (1979) performs much the same function. Bryan Holme's ADVERTISING (1982) is an excellent effort to look at changes in advertising content, styles, and media during the last one hundred years. Through this presentation one is made aware of the increasingly important role played by advertising in the American economy and our daily lives.

More recent illustration epiphenomena have been book jackets, paperback book covers, and record covers. Kurt Weidemann's BOOK JACKETS AND RECORD COVERS (1969) is a brief history of illustration in those two areas, while Brad Benedict and Linda Barton's PHONOGRAPHICS: CONTEMPORARY ALBUM COVER ART AND DESIGN (1977) provides an insightful history (with examples) of rock music record albums. There are several good histories of paperback cover art. Piet Schreuders's book, PAPERBACKS, U.S.A.: A GRAPHIC HISTORY, 1939–1959 (1981), while dealing with the paperback book industry in general, devotes an enormous amount of space to paperback art and is more comprehensive in scope although more limited in time coverage than Geoffrey O'Brien's HARD-BOILED AMERICA: THE LURID YEARS OF PAPERBACKS (1981), which is concerned more broadly with the development of the "tough-guy" genre of paperback books and their artwork. A number of writers have dealt with science fiction and pulp magazines but Peter Haining's book TERROR!: A HISTORY OF HORROR ILLUSTRATIONS FROM THE PULP MAGAZINES (1976) stands alone in its examination of illustration artwork. Ian Summers's TOMORROW AND BEYOND: MASTERPIECES OF SCIENCE FICTION ART (1978) provides a similar historical overview of science fiction artwork, although Anthony Frewin's ONE HUNDRED YEARS OF SCIENCE FICTION ILLUSTRATION: 1840–1940 (1974) provides a longer historical perspective, albeit with a more continental focus.'

The history of lithography and chromolithography as illustration media and the major publishers of such media have recently received increased attention. Early lithographs and chromolithographs were the first media that brought color artwork to the masses. Principal among the major lithographers was the firm of Currier and Ives, founded in 1834 and surviving until 1907. During that period it published millions of copies of more than seven thousand prints, most of which sold for twenty-five cents or less. Harry T. Peters's CURRIER AND IVES: PRINTMAKERS TO THE AMERICAN PEOPLE (1942) is an excellent analysis of the firm's artwork; the book's strength comes from its understanding of what made Currier and Ives so successful—their understanding of new methods of color reproduction and their sense of public taste—and its discussion of the firm's artists. The latter is important since many of the Currier and Ives prints were not signed and a number of important artists and illustrators at one time or another worked for the firm. In addition, Peters reproduces several hundred of the more popular Currier and Ives prints, grouped by topical category. Russell Crouse's book, MR. CURRIER AND MR. IVES (1941) provides a briefer history of the firm and more color reproduction of the firm's artwork. Walton Rawls's THE GREAT BOOK OF CURRIER AND IVES' AMERICA (1978) may be the most definitive work yet published on the firm and its artwork. Rawls discusses in meticulous detail the training of Nat Currier and the development of the firm. Of particular importance is his analysis of Currier and Ives as a business—which sold pictures and prints rather than art, its relationship with comparable businesses—Louis Prang and the Art Union, and the firm's understanding of what kinds of pictures would appeal to a mass audience. All three of these factors were important in Currier and Ives's longevity. The remainder of the book deals with a selection of Currier and Ives's prints organized by topic: historical prints, New York City, children, the West, home life, politics, nature, landscapes, horses and sports, and social issues.

Of the books on chromolithography Peter Marzio's excellent book, THE DEMOCRATIC ART: PICTURES FOR A 19TH CENTURY AMERICA (1979), provides the broad overview that this topic deserves, focusing on the development of chromolithography from 1840 to 1900—the period he describes as "chromo civilization." After an extensive discussion of the chromolithography process Marzio then introduces and analyzes the work of the early chromolithography publishers—Duval, Prang, Sinclair, Hoover, Sarony, Currier and Ives, Wagner and McGuinan, Rosenthal, Schoolcraft, Endicott, and Bien—many of whom were located in Cincinatti, which became the chromolithography center of the early period. The most successful American chromolithographer was Louis Prang, whose firm worked from 1866 to 1897. Prang's success, according to Marzio, was due to his ability to understand popular taste, to understand how Victorian values and sentiments could be translated into chromolithographic art that would sell in a mass market. Katherine Morrison McClinton's book, THE CHROMO-LITHOGRAPHY OF LOUIS PRANG (1973), makes the same point, devoting eight chapters in color and black and white to a discussion and analysis of leading examples of Prang's commercial artwork. McClinton's book gives ample evidence of Marzio's assertion of Prang's artistic skill and ability to read popular tastes. By the turn of the century chromolithography was "big" business—but the end was in sight; the publication of four-color artwork in the major illustrated magazines, which began in 1900, dealt an economic blow to the more expensive and cumbersome chromolithography process.

Surprisingly little attention has been paid to the illustration media. Many of the contemporary books on illustration media are of the "how to" variety, without discussing "when," "where," and "what" to do. To learn how to use the airbrush, without learning when and where its use is most appropriate, may be to learn an empty lesson. Equally lacking has been any useful exploration of the various illustration media and the quality and quantity of artwork produced. Wood engraving, for example, produced a set of requirements that made illustration appealing to a given set of illustrators. The shift to halftone and four-color reproduction, on the other hand, made some of the skills that were relevant for wood engraving irrelevant to the new technological processes. The impact of technological and reproduction changes on the quality of illustration and the people involved has been sadly neglected in the literature. In Rawls's otherwise excellent history of Currier and Ives, THE GREAT BOOK OF CURRIER AND IVES' AMERICA (1978), the reasons for the demise of the company are not clearly stated, but Rawls must have understood that the development of four-color printing made the color lithography of Currier and Ives outdated. As I have noted elsewhere, technological change had an important impact on the career longevity of a number of illustrators. Some, for example, could not make the transition from pen-and-ink illustration to working in oils; trained and experienced in thinking in black-and-white, linear terms, they were suddenly faced with working in another medium with a different set of assumptions about what would be artistically attractive. In fact, one reason for Howard Pyle's success as a teacher was his understanding of the various publication media, and his ability to show his students how to best use various media to deal with their illustration problems.

The various media histories suffer from one major defect, an unwillingness to examine the interrelationship between technology and illustration, particularly technological changes that had an impact on the nature and quality of American illustration. By the late 1920s, for example, SCRIBNER'S and HARPER'S were no longer illustrated magazines, although there is little evidence in their company histories why the change in emphasis occurred. One can surmise that the economics of magazine publishing and changes in magazine audiences played a role, but there is little direct or concrete evidence.

BIBLIOGRAPHY

Abbe, Dorothy, comp. STENCILLED ORNAMENT AND ILLUSTRATION. Hingham, Mass., Puterscheim-Hingham, 1979.

Atwar, Robert, Donald McQuade, and John W. Wright. EDSELS, LUCKIES, AND FRIGIDAIRES. New York, Delacorte Press, 1979.

Audsley, George Ashdown. THE ART OF CHROMOLITHOGRAPHY. New York, Charles Scribner's Sons, 1883.

Benedict, Brad, and Linda Barton, eds. PHONOGRAPHICS: CONTEMPORARY ALBUM COVER ART AND DESIGN. New York, Collier Books, 1977.

Berg, Andrew S. MAX PERKINS, EDITOR OF GENIUS. New York, E. P. Dutton, 1978.

Best, James J. "The Brandywine School and Magazine Illustration, HARPER'S, SCRIBNER'S, and CENTURY, 1906–1910." JOURNAL OF AMEICAN CULTURE, no. 3 (1980), 128–44.

———— "Editors and Illustrators During the Golden Age of American Illustration." Unpublished manuscript, 1982.

———— "Pay Rates and Incomes for Illustrators: 1888–1938." Unpublished manuscript, 1982.

Brenni, Vito J. BOOK ILLUSTRATION AND DECORATION. Westport, Conn., Green-
    wood Press, 1980.

Burlingame, Roger. OF MAKING MANY BOOKS. New York, Charles Scribner's Sons,
    1946.

Cahn, Joel. "How Much Are Illustrators Worth?" PRINT, May 1974, 42–45, 90, 97–100.

JOSEPH HAWLEY CHAPIN, 1869–1939: ARTIST, ART DIRECTOR, FRIEND. New
    York, Friends of Joseph Hawley Chapin, 1939.

Coleman, Morris. "Some Technical Notes on Book Illustration." AMERICAN ARTIST,
    January 1953, 48–56.

Crouse, Russell. MR. CURRIER AND MR. IVES. Garden City, N.Y., Garden City
    Publishing Co., 1941.

Dance, S. Peter. THE ART OF NATURAL HISTORY. Woodstock, N.Y., Overlook
    Press, 1978.

Didinger, Ray, and Tex Maule. THE PROFESSIONALS. New York, New American
    Library, A National Football League Book, 1980.

Elzea, Rowland, ed. HOWARD PYLE: DIVERSITY IN DEPTH. Wilmington, Delaware
    Art Museum, 1973.

Exman, Eugene. THE BROTHERS HARPER. New York, Harper and Row, 1965.

Finley, Ruth E. THE LADY OF GODEY'S: SARAH JOSEPHA HALE. Philadelphia,
    J. B. Lippincott, 1931.

Frewin, Anthony. ONE HUNDRED YEARS OF SCIENCE FICTION ILLUSTRATION:
    1840–1940. London, Jupiter Books, 1974.

Furst, Herbert. THE MODERN WOODCUT. New York, Dodd, Mead, 1924.

Gullano, Charles, and John Esprey. "American Trade Bindings and Their Designers,
    1880–1915." In Jean Peters, ed., COLLECTIBLE BOOKS. New York, R. R.
    Bowker, 1979, 32–67.

Guptill, Arthur L. "Mead Schaeffer Paints a Post Cover." AMERICAN ARTIST, De-
    cember 1945, 12–15, 28.

Halsey, Ashby, Jr. ILLUSTRATING FOR THE SATURDAY EVENING POST. Boston,
    Arlington House, 1951.

Haining, Peter. TERROR!: A HISTORY OF HORROR ILLUSTRATIONS FROM THE
    PULP MAGAZINES. N.p., A and W Visual Library, 1976.

Harper, J. Henry. THE HOUSE OF HARPER. New York, Harper's, 1912.

Hillier, Bevis. THE DECORATIVE ARTS OF THE FORTIES AND FIFTIES. New
    York, Clarkson N. Potter, 1975.

Holme, Bryan. ADVERTISING: REFLECTIONS OF A CENTURY. New York, Viking
    Press, 1982.

Hornung, Clarence P. HANDBOOK OF EARLY ADVERTISING ART, VOLS. I, II.
    New York, Dover Publications, 1947.

Hydeman, Sid. HOW TO ILLUSTRATE FOR MONEY. New York, Harper and Bros.,
    1936.

"Illustration Today." PRINT, July 1967, 8–63.

Jaques, Robin. ILLUSTRATORS AT WORK. London, Studio Books, 1963.

John, Arthur. THE BEST YEARS OF THE "CENTURY." Urbana, University of Illinois
    Press, 1981.

Johnson, Robert Underwood. REMEMBERED YESTERDAYS. Boston, Little Brown,
    1923.

Kingman, Lee, ed. THE ILLUSTRATOR'S NOTEBOOK. Boston, Horn Book, 1978.

Kirsch, Francine. CHROMOS: A GUIDE TO PAPER COLLECTIBLES. New York, A. S. Barnes, 1981.

Klemin, Diana. THE ILLUSTRATED BOOK: ITS ART AND CRAFT. New York, Bramhall House, 1970.

Kuhn, Bob. THE ANIMAL ART OF BOB KUHN. Westport, Conn., Northern Lights Publishers, 1973.

Lankes, J. J. A WOODCUT MANUAL. New York, Henry Holt and Co., 1932.

Linton, W. J. THE HISTORY OF WOOD-ENGRAVING IN AMERICA. Boston, Estes and Laureate, 1882.

Loomis, Andrew. CREATIVE ILLUSTRATION. New York, Viking Press, 1947.

Ludwig, Coy. MAXFIELD PARRISH. New York, Watson-Guptill, 1973.

Lyon, Peter. SUCCESS STORY: THE LIFE AND TIMES OF S. S. McCLURE. Deland, Fla., Everett/Edwards, Inc., 1963.

McClinton, Katherine Morrison. THE CHROMOLITHOGRAPHY OF LOUIS PRANG. New York, Clarkson N. Potter, 1973.

McMullan, James. REVEALING ILLUSTRATIONS. New York, Watson-Guptill, 1981.

Margolin, Victor, Ira Brichta, and Vivian Brichta. THE PROMISE AND THE PRODUCT: 200 YEARS OF AMERICAN ADVERTISING POSTERS. New York, Macmillan, 1979.

Marzio, Peter C., THE DEMOCRATIC ART: PICTURES FOR A 19TH CENTURY AMERICA. Boston, Godine, 1979.

Maurello, S. Ralph. THE COMPLETE AIRBRUSH BOOK. New York, William Penn Publishing Co., 1955.

Meyer, Susan E. NORMAN ROCKWELL'S PEOPLE. New York, Henry Abrams, 1981.

Mott, Frank Luther. A HISTORY OF AMERICAN MAGAZINES, VOLS. I–V. Cambridge, Mass., Harvard University Press, 1938–1968.

Muller, Marion. "Connecting the Dots." U&LC, September 1982, 36–44.

O'Brien, Geoffrey. HARD-BOILED AMERICA: THE LURID YEARS OF PAPERBACKS. New York, Van Nostrand, 1981.

Pennell, Joseph. THE GRAPHIC ARTS. Chicago, University of Chicago Press, 1920.

——— THE ILLUSTRATION OF BOOKS. New York, Century Co., 1896.

——— PEN DRAWING AND PEN DRAUGHTSMEN. New York, Macmillan, 1920.

Peters, Harry T. CURRIER AND IVES: PRINTMAKERS TO THE AMERICAN PEOPLE. Garden City, N.Y., Doubleday, Doran and Co., 1942.

Pitz, Henry C. ILLUSTRATING CHILDREN'S BOOKS. New York, Watson-Guptill, 1963.

——— HOWARD PYLE. New York, Clarkson N. Potter, 1975.

Portenaar, Jan. THE ART OF THE BOOK AND ITS ILLUSTRATION. Philadelphia, J. B. Lippincott, 1935.

Price, Matlack. "Henry Quinan, an Artist's Dream of an Art Director." AMERICAN ARTIST, June 1945, 21–24, 35.

Rawls, Walton. THE GREAT BOOK OF CURRIER AND IVES' AMERICA. New York, Abbeville Press, 1978.

Reed, Walt, comp. THE MAGIC PEN OF JOSEPH CLEMENT COLL. West Kingston, R.I., Donald M. Grant, 1978.

Richard H. Childers Productions. AIR POWERED. New York, Random House, 1979.

Richardson, Fred. BOOK OF DRAWINGS, BEING A SELECTION OF THOSE DONE FOR THE CHICAGO DAILY NEWS. Chicago, Lakeside Press, 1899.

Rix, Martyn. THE ART OF THE PLANT WORLD. Woodstock, N.Y., Overlook Press, 1980.

Schmidt, Dorie, ed. THE AMERICAN MAGAZINE: 1890–1940. Wilimington, Delaware Art Museum, 1979.

Schreuders, Piet. PAPERBACKS, U.S.A.: A GRAPHIC HISTORY, 1939–1959. San Diego, Blue Dolphin Enterprises, 1981.

Schwarz, Joseph. WAYS OF THE ILLUSTRATOR: VISUAL COMMUNICATIONS IN CHILDREN'S LITERATURE. Chicago, American Library Association, 1982.

Seton, Ernest Thompson. STUDIES IN THE ART ANATOMY OF ANIMALS. London and New York, Macmillan and Co., 1896.

Simon, Howard. 500 YEARS OF ART AND ILLUSTRATION. Cleveland and New York, World Publishing Co., 1942.

"Sports Illustration." AMERICAN ARTIST, July 1977.

Spurrier, Steven. BLACK AND WHITE ILLUSTRATION. New York, Pitman, 1958.

Summers, Ian, ed. TOMORROW AND BEYOND: MASTERPIECES OF SCIENCE FICTION ART. New York, Workman Publishing Co., 1978.

Tate, Sharon Lee, and Mona Shafer Edwards. THE COMPLETE BOOK OF FASHION ILLUSTRATION. New York, Harper and Row, 1982.

Tebbel, John. THE AMERICAN MAGAZINE: A COMPACT HISTORY. New York, Hawthorne Books, 1969.

——— A HISTORY OF BOOK PUBLISHING IN THE UNITED STATES, VOL. I. New York, R. R. Bowker, 1972.

——— GEORGE HORACE LATIMER AND THE SATURDAY EVENING POST. Garden City, N.Y., Doubleday and Co., 1948.

Tedesco, A. P. THE RELATIONSHIP BETWEEN TYPE AND ILLUSTRATION IN BOOKS AND BOOK JACKETS. Brooklyn, N.Y., George McKibben, 1948.

Tomsich, John. A GENTEEL ENDEAVOR. Stanford, Stanford University Press, 1971.

Watson, Ernest. FORTY ILLUSTRATORS AND HOW THEY WORK. New York, Watson-Guptill, 1946.

Weidemann, Kurt, ed. BOOK JACKETS AND RECORD COVERS: AN INTERNATIONAL SURVEY. New York, Praeger, 1969.

Weitenkampf, Frank. AMERICAN GRAPHIC ART. New York, Henry Holt and Company, 1912. Reprint. New York, Johnson Reprint Series, 1970.

Magazines and Periodicals

Comparatively few magazines and periodicals deal exclusively with illustration or illustrated materials. The following list should be viewed as suggestive rather than definitive.

AB BOOKMAN'S WEEKLY. Clifton, N.J., 1947–present. This is the antiquarian bookseller's trade publication, which contains periodic articles on children's and illustrated books by knowledgeable book dealers and collectors.

AMERICAN ARTIST. New York, 1937–present. Under the editorship of Ernest Watson and Susan Meyer, this magazine has published periodic articles about American illustrators. From 1937 until the mid-1970s it was the one consistent source of information about Golden Age illustrators, including many interviews with still-living illustrators.

ANNUAL OF ADVERTISING, EDITORIAL, TV, ART AND DESIGN. New York, 1972–present. This is a yearly compendium of the "best" of American commercial art, especially useful for keeping up with trends in contemporary American illustration.

ARCHIVES OF AMERICAN ART JOURNAL. New York, 1960–present. This journal, published by the Archives of American Art, publishes articles based on material in the Archives or associated with them. Since the Archives contain a great deal of material relating to American illustration, the JOURNAL occasionally publishes useful material.

GRAPHIS. Zurich, 1944–present. This periodical publishes articles and examples of the latest in European illustration.

GRAPHIS ANNUAL, INTERNATIONAL ADVERTISING ART. New York, 1952/1953–present. This annual presents the "best" of European illustration during the year; it is the counterpart of the ANNUAL OF ADVERTISING, EDITORIAL, TV, ART AND DESIGN and ILLUSTRATORS, THE ANNUAL OF AMERICAN ILLUSTRATION.

ILLUSTRATORS, THE ANNUAL OF AMERICAN ILLUSTRATION. New York, 1959–present. A yearly collection of the "best" of American illustration, as selected by the Society of Illustrators. A review of each year gives insights into how much (or how little) American illustration changes over time. Comparison with GRAPHIS ANNUAL shows the similarities and differences between American and European illustration.

INTERNATIONAL STUDIO. New York, 1897–1931. One of the better magazine sources of information on "quality" illustration and the fine arts in Great Britain and the United States. Excellent coverage of the Art Nouveau movement during the period 1897–1920, with excellent review articles of major figures, particularly European illustrators.

MONTHLY ILLUSTRATOR. New York, 1895–1897. Unfortunately short-lived successor to the QUARTERLY ILLUSTRATOR, it contains reviews of who was doing illustrations in which magazines, articles on now-unknown illustrators, and even a series on major publishers of illustrations. It is very difficult to find copies of this and the QUARTERLY ILLUSTRATOR, however.

PRINT. New York, 1946–present. The best source of information on contemporary American illustrators, with biographical sketches and examples of artwork by leading artists. It covers the entire range of American illustration—anything that appears in "print."

QUARTERLY ILLUSTRATOR. New York, 1893–1895. The predecessor of the MONTHLY ILLUSTRATOR, containing many excellent articles on work styles and examples of art from now-unknown illustrators.

U&LC. New York, 1973–present. A trade publication of the typographical industry, it frequently contains articles on American illustration, both contemporary and older.

APPENDIX 2

Research Collections

There are three basic types of materials essential to any research on American illustration: the original artwork used for illustrations, the published illustrations, and the correspondence or records of the various illustrators and their publishers. Surprisingly little original artwork, particularly those commissions executed prior to 1910, still exists. Until the early 1900s, illustrations were the property of the publisher rather than the artist, and many publishing houses had vast and fast-growing collections, which were periodically weeded out, editors and publisher keeping choice pieces and disposing of the remainder to friends, the public, or the trash heap. Even when the original artwork was returned to the illustrator, the illustrator frequently did not keep it. Many illustrators were unaware of postpublication sale possibilities and frequently destroyed their artwork after it was published; Cortland Schoonover found that his father Frank Schoonover kept only eight hundred of the approximately six thousand illustrations he had published during his lifetime.

In addition, much of the illustration artwork still extant is in private hands. In recent exhibitions mounted by the Delaware Art Museum, fifty-four of fifty-five pieces by Douglas Duer came from private collections, thirty-nine of forty illustrations by W.H.D. Koerner were donated by private collections, and in a major exhibition of one of Howard Pyle's leading students, Stanley Arthurs, only nine of the seventy-two illustrations came from the museum's holdings.

There are few large-scale public collections of illustration artwork. Few of these collections are complete or comprehensive—invariably the illustration artwork in public collections must share space with the fine arts. The Delaware Art Museum, which contains over seven hundred sketches and almost five hundred pieces of illustration artwork by Howard Pyle, for example, does not have several of the most important Pyle pieces, which are located in the Brandywine River Museum, the Philadelphia Free Library, or in private collections. The Brandywine River Museum, when mounting an N. C. Wyeth exhibit, must augment its holding of less than twenty oils with loans from the Delaware Art Museum, the Children's Room of the Philadelphia Free Library, and private collections. These two museums, located forty miles apart, contain the best collections of original artwork by Howard Pyle and his students and their catalogs are constantly expanding our knowledge of this group.

Other museums have broader collections but with less depth. The Brooklyn Museum, the Thornton Oakley Collection of the Philadelphia Free Library, the Philadelphia Art Museum, the New York Public Library, the Grunwald Center for the Graphic Arts at UCLA, the F. R. Gruger Collection at the University of Oregon, and the Museum of American Art in New Britain, Connecticut, contain major and important collections of illustration artwork. The Amon Carter Museum of Art in Fort Worth, Texas, and the Buffalo Bill Cody Museum in Cody, Wyoming, are two important research centers for western art. The Society of Illustrators in New York City has well over three hundred paintings, drawings, and sketches by twentieth-century American illustrators, and their annual show of contemporary illustration artwork is a major presentation of award winning illustrations for the preceding year. The Print Division of the Library of Congress contains over forty thousand lithographs, engravings, woodcuts, and original prints from the eighteenth and nineteenth centuries, as well as sixty thousand American and foreign posters dating from 1850 to the present. The poster collection is one of the most complete and comprehensive in the nation.

The best collections of published illustrations are in libraries. The largest single collection is in the Library of Congress, which contains copies of all copyrighted materials. In addition, the Library of Congress has several specialized collections of interest to students of American illustration. The Juvenile Collection contains approximately fifteen thousand volumes, many of them illustrated, cataloged chronologically by author, and the Lessing J. Rosenwald collection of incunabula, illustrated books, and fine printed and bound books is one of the largest and best collections in the world. The Pierpont Morgan Library in New York City also has an extensive collection of children's and illustrated books. Other major holdings can be found in the Spencer Collection of the New York Public Library, the Philadelphia Free Library, the Newberry Library in Chicago, the Detroit Public Library, the library of the Metropolitan Museum of Art in New York, as well as university collections at UCLA, Princeton, Johns Hopkins, Columbia, and the University of Chicago. The Popular Culture Library at Bowling Green University in Ohio has some illustration ephemera of interest. Several museums also have important library holdings. The Delaware Art Museum, for example, has the books used by Morse and Brinkle to compile their comprehensive bibliography of Howard Pyle's published illustrations. The Brandywine River Museum has a solid collection of books illustrated by N. C. Wyeth and other Pyle students, and is attempting to systematically collect their magazine illustrations as well. If successful in this latter effort, the resultant bibliography will be immensely valuable. As with illustration artwork, however, some of the largest and best collections are in the hands of book dealers and collectors. A few of these specialized collectors have organized into clubs, like the Harrison Fisher Society in California, but most of the specialty collections are known only to book dealers and other collectors. The size and comprehensiveness of some of these private collections can be surprising; the auction of Justin Schiller's collection of Oziana (see L. FRANK BAUM AND RELATED OZIANA [1978]) was composed of over five hundred pieces, and the auction catalog remains an important bibliographic and price reference for this material.

The scholar who seeks to go beyond the artwork and published materials will find the task very difficult indeed. Records, correspondence, diaries, and daybooks of individual illustrators, editors, and publishers have been fragmented or destroyed. Much of Howard Pyle's correspondence was destroyed after his death. The diary of Joseph Chapin, art editor of Scribner's for forty years, is missing. Some of Frank Schoonover's papers are at the Delaware Art Museum, some at the Philadelphia Free Library, and still others are in the hands of private collectors. F. R. Gruger's correspondence is housed at the University of Oregon and Norman Rockwell's correspondence and documents are currently being collected. The incomplete correspondence from a number of illustrators is available by microfilm through the Archives of American Art in Washington, D.C. The Society of Illustrators has an archive of material from Arthur William Brown, Wallace Morgan, Rene Clarke, William Meade Prince, Charles Dana Gibson, and James Montgomery Flagg, who were founders, members, early presidents, or benefactors of the Society.

Publishing company correspondence and records are woefully incomplete or missing. The Archives of American Art has very limited correspondence between CENTURY and HARPER'S magazines and their illustrators. The early company records of Scribner's are now on deposit in the Firestone Collection at Princeton University, but the collection has not been cataloged completely and some of the more vital material—the letter books of art editor Joseph Chapin—is missing. And what has happened to the early company records of publishers like McCLURE'S, THE SATURDAY EVENING POST, and LESLIE'S? Without these records it will be difficult, if not impossible, to determine why some illustrators worked for some publishers.

APPENDIX 3

Bibliography of Illustrated Books

The following bibliography of illustrated books is arranged alphabetically by illustrator.

Abbey   Herrick, Robert. SELECTIONS FROM THE POETRY OF ROBERT HERRICK. New York. Harper's, 1882.

Artzybasheff   Artzybasheff, Boris. POOR SHAYDULLAH. New York, Macmillan, 1931.

Colum, Padraic. THE FORGE IN THE FOREST. New York, Macmillan, 1925.

Aulaire   Aulaire, Ingre. ABRAHAM LINCOLN. New York, Doubleday, 1939.

Bemelmans   Bemelmans, Ludwig. MADELINE. New York, Simon and Schuster, 1939.

Bradley   Bradley, Will. PETER POODLE: TOY MAKER TO THE KING. New York, Dodd, Mead, 1906.

Bramson   London, Jack. THE CALL OF THE WILD. New York, Macmillan, 1912.

Bull   London, Jack. THE CALL OF THE WILD. New York, Macmillan, 1903.

Burkert   Burkert, Nancy Eckholm. SNOW WHITE AND THE SEVEN DWARFS. New York, Farrar, Strauss, and Giroux, 1972.

Darley   COOPER'S NOVELS ILLUSTRATED BY DARLEY. New York, W. A. Townsend, 1859–1861, 32 vols.

Darley, F.O.C. COMPOSITIONS IN OUTLINE BY FELIX O.C. DARLEY FROM JUDD'S MARGARET. New York, Redfield, 1856.

Darley, F.O.C. ILLUSTRATIONS OF THE LEGEND OF SLEEPY HOLLOW. New York, American Art-Union, 1849.

Darley, F.O.C. ILLUSTRATIONS OF RIP VAN WINKLE. New York, American Art-Union, 1848.

Darley, F.O.C. SCENES IN INDIAN LIFE. Philadelphia, J. R. Colon, 1843.

Darley, F.O.C. SKETCHES ABROAD WITH PEN AND PENCIL. New York, Hurd and Houghton, 1868.

Irving, Washington. THE ALHAMBRA. New York, Putnam, 1851.

Irving, Washington. A HISTORY OF NEW YORK. New York, Putnam, 1850.

Irving, Washington. THE LIFE OF GEORGE WASHINGTON. New York, Putnam, 1855–1859.

Irving, Washington. THE SKETCH BOOK OF GEOFFREY CRAYON, GENT. New York, Putnam, 1848.

LIBRARY OF HUMOROUS AMERICAN WORKS. Philadelphia, Carey and Hart, 1846–1849.

Parkman, Francis. THE CALIFORNIA AND OREGON TRAIL. New York, Putnam, 1849.

Denslow   Baum, L. Frank. FATHER GOOSE, HIS BOOK. Chicago, G. M. Hill, 1899.

Baum, L. Frank. THE WONDERFUL WIZARD OF OZ. Chicago, G. M. Hill, 1900.

Denslow, W. W. DENSLOW'S MOTHER GOOSE. New York, McClure Phillips, 1901.

Dulac   Housman, Lawrence. STORIES FROM THE ARABIAN NIGHTS. London, Hodder and Stoughton, 1907.

Duvoisin   Duvoisin, Roger. DONKEY-DONKEY. Racine, Wis., Whitman, 1933.

Duvoisin, Roger. PETUNIA. New York, Knopf, 1950.

Tresselt, Alvin. WHITE SNOW, BRIGHT SNOW. New York, Lothrop, Lee and Shepard, 1947.

Frost   Harris, Joel Chandler. UNCLE REMUS. New York, Appleton, 1895.

Frost and   Harris, Joel Chandler. THE TAR-BABY. New York, Appleton, 1904.
Kemble

Gibson   Gibson, Charles Dana. EVERYDAY PEOPLE. New York, Charles Scribner's Sons, 1904

Gibson, Charles Dana. SKETCHES IN EGYPT. New York, Doubleday and McClure, 1899.

Gibson, Charles Dana. THE SOCIAL LADDER. New York, R. H. Russell, 1902.

Green   Duncan, Norman. THE SUITABLE CHILD. New York, F. H. Revell, 1909.

LeGalliene, Richard. AN OLD COUNTRY HOUSE. New York, Harper and Bros., 1902.

Guerin   Hichens, Robert. EGYPT AND ITS MONUMENTS. New York, Century Co., 1908.

Lansdale, Maria Nornor. THE CHATEUX OF TOURAINE. New York, Century Co., 1906.

Hurd   Baldwin, James. THE STORY OF ROLAND. New York, Charles Scribner's Sons, 1930.

Baldwin, James. THE STORY OF SIEGFRIED. New York, Charles Scribner's Sons, 1931.

James   James, Will. THE LONE COWBOY. New York, Charles Scribner's Sons, 1930.

James, Will. SMOKY. New York, Charles Scribner's Sons, 1928.

Kemble   Kemble, Edward. COMICAL COONS. New York, R. H. Russell, 1898.

Kemble, Edward. KEMBLE'S COONS. New York, R. H. Russell, 1896.

Kent   BEOWULF. New York, Random House, 1932.

Kent, Rockwell. N BY E. New York, Brewer and Warren, 1930.

Kent, Rockwell. WILDERNESS. New York, Putnam, 1920.

Melville, Herman. MOBY DICK. New York, Random House, 1930.

Lawson   Bianco, Margery. THE HURDY-GURDY MAN. New York, Oxford University Press, 1933.

Leaf, Munro. THE STORY OF FERDINAND. New York, Viking Press, 1936.

Macaulay   Macaulay, David. CASTLE. Boston, Houghton Mifflin, 1977.

Macauley, David. CATHEDRAL. Boston, Houghton Mifflin, 1973.

Nielsen   Asbjornsen, Peter C. EAST OF THE SUN AND WEST OF THE MOON. London, Hodder and Stoughton, 1914.

Parrish   Field, Eugene. POEMS OF CHILDHOOD. New York, Charles Scribner's Sons, 1904.

Grahame, Kenneth. DREAM DAYS. New York, Dodd, Mead, 1898.

Grahame, Kenneth. THE GOLDEN AGE. New York, John Lane, 1900.

Saunders, Louise. THE KNAVE OF HEARTS. New York, Charles Scribner's Sons, 1925.

Penfield   Penfield, Edward. HOLLAND SKETCHES. New York, Charles Scribner's Sons, 1907.

Penfield, Edward. SPANISH SKETCHES. New York, Charles Scribner's Sons, 1911.

Petersham   Petersham, Maud. MIKI. Garden City, N.Y., Doubleday Doran, 1925.

Pyle   Holmes, Oliver Wendell. THE ONE HOSS SHAY. New York, Houghton Mifflin, 1892 and 1905.

Johnson, Merle, comp. HOWARD PYLE'S BOOK OF THE AMERICAN SPIRIT. New York, Harper and Bros., 1923.

Johnson, Merle, comp. HOWARD PYLE'S BOOK OF PIRATES. New York, Harper and Bros., 1921.

Pyle, Howard. THE MERRY ADVENTURES OF ROBIN HOOD OF OF GREAT RENOWN IN NOTTINGHAMSHIRE. New York, Charles Scribner's Sons, 1883.

Pyle, Howard. OTTO OF THE SILVER HAND. New York, Charles Scribner's Sons, 1888.

Pyle, Howard. PEPPER AND SALT. New York, Harper and Bros., 1886.

Pyle, Howard. THE STORY OF THE CHAMPIONS OF THE ROUND TABLE. New York, Charles Scribner's Sons, 1905.

Pyle, Howard. THE STORY OF THE GRAIL AND THE PASSING OF ARTHUR. New York, Charles Scribner's Sons, 1910.

Pyle, Howard. THE STORY OF KING ARTHUR AND HIS KNIGHTS. New York, Charles Scribner's Sons, 1903.

Pyle, Howard. THE STORY OF SIR LANCELOT AND HIS COMPANIONS. New York, Charles Scribner's Sons, 1907.

Pyle, Howard. THE WONDER CLOCK. New York, Harper and Bros., 1888.

Rackham Barrie, J. M. PETER PAN IN KENSINGTON GARDENS. London, Hodder and Stoughton, 1906.

Grahame, Kenneth. THE WIND IN THE WILLOWS. New York, Limited Editions Club, 1940.

Remington Remington, Frederic. DONE IN THE OPEN. New York, R. H. Russell, 1902.

Remington, Frederic. PONY TRACKS. New York, Harper and Bros., 1895.

Roosevelt, Theodore. RANCH LIFE AND THE HUNTING TRAIL. New York, Century Co., 1915.

Rockwell Twain, Mark. THE ADVENTURES OF HUCKLEBERRY FINN. New York, Heritage Press, 1940.

Twain, Mark. THE ADVENTURES OF TOM SAWYER. New York, Heritage Press, 1940.

Russell Linderman, Frank. INDIAN OLD-MAN STORIES. New York, Charles Scribner's Sons, 1920.

Linderman, Frank. INDIAN WHY STORIES. New York, Charles Scribner's Sons, 1915.

Sendak   Sendak, Maurice. IN THE NIGHT KITCHEN. New York, Harper and Row, 1970.

Sendak, Maurice. WHERE THE WILD THINGS ARE. New York, Harper and Co., 1963.

Seton   Seton, Ernest Thompson. LIVES OF THE HUNTED. New York, Charles Scribners's Sons, 1901.

Seton, Ernest Thompson. THE TRAIL OF THE SANDHILL STAG. New York, Charles Scribner's Sons, 1899.

Seton, Ernest Thompson. WILD ANIMALS I HAVE KNOWN. New York, Charles Scribner's Sons, 1898.

Seuss   Seuss, Dr. IF I RAN THE ZOO. New York, Random House, 1950.

Timlin   Timlin, William. THE SHIP THAT SAILED TO MARS. London, George G. Harrap, 1923.

Ward   Ward, Lynd. THE BIGGEST BEAR. New York, Scholastic Book Service, 1952.

Ward, Lynd. GOD'S MAN. New York, P. Smith. 1929.

Ward, Lynd. MADMAN'S DRUM. New York, Jonathan Cape, 1930.

Weise   Salten, Felix. BAMBI. New York, Simon and Schuster, 1928.

Weise, Kurt. LIANG AND LO. New York, Doubleday, 1930.

Wyeth   Boyd, James. DRUMS. New York, Charles Scribner's Sons, 1928.

Cooper, James Fenimore. THE DEERSLAYER. New York, Charles Scribner's Sons, 1925.

Cooper, James Fenimore. THE LAST OF THE MOHICANS. New York, Charles Scribner's Sons, 1919.

Rawlings, Marjorie Kinnan, THE YEARLING. New York, Charles Scribner's Sons, 1939 and 1940.

Stevenson, Robert Louis. THE BLACK ARROW. New York, Charles Scribner's Sons, 1916.

Stevenson, Robert Louis. DAVID BALFOUR. New York, Charles Scribner's Sons, 1924.   .

Stevenson, Robert Louis. KIDNAPPED. New York, Charles Scribner's Sons, 1913.

Stevenson, Robert Louis. TREASURE ISLAND. New York, Charles Scribner's Sons, 1911.

Verne, Jules. MICHAEL STROGOFF. New York, Charles Scribner's Sons, 1927.

Verne, Jules. THE MYSTERIOUS ISLAND. New York, Charles Scribner's Sons, 1918.

Various
artists

Bryant, William Cullen. PICTURESQUE AMERICA. New York, Appleton, 1872–1874.

Bryant, William Cullen. PICTURESQUE EUROPE. New York, Appleton, 1874.

Index

Abbe, Dorothy, 138, 147
Abbey, Edwin Austin, 5, 7, 24, 51, 59, 76-
    77, 83, 110, 117, 120, 124, 130, 157
Abbott, Charles, 79, 82, 110, 124, 130
Afro-American artist-illustrators, 25
Airbrush, 137
Aldren, Henry, 142
Alexander, Charles, 37, 38, 41, 124, 125,
    130
Alexander, J. W., 76
Alexander, John, 72
Allen, Douglas, 48, 52, 84, 87, 92, 110
Allen, Douglas, Jr., 48, 52, 84, 87, 110
Amaral, Anthony, 102, 106, 109, 110
American Institute of Graphic Arts, 35, 41
Amon Carter Museum of Art, 153
Anderson, Alexander, 3-4, 22, 50-51, 57,
    71-72, 117, 123, 134, 142
Animal illustration, 10-11, 61, 139
Apgar, Frank, 53, 87, 110
Archives of American Art, 154, 155
Ardizzone, Edward, 39
Armstrong, Margery, 138
Art editors, 7, 117-18, 121-22, 123, 137,
    144
Art Students League, 80, 100, 118-19, 120,
    121
Arthurs, Stanley, 8, 82, 87-88, 110, 153
Artzybasheff, Boris, 64, 157
Ash Can school, 38, 96, 108, 125
Ashley, Clifford, 53, 88, 121
Atwar, Robert, 32, 42, 147, 185
Audsley, George Ashdown, 134-35, 147
Audubon, James, 22, 139
d'Aulaire, Edgar Parin, 64
d'Aulaire, Ingri, 64, 157

Avati, James, 31, 65

Bacher, Otto, 84, 120
Bacon, Peggy, 125
Bader, Barbara, 28, 42, 128, 130
Baigell, Matthew, 110
Baker, Douglas, 110
Bama, James, 107
Barber, John W., 72
Barton, Linda, 32, 42, 65, 67, 137, 145,
    147
Bates, Bertha Corson Day, 53
Baum, L. Frank, 55, 99-100, 154
Beam, Phillip C., 51, 75, 78, 110
Beard, Daniel C., 25
Beardsley, Aubrey, 127
Becker, Maurice, 103
Beeler, Joe, 107
Beggarstaff brothers, 33, 40, 41, 126
Bellows, George, 15-16, 125
Bemelmans, Ludwig, 16, 63-64, 157
Benedict, Brad, 32, 42, 65, 67, 137, 145,
    147
Bennett, Whitman, 39, 42, 48, 67
Benton, Thomas Hart, 125
Berg, Andrew S., 143, 147
Berman, Avis, 86, 110
Best, James J., 50, 83, 99, 110, 118, 137,
    142, 144, 147
Bewick, Thomas, 123
Birch, Reginald, 84, 120
Blake, William, 39
Blanck, Peter, 42, 48, 67
Bland, David, 24, 42
Blechman, Robert, 42
Blegved, Erik, 106, 110

Blum, Edward, 84
Blum, Robert, 118
Bolton, Theodore, 47-48, 50, 54, 55, 57, 72, 110
Bonn, Thomas, 31, 42
"Book Beautiful" movement, 23-24
Borein, Harold, 93-94, 122
Boston Museum of Fine Arts, 26, 42
Bowen, Abel, 72
Bowers, Christine, 105, 110
Bowers, Q. David, 105, 110
Bradley, Will, 11, 12, 22, 24, 33, 62, 66, 121, 127, 138, 157
Bramson, Paul, 10, 61, 157
Brandywine River Museum, 25, 53, 79, 89, 153, 154
Brandywine School, 8
Brenni, Vito J., 140, 148
Brewer, Francis J., 42
Brichta, Ira, 32, 44, 130, 145, 149
Brichta, Vivian, 32, 44, 130, 145, 149
Briggs, Austin, 26
Brinckle, Gertrude, 52, 154
Broder, Patricia Janis, 103, 110
Brooklyn Museum of Arts and Sciences, 23, 26, 42, 153
Brooks, V., 130
Brothers Hildebrandt, 129
Brown, Ann Barton, 25, 42, 82, 110
Brown, Arthur William, 26, 110, 154
Brown, Marcia, 40, 138
Brown, Steven, 41, 42
Buechner, Thomas, 55, 110
Buffalo Bill Cody Museum, 153
Bull, Charles Livingston, 61, 157
Bunce, William Gidney, 120
Burchfield, Charles, 125
Burkert, Nancy Eckholm, 28, 64, 106, 107, 157
Burlingame, Roger, 137, 142-43, 144, 148
Burr, Frederic M., 110

Cady, Harrison, 66
Cahn, Joel, 148
Caldecott awards, 29, 64, 67
Calder, Alexander, 125, 126
Carroll, John, 48, 56, 102, 111

Carroll, Lewis, 39
Castaigne, Andre, 10, 98
Cate, Phillip Dennis, 111
Catlin, George, 23
Century Club, 4
Chamberlin, K. R., 103
Chamberlin-Hellman, M., 114
Chapin, Joseph H., 78, 118, 138, 143, 144, 148, 154, 155
Chapman, Conrad Wise, 74
Chappell, Warren, 40, 138
Chase, William Merritt, 118
Cheret, Jules, 33, 40, 126
Childs, Benjamin F., 72
Christ-Janer, Albert, 103, 110
Christy, Howard Chandler, 6, 9, 11, 22, 23, 26, 34, 54, 61, 62, 94, 95-96, 98, 100, 105, 118, 125; Christy Girl, 9, 95, 96
Chromolithography, 134-35, 146
Church, F. S., 119
Cirker, Blanche, 126-27, 130
Cirker, Haywood, 127, 130
Clark, Walter Appleton, 99, 118, 119, 125
Clarke, Harry, 127
Clarke, Rene, 154
Cliendienst, B. W., 120
Clymer, John, 102
Cober, Alan, 35, 42, 65
Cogslea, 53, 88, 121
Cohen, Margaret, 142
Coleman, Morris, 148
Coll, Joseph Clement, 102, 135
Color plate books, 48
Cooney, Barbara, 138
Cornwell, Dean, 9, 87, 103
Coughlan, Margaret, 28, 43
Cox, Kenyon, 118
Crawford, Elizabeth, 49
Croone, William, 72
Crouse, Russell, 146, 148
Cruickshank, George, 123
Cummins, D. Duane, 93, 111
Currier and Ives, 135, 145-46, 147
Curry, John Stewart, 125

Dali, Salvador, 39
Dalley, Terrence, 130

Dalphin, Marcia, 27, 45, 49, 69
Dance, S. Peter, 139, 148
Darley, Felix Octavius Carr (F.O.C.), 4, 22, 23, 50, 51, 57, 58, 72, 73, 117, 123, 157-58
Darracott, Joseph, 42
Darton, F. J. Harvey, 35, 42
Davidson, Harold, 93-94, 111
Davidson, Jo, 16
Davis, Floyd, 26
Davis, Theodore, 76, 84
Dearborn, Nathaniel, 72
Deland, Clyde, 121
Delaware Art Museum, 25, 38, 53, 54, 72, 89, 97, 142, 153, 154
Delessert, Etienne, 65
De Montreville, Doris, 49
Demuth, Charles, 125
Dennis, Wesley, 107
Denslow, W. W., 55, 62, 98-99, 121, 158
Deshazo, Edith, 97, 111, 119, 130
Detroit Public Library, 154
DeVictor, Richard P., 52
Dickason, David, 124, 130
Didinger, Ray, 139, 148
Dillenberger, Jane, 83-84
Dippie, Brian, 90-91, 92, 93, 111, 126, 130
Dodd, Loring H., 111
Dohanos, Steve, 19, 21, 57, 65, 68, 79, 108, 109, 111, 129
Dove, Arthur, 38, 97, 125
Downey, Fairfax, 54, 94, 95, 111, 126, 130
Drake, William, 84, 118, 143, 144
DuBois, June, 93, 111
Duer, Douglas, 111, 153
Dulac, Edmund, 127, 158
DuMond, Frank V., 76, 120, 125
Dunn, Harvey, 9, 87, 88, 102, 103
Dürer, Albrecht, 124
Duvoisin, Roger, 16, 64, 158
Duyckinck, Everett, 50-51, 71, 72, 111
Dwiggins, W. A., 138
Dykes, Jeff, 27, 42, 48, 52, 53, 54, 68, 85, 111

Eastman, Max, 111
Edwards, Mona Shafer, 139

Eichenberg, Fritz, 138
Ellis, William Richardson, 43
Elzea, Rowland, 24, 25, 43, 54, 57, 68, 80, 81, 82, 88, 89, 110, 140, 142, 148
English, Mark, 65
Ernst, Max, 39
Esherick, Wharton, 125
Esprey, John, 138
Ewer, J. E., 111
Exman, Eugene, 117-18, 130, 142, 143, 148

Falls, C. B., 28, 62
Fenn, Harry, 83, 84, 99
Field, Elinor Whitney, 44, 59
Finch, Christopher, 55, 63, 100-101, 111
Finley, Ruth E., 148
Fisher, Harrison, 6, 9, 11, 22, 23, 38, 54, 55, 62, 96, 100, 105, 125; Fisher Girl, 9, 96
Fitzgerald, Richard, 103, 111
Flagg, James Montgomery, 9, 11, 22, 26, 34, 54, 60, 61, 62, 94, 95, 96, 100, 105, 111, 125, 154; Flagg Girl, 95
Fleming, Henry, 120
Fogarty, Thomas, 48, 118
Folmsbee, Beulah, 27, 44, 69
Foster, Joanna, 27, 44, 50, 68
Frazetta, Frank, 18, 107, 108
Freas, Frank Kelly, 107-8, 112
Freeman, Larry, 33, 43, 126, 130
Freeman, Ruth, 28-29, 43, 53, 68, 89, 111
Frewin, Anthony, 30, 43, 105, 111, 145, 148
Frost, Arthur Burdette (A. B.), 5, 6, 11, 24, 51-52, 59, 76, 77, 78, 83, 118, 120, 122, 124, 125, 158
Fuchs, Bernard, 26, 65
Fuller, Muriel, 49
Furst, Herbert, 135, 148

Gag, Wanda, 16
Gallati, Barbara, 97, 112
Gallo, Max, 33, 43
Gambee, Bud, 73, 112
Gamble, Kathryn, 76
Gardner, Albert Ten Eyck, 78, 112

Geisel, Theodor Seuss (Dr. Seuss), 16, 28, 64, 161
Genteel Tradition, 37-38, 124, 125, 126, 144
Gibson, Charles Dana, 7, 9, 10, 11, 12, 13, 22, 23, 24, 26, 54, 60-61, 78, 94-95, 96, 99, 100, 105, 118, 120, 125, 126, 135, 154, 158; Gibson Girl, 9, 94, 95, 96
Gilded Age, 22, 37
Gilder, Richard Watson, 143, 144
Gilray, James, 120
Glackens, William, 12, 15, 38, 97, 103, 119, 125, 126. *See also* "Philadelphia Four"
Glaser, Milton, 65
Glitenkamp, H. L., 24
Golden Books, 28
Gorman, Joan H., 24
Gowans, Alan, 35-37, 43
Grandville, Jean, 123
Green, Elizabeth Shippen, 7-8, 9, 53, 55, 60, 120, 121, 158
Greenaway, Kate, 39, 40
Greene, Douglas, 55, 99, 112
Grossman, Julian, 75, 112
Grossman, Robert, 65
Grosz, George, 103, 125
Gruger, F. R., 38, 125; Collection, 153, 154
Grunwald Center for the Graphic Arts, 25, 153
Guerin, Jules, 10, 61, 98, 158
Guipon, Leon, 98
Gullano, Charles, 138, 148
Gunn, James, 43
Guptill, Arthur, 101-2, 112, 139, 148

Haggerty, Mick, 65
Hahler, Christine Anne, 51, 72, 112, 123, 130
Haining, Peter, 30, 43, 145, 148
Hall, John H., 72
Halsey, Ashby, 139, 148
Hambridge, Jay, 99, 118
Hanff, Peter, 55
Hardy, John, 126
Harper, J. Henry, 76, 112, 117, 130, 143, 148

Harper and Bros., publishers, 5, 76-77, 117, 133, 142
Harthan, John, 23, 43
Hartley, Joseph, 119
Haskell, Ernest, 99
Hassrick, Peter, 27, 43, 90, 112
Hassrick, Royal B., 112
Haugh, Georgia S., 72, 112
Haviland, Virginia, 28, 43
Hawkes, Elizabeth, 53, 54, 57, 81, 88, 89, 112, 142
Haycroft, Howard, 49
Hearn, Michael, 55, 99, 106, 112
Hedgpeth, Donald, 107, 112
Held, John, Jr., 13, 15, 26, 95, 105; Flapper Girls, 13
Heller, Steve, 66
Hendrick, Gordon, 51, 75, 78-79, 112
Henri, Robert, 96, 97, 104
Henry, Marguerite, 107, 112
Herford, Oliver, 66, 118
Hermann, Hans, 99
Hill, Donna, 49
Hillcourt, William, 55
Hillier, Bevis, 33, 43, 127, 130, 148
Hitchcock, Louis, 10, 98
Hockney, David, 43
Hodgson, Pat, 74, 112
Hofer, Phillip, 28
Hogarth, Grace Allen, 27, 43, 50, 68
Holland, Brad, 65
Holme, Bryan, 32, 34, 43, 145, 148
Homer, Winslow, 5, 51, 58, 74, 75, 76, 78-79
Hoole, Stanley, 74, 112
Hopper, Edward, 12, 56, 97, 103, 104, 108, 119, 125
Hornung, Clarence, 22, 32, 43, 51, 68, 72, 112, 127, 130, 144-45, 148
Howard, James K., 107, 113
Hurd, Peter, 62, 159
Hutchinson, W. H., 88, 113
Hutt, Henry, 120
Hydeman, Sid, 137, 148
Hyman, Trina Shart, 106, 112

Illustration: advertising, 32-33, 144-45;

changes after World War II, 17-19; changes in, as a profession, 18-19, 122-23, 129; changes in technique, 20, 23, 134-35; children's books, 16, 27-29, 49-50, 56, 62, 63-64, 99-100; computer-generated, 137; differences between British and American, 11-12; ephemera, 31-32, 65, 145; fashion, 139; first American, 3; Golden Age of, 6, 11-12, 22, 23, 24, 38, 57, 84, 109, 121, 129, 136, 137; how differs from fine art, 36, 128; impact of British, 127-28; impact of European, 11-12, 127-28; impact of technology, 6, 12-13, 18, 19-30, 24, 32; incomes from, 6-7, 38; livre d'artiste, 128; of paperbacks, 30-31, 65, 145; pen-and-ink drawing, 135; political, 103; poster art, 11, 12, 17-18, 32, 33-35, 40-41, 62, 126-27; of pulps, 16-17, 30, 63; reasons for decline after World War I, 12-14; role of art editors, 7, 121-22, 123; science fiction, 10, 29-30, 107-8, 145; Silver Age, 38, 125; tech-nique, 32, 123, 136-37

Illustration schools: Art Deco movement, 128; Art Nouveau movement, 12, 33, 126; Arts and Crafts movement, 12, 124; "common sense" Realism, 100; Photo-Realism, 108, 126; Pre-Raphaelites, 12, 124, 125; Realism, 19, 126, 129; Regionalists, 125; Romantic Realism, 11, 81; Social Realists, 38, 125; urban realism, 103-4

Illustrators: "American Beauty," 9, 54, 60-61, 94-96, 105, 125; artist-illustrators, 25, 84, 96-97, 119, 122, 124, 125; contemporary, 57, 64; great, 38; role in World War I, 11; special artists, 5-6, 25, 73-76, 133-34; western, 10, 16, 27, 54, 61, 89-93, 102, 107; women, 9, 25, 88-89

Ivanowski, Sigismund, 98

James, Will, 16, 62, 102, 106, 122, 159
Jaques, Robin, 136, 148
John, Arthur, 142, 143-44, 148
Johnson, Diane, 127, 130
Johnson, Fridolph, 22, 43, 56, 68, 72, 104, 113, 127

Johnson, Merle, 59
Johnson, Robert Underwood, 148
Jonas, Robert, 65
Jones, Helen, 106, 113

Kagan, Daniel, 35, 43, 57, 68, 108, 113
Karolevitz, Robert, 87, 113
Kastel, Roger, 18
Kauffer, Edward M., 125
Keller, A. I., 5, 27, 48, 125
Kemble, Edward, 24, 51, 59, 83, 84, 117, 124, 158, 159
Kent, Norman, 113
Kent, Rockwell, 15, 26, 38, 56, 63, 66, 68, 103, 104-5, 113, 125, 126, 135, 136, 159
King, Ethel, 72, 113
Kingman, Lee, 27, 29, 40, 44, 50, 68, 136, 138, 148
Kirsch, Francine, 135, 149
Klemin, Diane, 136, 138, 149
Knauft, Ernest, 77, 79, 84, 113
Koch, Robert, 44
Koerner, W.H.D., 56, 88, 113, 153
Kuhn, Bob, 138-39, 149
Kunitz, Stanley J., 49
Kyle, David, 29, 44

Landgren, Marchal, 118, 130
Lanes, Selma, 40, 44, 56, 69, 106, 109, 113
Laning, Edward, 104, 113
Lankes, J. J., 149
Lansing, Garrett, 72
Larkin, David, 106, 113
Latimer, George Horace, 142, 144
Latimer, Louise, 27, 44, 49, 69
Lawson, Robert, 16, 64, 106, 159
Leigh, William Robinson, 93
Levin, Gail, 56, 97, 113, 119, 130
Levine, David, 35, 44
Lewis, Benjamin, 113
Lewis, John, 39, 44, 50, 51, 72
Leyendecker, Frank, 99, 120
Leyendecker, J. C., 11, 14, 26, 33, 34, 38, 55, 62, 63, 99, 100, 120, 128, 144; Arrow Shirt man, 14-15, 99

Library of Congress, 29; Juvenile Collection, 154; Lessing J. Rosenwald Collection, 154; Print Division, 154
Linton, W. J., 71, 72, 113, 123, 133, 149
Lithography, 134
Littlefield, William, 125
Lloyd, Peter, 65
Loeb, Louis, 120
Lontoft, Ruth Giles, 27, 44, 50, 68
Loomis, Andrew, 136, 138, 149
Lougheed, Robert, 107
Low, Will, 83, 84, 113, 119
Lucas, E. V., 76-77, 113
Ludwig, Coy, 52, 59, 60, 85-86, 87, 113, 121, 130, 140, 149
Luks, George, 97, 103. *See also* "Philadelphia Four"
Lyon, Peter, 142, 144, 149

Macaulay, David, 18, 64, 159
McClinton, Katherine Morrison, 134-35, 146, 149
McClure, S. S., 142
McConnell, Gerald, 64
McCracken, Harold, 48, 54, 56, 89-90, 91, 92, 113
McCutcheon, George, 119
McHendry, John J., 39, 44
McKay, G. L., 44
McLanathan, Richard, 81, 85
McLean, Wilson, 65
McMein, Neysa, 34
McMullan, James, 18, 35, 44, 57, 69, 108, 109, 114, 139-40, 149
McQuade, Donald, 32, 42, 145, 147
Magritte, Rene, 129
Mahoney, Bertha M., 27, 44, 49, 69, 70
Manso, Leo, 31
Margolin, Victor, 32, 33, 34, 44, 127, 130, 145, 149
Marquardt, Dorothy, 49
Marsh, Reginald, 104
Marx, Robert, 128
Marzio, Peter, 146, 149
Masereel, Franz, 128, 135
Mason, William, 72
Mathews, Alfred, 84
Maule, Tex, 139, 148

Maurello, S. Ralph, 137, 149
Maxwell, John, 114
Meglin, Nick, 94, 108, 114, 130
Mehlman, Robert, 44
Mellquist, Jerome, 37-38, 44, 124, 130
Merrill, F. T., 39
Metropolitan Museum of Art, 39, 72, 154
Metzl, Ervine, 33, 40-41, 44, 127, 131; aesthetic theory for posters, 40-41
Metzoff, Stanley, 31
Meyer, Susan, 26, 38, 44, 54, 69, 79, 80, 81, 83, 84, 85, 86, 90, 94, 95, 100, 101, 109, 114, 122, 131, 140, 149
Micklewright, Robert, 39
Milcher, Gari, 34
Miller, Bertha Mahoney. *See* Mahoney, Bertha M.
Minor, Robert, 103
Mitchell, Breon, 128, 131
Mitchell, Gene, 89, 114
Moline, Mary, 55-56
Montclair, New Jersey, Art Museum, 76
Mora, F. Luis, 125
Morgan, Wallace, 34, 38, 154
Morse, Willard S., 52, 154
Mott, Luther, 140, 141, 142, 149
Mullen, Chris, 31, 44
Muller, Marion, 137, 149
Museum of American Art, 153

Nast, Thomas, 5, 74, 76
National Academy of Design, 117
National School of the Graphic Arts, 136
Neil, John R., 62
Newberry Library, 154
New Britain Museum of American Art, 45
Newell, Peter, 66
Newlove, Donald, 107-8, 114
Newman, Sasha, 97, 114
New York Public Library, 153, 154
Nielsen, Kay, 127, 159
North, Ernest Dressel, 99, 114

Oakley, Thornton, 7, 8, 9, 84, 121
Oakley, Violet, 9, 53, 88, 120, 121
O'Brien, Geoffrey, 30, 31, 44, 145, 149
Ovendon, Graham, 39, 44

Palombi, Peter, 65
Parker, Al, 26
Parker, Robert Andrew, 128
Parrish, Maxfield, 7, 8, 9, 11, 12, 13, 24, 26, 33, 52-53, 59-60, 66, 81, 82, 84, 85-87, 98, 121, 129, 140, 159; and dynamic symmetry, 86
Parry, E. C., 114
Parsons, Charles, 5, 51, 76, 78, 79, 114, 117, 118, 120, 123, 131, 143, 144
Patterson, Ruth, 83, 114
Paul, Frank R., 30
Peak, Bob, 65
Peake, Mervyn, 39
Peixotto, Ernest, 84, 99
Penfield, Edward, 10, 11, 12, 33, 40-41, 61, 62, 82, 120, 127, 159
Pennell, Elizabeth Robins, 97-98, 114
Pennell, Joseph, 79, 97-98, 114, 135, 136, 149
Perkins, Max, 143
Perlman, Bernard B., 114
Peters, Harry T., 145, 149
Peters, Jean, 138
Petersham, Maude, 63, 159
Petersham, Miska, 63
Philadelphia Art Museum, 153
"Philadelphia Four," 25. *See also* Glackens, William; Luks, George; Shinn, Everett; Sloan, John
Philadelphia Free Library, 153, 154
Phillips, Cole, 9, 11, 34, 54, 62, 67, 86, 105; "Fadeaway Girl," 9, 96
"Phiz," 123
Pierpont Morgan Library, 42, 154
Pitaja, Emile, 131
Pitz, Henry, 21, 25, 26, 44, 52, 69, 73, 79, 80, 81, 83, 87, 114, 118, 121, 122, 124, 131, 140, 149
Poltarness, Welleran, 39, 45
Poortvliet, Rien, 129
Popular Culture Library, 154
Popular illustration, definition, 3
Portenaar, Jan, 136, 149
Prang, Louis, 146
Pratt, Fletcher, 74, 115
Preston, May Wilson, 98, 103, 120
Price, Matlack, 45, 138, 149

Price, Norman, 120, 131
Prince, William Meade, 154
Pyle, Howard, 5, 7-9, 12, 22, 23, 24, 25, 26, 28, 38, 48, 52, 53, 54, 57, 58-59, 66, 76, 79-83, 84, 85, 87, 88, 89, 98, 117, 118, 119, 120, 121, 122, 123, 124, 127, 129, 135, 136, 137-38, 144, 147, 153, 154, 159-60; illustration style of, 58-59, 80-81, 83, 124; impact of Impressionism on, 80-81, 125; sources of inspiration, 80; students of, 7-9, 52-54, 59-60, 84-89, 102-3; teaching style of, 8, 79, 81-83, 140

Quick, Michael, 124
Quimby, Harriet, 27, 43, 50, 68
Quinan, Harry, 138

Rackham, Arthur, 39, 40, 68, 127, 129, 160
Raleigh, Henry, 34, 38
Rawls, Walton, 146, 149
Ray, Frederick, 74, 75, 115
Reed, Henry, 77-78, 115
Reed, Walt, 26, 35, 45, 54, 69, 78, 79, 102, 115, 135, 149
Reedish, Rich, 107
Reinhart, C. S., 51, 76, 83
Remington, Frederic, 6, 10, 24, 26, 27, 38, 48, 54, 61, 67, 76, 88, 89-92, 93, 94, 95, 102, 120, 126, 129, 160; impact of Impressionism on, 91
Renner, Frederick G., 45, 48, 54, 56, 70
Renwick, Stephen Lee, 115
Rhead, Louis, 62
Richard Childer Productions, 137, 149
Richardson, Darrell, 99
Richardson, Frederic, 135, 149
Rix, Martyn, 139, 150
Robinson, Boardman, 16, 38, 103, 125, 126
Robinson, Robert, 105
Robinson, W. Heath, 127
Rockwell, Norman, 14-15, 16, 38, 55, 63, 65, 67, 99-102, 115, 122, 126, 140, 144, 154, 160
Rogers, William, 118
Rowlandson, Thomas, 123

Russell, Charles M., 10, 24, 27, 48, 54, 61, 67, 89, 92-93, 94, 102, 107, 129, 160

St. Gaudens, August, 120
St. John, Bruce, 96, 115, 119, 131
St. John, J. Allen, 99
Salmagundi Club, 119-20
Samuels, Harold, 91-92, 115
Samuels, Peggy, 91-92, 115
San Diego Museum of Art, 42
Sarkissian, Adele, 50
Sarony, Napoleon, 120
Schaefer, Meade, 16, 122, 139
Schau, Michael, 54, 55, 96, 99, 115, 128, 131
Schiller, Justin, 66, 154
Schmidt, Dorie, 121, 131, 142, 150
Schnessel, S. Michael, 53, 88, 115, 121, 131
Schoonover, Cortland, 53, 87, 153
Schoonover, Frank, 7, 8, 9, 13, 53, 82, 84, 87, 88, 99, 103, 115, 121-22, 153, 154
Schorre, Charles, 65
Schreuders, Piet, 31, 45, 145, 150
Schreyvogel, Charles, 27
Schwartz, David, 65
Schwartz, Joseph, 149
Scribner and Sons, publishing company, 78, 85, 133, 142, 143, 155
Scribner's ILLUSTRATED CLASSICS, 60, 62-63, 67, 84-85
Sears, Stephen, 75, 115
Sendak, Maurice, 40, 56, 64, 106, 161
Seton, Ernest Thompson. *See* Thompson, Ernest Seton
Sewell, Helen, 16
Shaw, John, 50
Shelton, W. H., 119-20, 131
Shepard, E. H., 39
Shinn, Everett, 97, 103, 115, 119, 125
Simon, Howard, 24, 45, 135, 150
Skeeter, Paul W., 86, 115
Sloan, John, 12, 15, 38, 96-97, 103, 104, 119, 122, 125, 126. *See also* "Philadelphia Four"
Smedley, W. T., 115

Smith, E. Boyd, 27, 28, 48, 69
Smith, Elva, 49
Smith, F. Hopkinson, 76, 79, 83, 115, 120, 131
Smith, Jessie Wilcox, 7, 9, 53, 60, 84, 88, 89, 120, 121
Society of Illustrators, 7, 19, 21, 35, 44, 45, 56-57, 63-64, 109, 119, 120-21, 131, 154
Solt, Mary Ellen, 128
Soria, Regina, 83, 115
Spurrier, Steven, 150
Stedman, Ralph, 39
Steele, Frederic Door, 10, 98
Stern, Phillip Van Doren, 73, 74, 75, 115
Sterner, Albert, 118, 120
Stevens, William G., 10, 98
Stillwell, Sarah, 9, 53, 84, 89
Stoltz, Donald, 55, 101, 115, 116
Stoltz, Marshall, 55, 101, 115, 116
Strahan, Edward, 120
Street, Julian, 34, 45
Stryker, Cathryn Connell, 53, 88, 116, 121, 131
Summers, Ian, 30, 45, 105, 116, 129, 145, 150
Szyk, Arthur, 66

Taber, Walton, 76
Taft, Robert, 27, 45, 84, 116
Tate, Sharon Lee, 139, 150
Taylor, F. W., 10, 98
Tebbel, John, 140, 141-42, 144, 150
Tedesco, A. P., 137, 150
Tenniel, John, 39
Thackeray, William, 123
Thayer, Gerald, 104
Thompson, Ernest Seton, 10, 61, 138, 150, 161
Thompson, W. Fletcher, 73, 74, 75, 116
de Thulstrup, Thure, 25
Tile Club, 120, 130
Timlin, William, 161
Tinkelman, Murray, 18, 57, 108
Tomsich, John, 37, 38, 45, 144, 150
de Toulouse-Lautrec, Henri, 33, 126
Traxel, David, 104-5, 116
Treidler, Adolph, 34

Trimble, Jessie, 88, 116
Tudor, Bethany, 106, 116
Tudor, Tasha, 106-7

Ungerer, Tomi, 39

Van Hamersveld, John, 65
Van Stockum, Hilda, 40, 138
Vedder, Elihu, 24, 83, 84, 120
Viguers, Ruth Hill, 27, 45, 49, 69
Vizetelly, Frank, 74
Volck, John Adalbert, 74
Von Schmidt, Harold, 16, 26, 48, 56, 63, 79, 102, 122
Vorpahl, Ben, 91, 92, 109, 116

Walton, Donald, 116
Ward, Lynd, 15, 38, 56, 63, 69, 105, 107, 116, 128, 135, 161
Ward, Martha, 49
Watson, Donald, 100
Watson, Ernest, 87, 116, 139, 150
Waud, Alfred, 74, 75, 84
Waud, William, 74
Weber, Max, 125
Weidemann, Kurt, 31, 45, 145, 150
Weinhardt, Carl, 105, 116
Weise, Kurt, 16, 64, 161
Weitenkampf, Frank, 23, 45, 116, 133, 150

Wenzell, A. B., 120
Whalley, Joyce Irene, 28, 45
Wheeler, Monroe, 125, 131
White, Charles, 65
White, G. Edward, 91, 92, 116
White, Stanford, 120
Whitney, Elias, 72
Willardson, David, 65
Wood, Grant, 125
Woodcuts, 135
Wood engraving, 133-34
Woolman, Bertha, 29, 45
Wright, George, 10, 98, 125
Wright, John W., 32, 42, 145, 147
Wyeth, Andrew, 85, 106
Wyeth, Betsy James, 8, 82, 84, 85, 109, 116
Wyeth, N. C., 7, 8, 9, 12, 13, 14, 16, 26, 27, 38, 39, 48, 52, 60, 62, 66, 82, 84, 85, 99, 103, 121, 153, 154, 161

Yale University Art Gallery, 77
Yanker, Gary, 34, 45
Yohn, F. C., 10, 98, 120, 125
Yost, Karl, 45, 48, 54, 56, 70
Young, Art, 15, 66, 103

Zeman, Zbynek, 34, 45

About the Author

JAMES J. BEST is Associate Professor of Political Science at Kent State University. His previous publications include *Public Opinion: Micro and Macro* and *The Washington State Legislative Handbook*. He has contributed chapters to various books including *The Handbook of American Popular Culture* (Greenwood Press, 1981).

www.ingramcontent.com/pod-product-compliance
Lightning Source LLC
Chambersburg PA
CBHW050228270326
41914CB00003BA/618